FOCUSED OPERATIONS MANAGEMENT

Achieving More with Existing Resources

BOAZ RONEN   SHIMEON PASS

John Wiley & Sons, Inc.

Published by John Wiley & Sons, Inc., Hoboken, New Jersey.

Published simultaneously in Canada.

For general information on our other products and services or for technical support, please contact our Customer Care Department within the United States at (800) 762–2974, outside the United States at (317) 572–3993 or fax (317) 572–4002.

Wiley also publishes its books in a variety of electronic formats. Some content that appears in print may not be available in electronic books. For more information about Wiley products, visit our web site at www.wiley.com.

Library of Congress Cataloging-in-Publication Data:

Ronen, Boaz.
  Focused operations management: achieving more with existing resources/Boaz Ronen, Shimeon Pass.
    p. cm.
  Includes bibliographical references.
  ISBN 978-0-470-14510-4 (cloth)
  1. Industrial management. 2. Production management. 3. Performance—Management.
  I. Pass, Shimeon, 1947–II. Title.
  HD31.R65 2008
  658—dc22

2007012351

10 9 8 7 6 5 4 3 2 1

To our families

Contents

Part III: Strategy and Value Creation

Part IV: Applying the Focused Management Approach

Part V: Perspective and Implementation

Preface

How can a company double its value in less than 18 months? How can an organization use existing resources to reduce the time to market in the research and development department by 40 percent and at the same time increase the product quality?

How can a company increase the throughput of the information technology department by 20 percent using the same resources?

Why do traditional cost-accounting methods prevent firms and other organizations from making better managerial decisions in pricing, costing, investment justification, and make-or-buy decisions? What are the alternatives that allow for better decision making?

Why do performance measures sometimes undermine value creation?

How can the removal of inexpensive bottlenecks easily increase throughput, reduce response time, and increase quality?

Why does adding personnel and capital investments usually fail to bring about improvements in service, in high-tech and in manufacturing organizations?

These topics and more are the theme of this book. The information should be of great value to all executive and managerial personnel in every organization, including service, research and development, manufacturing, health care, insurance, financial organizations, and government agencies. This book provides practical knowledge and tools for people in managerial as well as staff positions. Moreover, this book will be equally useful for non-profit and for-profit organizations, in every sector, public or private, service or industry.

This book explains how you can do *much more* with the *same resources* in terms of throughput, response time, and quality by using practical tools and techniques. We provide a systemic view and touch on issues of performance measures, operations management, quality, cost accounting, pricing, and, above all, value creation and value enhancement. We hope that after reading this book, you will be able to implement immediate actions resulting in improvement in most performance measures of your organization.

Each chapter presents simple tools and concepts for more effective management—highlighting the *how* aspect. These tools are accompanied by dozens of real-world examples of their successful use. Then Chapter 19 helps to identify value drivers and guide decision makers on *where* and *when* to implement various components of value creation. The final chapters enable managers to identify and deal first with the most important and easily implementable topics.

We include the use of methods such as the theory of constraints that yield fast improvement in systems such as service organizations, high-tech companies, and industrial organizations. We demonstrate how simple tools like the focusing table, the focusing matrix, the Complete Kit concept, and Pareto analysis can increase throughput, reduce response time, and create value in every industry.

Based on our extensive experience in improving systems and surveying the most recent improvements in dozens of organizations, we show how the use of these methods can increase throughput and reduce response time substantially while using *existing* resources.

This book is also useful as a text and reference in teaching management and business administration, both for graduate and undergraduate students.

Based on our broad experience in using and successfully implementing all of the components presented in the book in over

120 organizations worldwide, this book reflects our rich teaching experience with managers and students in various settings such as masters' of business administration (MBA) programs, executive MBA programs, and health care management programs. Our experience encompasses Harvard University (School of Public Health), Columbia University (Graduate School of Business), New York University (Stern School of Business), Tel Aviv University (Faculty of Management), Boston University (School of Management), Ben-Gurion University of the Negev (Department of Industrial Management, School of Management), in several Kellogg programs (Northwestern University) throughout the world, and in SDA-Bocconi University in Milan, Italy.

Thousands of executives and students have actively implemented the methods described in the book after taking our courses or participating in our workshops.

Our approach is application oriented, using new managerial approaches. It is not the typical quantitative management book, nor is it an organizational behavior one. It is mission or business oriented (or both), targeted to achieve immediate and substantial improvements in all types of organizations.

Acknowledgments

We would like to acknowledge the valuable contributions of Shany Karmy, Joseph S. Pliskin, Gali Ronen, Zvi Lieber, Nitza Geri, Deborah Schindlar, and Eitan Sharoni.

About the Authors

Boaz Ronen is a professor of technology management at Tel Aviv University, Faculty of Management, the Leon Recanati Graduate School of Business Administration. He holds a bachelor of science degree in electronics engineering from the Technion, Haifa, and a master's of science degree and a doctorate in business administration from Tel Aviv University, Faculty of Management. Before his academic career, he worked more than 10 years in the high-tech industry. His main areas of interest are value enhancement and improving performance. In his work, he combines value creation, management of technology, the strategic and tactical aspects of the theory of constraints, and advanced management philosophies.

Ronen has provided consultation services for numerous corporations, health care organizations, and government agencies worldwide. During the past 20 years, Ronen has led a team that successfully implemented focused management, theory of constraints, and advanced management practices of value creation in dozens of industrial, high-tech, information technology, health care, and service organizations.

Ronen teaches in the EMBA and MBA programs at Tel Aviv University. He has received the rectors' award for outstanding teaching. He was also a visiting professor at the schools of business of New York University; Columbia University; the Kellogg-Bangkok program in Bangkok, Thailand; Stevens Institute of Technology; and at SDA-Bocconi, Milan, Italy. He has published over a hundred articles in leading academic and professional journals and coauthored five books on value creation, focused management, managerial decision making, healthcare management and cost accounting.

Shimeon Pass, who is currently a partner in Focused Management Ltd., is an expert in applying the philosophy and tools of the focused management methodology and the theory of constraints in high technology, industrial, service, retail, banking, and nonprofit organizations. He holds an MBA from the faculty of management, Tel Aviv University; a MSc from the department of organic chemistry, the Weizmann Institute, Rehovot; and a BSc from the faculty of chemistry, Technion, Haifa. While an executive at IBM, he specialized in software solutions marketing and the implementation of advanced managerial methods to enterprise information systems.

He now specializes in applying focused management and theory of constraint practices in the management of research and development organizations and project management. Pass coauthored Focused Operations Management for Health Services Organization with Boaz Ronen and Joseph S. Pliskin. His papers on value creation and performance improvement have been published in leading practice and academic journals.

Part I

The Dynamic Management Environment

The Modern Business Environment

During the past two decades, the business environment in many sectors has been characterized by rapid changes. The main revolution has been the transition from a sellers' market to a buyers' market. The sellers' market, which was rather common in the past, refers to a somewhat monopolistic business environment where the supplier or service provider dictated the dimensions of a transaction:

- *Price:* Usually determined by a "cost-plus" approach where the customer is charged the full costs of the services rendered plus a "reasonable profit."

- *Response time:* Determined by the supplier ("We are doing our best and we are really trying.").

- *Quality:* Determined by the service/product provider ("We are doing the best we can under the circumstances.").

- *Performance:* Dictated to the customer ("We know better than the customers what they need. We are the professionals.").

From a Sellers' Market to a Buyers' Market

Today's business environment is that of a buyers' market. This trend is the result of international transitions and macroeconomic, technological, political, and social changes. This environment is characterized by:

- Globalization of the world economy
- Fierce competition among organizations within and across countries
- Global excess capacities in production, services, and in some areas of development
- Using new managerial approaches
- Availability and accessibility of data and knowledge
- Timely availability of materials and services
- Ease of global travel and conveyance
- Adoption of advanced technologies for production and development
- Extensive use of advanced computers and information systems
- The extensive use of cheap and rapid communication technology
- Shortened life cycles of products and services
- Democratization and customer empowerment

Globalization—The Small Global Village

The world is gradually becoming a *world without borders*. In most regions, particularly in the Western countries, people can travel freely without the need for entry visas. Similarly, customs and tariffs on goods transferred across borders have been reduced or totally eliminated. Travel between countries is easy, fast, and cheap, whether be it people, merchandise, or materials.

In the past decade, we witnessed a trend in the formation of *multinational firms*. Successful companies acquire partial or full ownership of firms in other countries, thus obtaining an advantage of access to additional markets and diversification of the product line of the parent company. Firms engage in *international coopera- tion* with foreign firms, resulting in mutual benefits. Many compa- nies have *excess capacity in production and services*, and it is essential to find additional market channels and better congruence with customers of the various world markets.

Communication has become global. Many television programs, radio broadcasts, and written media are readily transportable to other parts of the world. People in remote areas watch, for better or worse, the same television programs, laugh at the same jokes, and are exposed to messages of democracy and an open world.

The globalization trend is not coincidental. It is strongly affected by the end of global wars and the opening of borders, resulting in a shift of resources from military industries to civilian ones, including services such as health care and education, as well as privatization of economic activity. The world has opened up and we are witnessing a desire for individual and social welfare, customer empowerment, and awareness of environmental quality. The enhanced openness has made technological and managerial knowledge accessible to all.

A leading company in the field of electronic measurement equip- ment identified a short lead time as a competitive edge with respect to their (potential) customers. By cutting their lead time from the industry standard of three months to two weeks, the com- pany was able to deliver a variety of products to the customers in a

(continued)

short lead time. As a result, they became the industry's leader. Using the cash generated, they acquired a British company, a French company, and later a Chinese company and became a global company competing worldwide.

A buyers' market is characterized by:
A fierce local/global competition
Excess capacity
Short life cycle of services/products
High uncertainty
Mature and demanding customers
Antitrust regulations
High pressure from shareholders

In a buyers' market the customer or the market determines the:

- *Price:* Determined by the market. The manufacturer or service provider must adjust to market prices to survive. Customers are not interested in how much it costs the manufacturer or the service provider. The market dictates the price, leaving the manufacturer or the service provider with the cruel choice of adjusting to market prices or disappearing. In some cases, superior quality, unusual features, or performance can improve the price by 10 percent to 15 percent or more.

- *Response time:* Determined by the best response time in the market. For example, for film and photo developing, when one-hour developing emerged, stores with a lead time of a full day had no chance of survival.

- *Quality:* Determined by the best quality existing in the market. For example, automobiles and electronic equipment are compared to Japanese products that provide the standard for quality. Even lower prices cannot provide market survival for those who do not perform to standards.

- *Performance:* Customers determine their wishes and needs.

The process of globalization and the shift from a sellers' market to a buyers' market also caused shareholders to put pressure on management. A manager is evaluated by different criteria than in the past. He is dealing with shareholders who will not accept excuses, know alternative solutions to problems, and are aware of and demand new managerial approaches and up-to-date managerial standards. Globalization and strong competition result in many firms coping with survival.

In not-for-profit organizations, including government agencies and hospitals, there has been an *increase in demand* for services on the one hand, and *budget reductions* on the other. This situation results in much higher pressures on management. Using new managerial approaches and philosophies enables management to extract additional output from their organizations without increasing resources. For example, in one major hospital, operating room output has increased by 20 percent with the same resources and with better clinical and service quality.

The Remedy—Adoption of New Managerial Approaches

Advanced technology, professional personnel, and powerful information systems do not guarantee survival in the highly competitive market. They are perhaps necessary or supportive conditions, but definitely not sufficient. The main determinant in the ability of the organization to survive the competition is the adoption of advanced managerial approaches that are compatible with the new business environment.

Recently, new managerial approaches have been developed and successfully implemented in many organizations. In many instances, managerial decision-making processes have changed. The foundation for the development of these new approaches is the desire to be compatible with a new business environment and to engage relevant value drivers to improve and enhance the value of these organizations.

Organizations realize that in order to succeed in the global competitive environment, it is not enough to revert to technological innovation or to use cheaper resources and materials. It is essential to manage differently. New managerial approaches result in enhancing the value of the organization.

Value enhancement: *Increasing the value of the organization to its owners usually goes hand in hand with value creation for its workers and to the community.*

The new managerial approaches have several characteristics in common:

- They are based on common sense.

- They evolved out of practice; only later did they receive academic and scientific validation.

- They are simple and use the KISS ("Keep It Simple, Stupid") approach.

- They break down the myth of the input-output model (Figure 1.1).

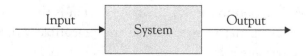

Figure 1.1 The Input-Output Model

The input-output model implies: "If we want to increase system outputs, we must increase inputs." For example, if we want to increase patient volume in a clinic by 20 percent, we may request more input in the form of personnel, space, advertising, and so on. If we ask the head of the development department to increase the throughput by 20 percent, we will usually get in return a request for more personnel and equipment. The modern managerial approaches show that this cycle can be broken. We can *increase output* without increasing input, just by changing the managerial approach. Evidence for better management of *existing resources* can be found in Mabin and Balderstone (2000) and in Coman and others (1996). An additional input has been added—a different and novel managerial approach.

Summary

The world has become a small village with global competition. The market faced by organizations is not only the region or the country in which they operate, but rather the whole world. On the one hand, this creates a threat from organizations outside the country, but on the other hand, it opens opportunities to penetrate huge outside markets. Management has become more difficult and more demanding in light of fierce competition, the increasing complexity and diversity of products and services, and the need to implement advanced technology. Past achievements are becoming obsolete as a result of competitors' improvements. An organization that does not improve will be driven out of the market. Technology, skilled personnel, and information systems are necessary but not sufficient conditions for survival. In addition, managerial approaches that are congruent with the competitive environment of today must be implemented.

Not-for-profit organizations, hospitals, government agencies, and others face increased demand for their services while budgets are shrinking. Implementation of new managerial approaches improves these organizations' performance.

The goal of management is to enhance the value of the firm (in business firms) or to improve organizational performance (in task-oriented and not-for-profit organizations). Many organizations are fighting for their survival. They need to identify relevant value drivers and improve them using innovative approaches based on common sense. The bottom line of these approaches is *doing more with what you have.*

2

Principles of Management in the Dynamic Environment

What Is a System?

A system is a collection of interconnected components acting together toward a common goal. It is a complex and holistic entity. It can be a biological system, an engineering system, or an organizational system (business, goal-oriented, or not-for-profit). A system has a goal that drives its activity. The overall goal generates defined quantitative objectives that must be achieved as well as a set of performance measures that enable management or owners to exercise control and judge whether they are on the right track to achieve the goal. The system has boundaries that partition it from the environment in which it operates. The system consists of subunits with a hierarchy and interactions. The system has a process that converts the inputs it receives from the environment into outputs the environment receives from the system. Some organizational systems have a feedback process by which the system corrects its activity and adjusts itself to environmental changes (see Figure 2.1).

W. E. Deming (1986), one of the pioneers of quality management, is responsible for the change in the modern perception of the organizational system. He emphasizes the people in the system and he includes suppliers and customers within the system definition, indicating that they are partners in the effective operation of the system. Hence, without a full dialogue

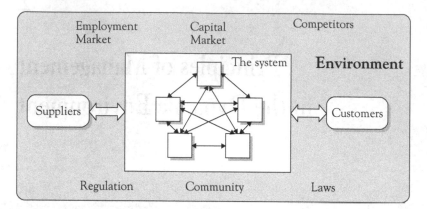

Figure 2.1 The classical model of an organizational system

between the organization and its customers on the one hand, and between the organization and its suppliers on the other hand, the system cannot improve performance. Without such a dialogue, the organization cannot comply with its customers' needs and will not receive from its suppliers adequate answers for those needs (Figure 2.2).

Goldratt added an important layer to system theory by simplifying the way we perceive the system and focusing on its constraints (Goldratt and Cox, 1988).

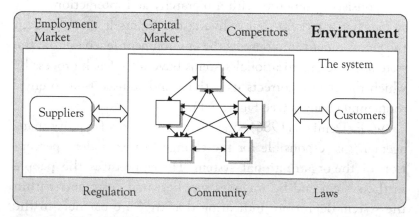

Figure 2.2 The "modern" model of an organizational system

According to this concept, the performance of the whole system depends on a few factors, designated as the *system constraints* (see Chapter 4).

System Optimization and Suboptimization

A major managerial failure emanates from the approach that "if every subunit in the system will perform optimally, then the whole system's performance will be optimal." However, an organization where every subunit is striving to improve its performance without examining its interactions with other subunits, or without examining the relation between these activities and the overall objectives and performance of the whole organization, may find there are adverse effects on organizational performance. This phenomenon, referred to as *local optimization*, may lead to the suboptimization of the system as a whole.

Suboptimization of a system: *Underachievement of the performance of the system relative to its potential. Local optimization caused by managerial decisions in some or all of its subsystems is a major reason for suboptimization.*

The purchasing department in an industrial company was measured by purchasing costs and discounts obtained from suppliers. The desire to minimize costs drove purchasing managers to buy inferior quality products. The poor quality caused manufacturing problems and high defective-product rates. Overall, the company's performance and reputation were compromised.

In a large insurance company, managers were rewarded according to the sales volume of insurance policies (production) and not

(*continued*)

according to the profit contributed by these sales. Consequently, the portfolio of many insurance agents caused losses to the company over the years, although the agents were highly rewarded (increasing those losses). Bottom line: This faulty reward system decreased the profitability of the company.

Suboptimization is usually caused by a local focus of the sub-organization, by measuring those suborganizations in a way that improvements in these local measures do not necessarily improve the organization as a whole, or using a local objective function that is not congruent with the overall objective function of the organization.

Satisficer versus Optimizer

Nobel laureate H. A. Simon revolutionized management by identifying a managerial phenomenon that causes decision-making failures. Simon (1957) claimed that executives, engineers, and decision makers are trying to become optimizers while making decisions.

Optimizer: *Executive, engineer, or decision maker who wants to make the best possible decision, without consideration of time constraints.*

To achieve the best possible decision, we must generate all the alternatives, gather all the information, and build a model that will evaluate the alternatives and choose the best among them. All this requires time, effort, and money. In the real world, there is no limit to the number of alternatives we can evaluate. We are all familiar with the situation where a group of executives and professionals gather and someone claims that we have not yet examined all the possibilities. There will always be someone who claims that there is a need to invest more time in additional options.

Information retrieval may not be easy. External information costs money and is not always readily available. Internal information is in many cases erroneous or biased. Hence, decision makers never have *all* the information needed to evaluate any given alternative.

Building the *optimal* model to evaluate alternatives is also time and labor intensive. Finding an optimal solution to a problem necessitates much preparation: defining all the decision variables, collecting all the relevant data (time studies, demand, labor resources, suppliers, customers, quantities, costs, batch sizes, delivery times, orders, inventory, and so on), building a model that will describe the real situation, identifying optimization and calculation methods, and locating the software and hardware to perform the optimization.

It is clear that the perfect solution sought by the optimizer may bring about a superior decision, but it may come too late. In our dynamic world, changes are frequent, and it is of utmost importance to make timely decisions that respond to market situations. Thus, optimal solutions, even if attainable, become irrelevant if they arrive late: the environment has changed, the competition has changed as have prices, laws, and regulations. Trying to behave as an optimizer results in the *analysis-paralysis syndrome.* Or in the medical world, "by the time the doctors decide, the patient may die."

Simon proposes an alternative approach and suggests that decision makers behave as "satisficers," that is, aspire to reach a "satisfactory solution," a "good enough solution," and not necessarily a perfect one (the "optimal" one).

Satisficer: *An executive or decision maker who is satisfied with a reasonable solution that will significantly improve the system and does not strive for the optimal solution.*

The satisficer sets a level of aspiration, a threshold he aspires to achieve. The objective is no longer to maximize or minimize some performance measure, but to achieve a solution that will improve the measure beyond the predefined level of aspiration. The satisficer need not examine all of the alternatives. He can examine some of them until he finds one that brings him over the threshold. Once the level of aspiration has been met, the satisficer may set a new aspiration level. This iterative process achieves a continuous improvement (Figure 2.3).

This approach is very time efficient. The satisficer does not waste precious time searching for the ultimate solution. He rather quickly identifies steps that may significantly improve his current situation.

The satisficer achieves excellence by complying with two principles:

1. Setting a high enough level of aspiration that is compatible with the market situation, competition, or investor expectations; and

2. Adopting an approach of continuous improvement.

The level of aspiration is set according to investor expectations for return on investment, the performance of the best competitor, market conditions, business opportunities, necessary conditions for survival, and so on.

Continuous improvement is essential for further value enhancement for the firm. A one-time improvement gives the firm a temporary

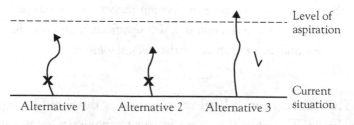

Figure 2.3 The satisficer approach

relative advantage over competitors. Without a process of continuous improvement, this relative advantage will be lost.

While the optimizer uses optimization techniques, the satisficer uses heuristics—decision rules that are not necessarily optimal but yield improvement (see Figure 2.4).

A large organization wanted to implement an enterprise resource planning (ERP) information system. A consulting firm was hired to analyze the system and its needs and to design and implement a new ERP system. The process took six years. After an additional two years, the technology changed and the system was obsolete. A competing organization in the same area adopted a standard ERP system that complied reasonably with its needs. The system was installed and adapted to the specific needs of the organization. Within one year, the system was operating successfully with concurrent implementations for more specific needs. The first organization tried to find the optimal solution and was without an ERP system for six years while incurring very high implementation development and consulting costs. The competitor settled for some achievable level of aspiration and had a satisfactory working system within one year at considerably lower costs.

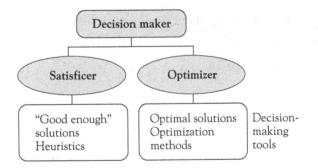

Figure 2.4 Decision-making process—optimizer versus satisficer

The managerial approaches presented in this book are based on the saticficer approach and on heuristics, hence their suitability for the dynamic managerial environment of today. We do not provide problem-free "perfect" solutions. However, there is no doubt that the suggested solutions are good and bring significant improvement. On a philosophical level, the organization need not be perfect; it only needs to perform better than its competitors.

The optimizer approach may occasionally generate better solutions to some problems. However, the assortment of tools and solutions presented in the book passed market and reality tests and are ready for immediate implementation.

There is a common wisdom among engineers and software professionals: "The enemy of good is better."

Elements of Focused Management

To survive today's fierce competition, an organization must continuously enhance its value and improve performance—doing more with the same resources. Organization performance can be enhanced by improving its value drivers using appropriate managerial approaches. Integration of managerial approaches and adapting their mix to organizational culture and environment improve the chances for better performance and value enhancement. The *focused management* methodology comprises the following managerial approaches:

- Constraint management using the theory of constraints (TOC)

- Methods for lead time reduction

- The "Compete Kit" concept

- New approaches for measurement and control

- The Global Decision-Making (GDM) model for decision making in pricing, determining transfer prices, and so on

- Approaches for formation of strategy

- Value focused management (VFM) approach

- Methods for quality improvement and process control

These approaches are discussed in subsequent chapters. Focused management thrives on improving organizational performance by adapting a mix of managerial approaches for each organization and identifying the relevant value drivers and focusing on them.

Value drivers: *Parameters whose improvement will significantly increase the value of the business firm or significantly enhance the performance measures of a not-for-profit organization.*

For a business organization, the value is defined as the discounted cash flow (see Chapter 19).

Examples of possible value drivers:

- Increasing contribution (to profit) from sales

- Reducing time to market in developing products and services

- Increasing throughput of operations and development activities units in the organization

- Strategic focus

- Quality improvement

Experience (including numerous organizations where the authors were involved) demonstrates that using a variety of managerial approaches and adapting them to specific needs brings significant performance improvements.

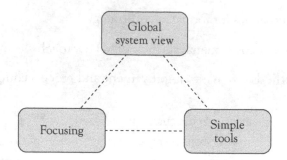

Figure 2.5 The focused management triangle

Focused Management Triangle

The focused management triangle (Figure 2.5) reflects the three basic approaches of focused management: (1) A global-system view, (2) focusing, and (3) simple view.

Global-System View

Appropriate management should consider the effect of a current decision on the whole system and not only on a single unit or subsystem. A global-system view (as opposed to a local view) will reduce organizational suboptimization.

Global vision requires expanding the system approach in two dimensions:

1. Expanding the system scope, and
2. Expanding the time frame.

Expanding the System Scope

A high-tech company developed a superior product with unique and innovative performance. Upon completion of the prototype, it was discovered that the developers used components that were very difficult to purchase, production was difficult, and the dimensions of the packaging were in excess of what major customers wanted. Performance is part of a global-system view. If decisions were made from a global perspective, it would have been clear that it was necessary to examine, as early as possible, customer requirements, performance, response times, and consider manufacturability, marketing, and sales issues.

❦

In a cellular phone company, sales personnel were rewarded by the number of new subscribers they brought in. The salesforce acquired large numbers of new customers that contributed very little to profit and also presented high risk in bill payment. This performance measure also led to selling new lines to existing customers with the gentle request to make their existing lines inactive. They were rewarded for generating new lines that in fact did not generate any new call volume. The bottom line result was increased costs to the company without addition of real sales.

❦

Expanding the Time Frame

One of the branches of a not-for-profit organization prepared medical emergency kits. Every item in the kit was chosen from a cost-effectiveness perspective. Within a short time, it was realized that one of the items, a tourniquet, had a very short shelf life of one year, while all other items had a shelf life of four years. The tourniquet was made of a plastic material and was very cheap (two cents each). This situation required refreshing the kit every year with a new tourniquet, necessitating disassembly of the whole kit and then reassembly. This annual maintenance was very costly. After some consideration, they decided to purchase a more expensive, high-quality elastic tourniquet with a shelf life of four years. This resulted in a longer shelf life for the whole kit and drastically reduced maintenance costs. The original decision looked at the very short-term purchasing costs, without looking to the longer life cycle cost of the whole kit.

In the decision-making process, every manager of a subsystem must evaluate everything from a global perspective to avoid suboptimization.

A proper process of development should consider the total life cycle of the developed product and includes issues of manufacturability, maintainability, testability, failure modes, and so on. Expansion of the time frame emphasizes the concept of life cycle cost (LCC). When purchasing materials and components or when choosing and buying equipment, you must globally evaluate the LCC of the component, product, or equipment to make better decisions for the whole system.

A logistics company was considering the purchase of new delivery vehicles. There were price differences in the quotations with no apparent differences in performance. The temptation was to purchase the cheapest vehicle. However, when the entire LCC was evaluated, the decision switched to buying the vehicle with the highest price tag that actually had the lowest LCC since the maintenance savings out weighed the extra purchasing cost. In subsequent purchases, suppliers were required to provide full LCC figures.

A health maintenance organization (HMO) started using a global-system view in the time dimension that resulted in a shift to invest more in disease prevention rather than in disease treatment. This solution led to better health for the insured customers and a drastic reduction in costs as a result in the decrease of utilization of medical services. This HMO recommended free flu immunizations to members above age 55. They initiated a measurement process of the percentage vaccinated in each clinic and provided feedback to the primary care physicians. The number of pneumonia hospitalizations during that year dropped significantly when compared to previous years.

In the decision-making process, a manager must consider not only the short-term issues but also medium and long-term issues.

Every system is actually a subsystem of a larger system. As such, it is vulnerable to suboptimization. Management must reduce sub-optimizations by exposing others to the sources of local optimization and working together to avoid them.

Focusing

The time of executives and managers is scarce. The organization is continually struggling with daily crises and the time devoted to extinguish fires does not leave enough time for change and improvement on all fronts. However, every issue that management wishes to improve will get priority and consideration and will frequently be implemented. Hence, management focus on a small number of important topics will yield significant improvements.

Focusing on essentials is one principle of successful management. The problems and tasks of a manager can be classified into four types (Figure 2.6), based on the Pareto principle (see Chapter 3).

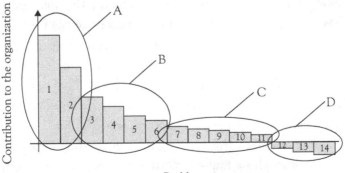

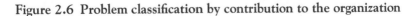

Figure 2.6 Problem classification by contribution to the organization

1. *Type A problems*. Very few but important problems; solving them will contribute much to the organization. These are usually difficult problems that require time and management resources.

2. *Type B problems*. Several problems with medium importance; solving them will contribute to the organization.

3. *Type C problems*. Many routine problems that are easy to deal with; solving them will contribute little.

4. *Type D problems*. Large collection of problems that are easy to deal with, but spending time on them will bring negative effects by wasting valuable management time that could have been better used in solving important problems.

Many executives spend much of their time dealing with type C problems rather than type A. This happens when the "urgent" (C) pushes aside the "important" (A). Management must focus on type A problems of the organization, that can substantially improve organizational performance. As we shall see, the manager must focus on system's constraints, its bottlenecks, critical tasks in projects, risk factors, and more. There is a need for a uniform language, determination, and managerial maturity to shift management to deal with what is important.

Due to the complexity of management, the manager does not have more than 10 percent to 15 percent of his time to deal with essentials and improve value drivers whose outcomes will be realized only several months down the road. Therefore, he must devote time to dealing with the problems that will enhance organizational value and improve the organization's performance.

The world of management is complicated. But, as we shall see in future chapters, this world can be made simpler if we focus on a few points whose improvement will improve the system as a whole.

In a large chemical enterprise, the purchasing manager realized that the purchasing personnel need not be involved in every purchase. He realized that 70 percent of purchases were for amounts less than $200. He changed the policy so that every purchase for less than $200 could be authorized by the manager of each department using a small purchases budget. Such purchases can be made over the phone (from a predetermined list of suppliers who agreed on special prices) without involving the purchasing department at all. The purchasing department deals only with orders in excess of $200. This freed valuable time for the purchasing experts to deal with other important issues.

Future chapters examine various focusing areas: type A items using Pareto analysis, constraints and bottlenecks, the critical chain in project management, and root problems of the organization.

Simple Tools

Complex managerial tools are not usually utilized in organizations, and the ones that are used do not significantly contribute to enhancing value. Using complex managerial tools has not brought remedy to managerial pains. The following chapters present simple tools that can be used in various managerial environments: The seven focusing steps of management by constraints, the focusing steps of the Pareto principle, the focusing table and focusing matrix, the current reality tree, the conflict resolution diagram, and additional tools.

Summary

- Today's business environment is dynamic and difficult to manage.

- The manager faces fierce competition and uncertainty.

- To reach effective decisions, the manager must view the system globally, focus on the essentials, and use simple tools.

- The manager of a subsystem can apply a global-system view by considering a broader system than the one he or she is heading, and by considering a longer time horizon.

- Focusing on essentials involves focusing on system constraints, type A items in the Pareto analysis, and the root problems of the organization.

- Implementation of simple tools is effective. The simple tools help managers focus on essentials and work more effectively.

- Modern managerial approaches are based on several principles:

  —The satisficer approach that aims at achieving a significant improvement and not an endless search for the perfect (optimal) solution.

  —Doing more with what you have—increasing output using existing resources.

  —Applying common sense and daily experience.

3

The Pareto Rule, the Focusing Table, and the Focusing Matrix

The Pareto Rule

Only a few simple principles of management have the potential to make an enormous contribution through intelligent use. Among these, the Pareto rule deserves special attention and is one of the most important principles of management.

Vilfredo Pareto was an economist of Italian ancestry who lived from 1848 to 1923. He discovered that roughly 20 percent of the population possesses 80 percent of the world's wealth. This is referred to as the "20/80 rule" or the "principle of the vital few and the trivial many."

Many phenomena in the world of management follow the Pareto rule, for example:

- 20 percent of stores in a supermarket chain account for 80 percent of the chain's profits.

- 20 percent of bank customers account for 80 percent of the bank's profits.

- 20 percent of patients in a hospital ward require 80 percent of the staff's attention.

- 20 percent of suppliers provide about 80 percent of the value of products, materials, and components.

- 20 percent of a company's projects produce about 80 percent of the contribution to profit.

- 20 percent of the inventory items constitute about 80 percent of the total inventory value.

- 20 percent of the salesforce is responsible for 80 percent of company sales.

- 20 percent of failure causes account for about 80 percent of all failures.

- 20 percent of a firm's customers generate 80 percent of the firm's revenues.

In the 1940s, the 20/80 rule was expanded to the three-way classification known today as the *ABC classification*. For example, ABC classification of a phenomenon would be:

Group A—20 percent of phenomenon factors responsible for 80 percent of phenomenon outcomes.

Group B—30 percent of phenomenon factors responsible for 10 percent of outcomes.

Group C—50 percent of phenomenon outcomes responsible for 10 percent of outcomes.

Group A—20 percent of the taxpayers account for 80 percent of the tax collection.

Group B—30 percent of the taxpayers account for 10 percent of the tax collection.

Group C—50 percent of the taxpayers account for the remaining 10 percent of the tax collection.

The Pareto Diagram

A Pareto diagram displays the Pareto rule visually and enables better communication of classification and analysis. It is a simple and clear instrument.

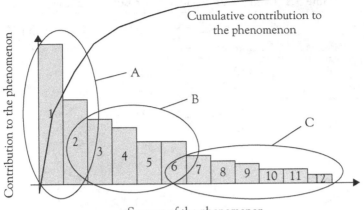

Figure 3.1 Pareto diagram

To derive the Pareto diagram for a managerial situation:

1. List all the sources of the phenomenon along with their contributions to the phenomenon.
2. Sort sources in descending order of contribution from the
   most important to the least important.
3. Draw a histogram of all situation sources as shown in
   Figure 3.1.

Example: Pareto Analysis of Product Contribution Volume

Let us consider a company that sells a variety of 12 products as presented in Table 3.1. Each product's monthly *contribution volume* is
evaluated; that is, the contribution of every product multiplied by
the number of units of that product sold per month.

Now sort the products in descending order from the product
with the highest contribution volume to the product with the lowest contribution volume as shown in Table 3.2.

We are now ready to prepare the Pareto diagram (Figure 3.2.)
using the information from Table 3.2.

Table 3.1 Example of product contribution volume

Product	Contribution per Unit ($)	Units Sold per Month	Contribution Volume ($K)
1	180	361	65
2	250	160	40
3	950	347	330
4	90	389	35
5	75	267	20
6	560	89	50
7	1350	11	15
8	650	169	110
9	220	114	25
10	15	1333	20
11	56	1518	85
12	150	1367	205

Table 3.2 Classification by product contribution volume

Product	Contribution Volume ($K)
3	330
12	205
8	110
11	85
1	65
6	50
2	40
4	35
9	25
5	20
10	20
7	15

The Pareto analysis as described in Figure 3.2 is followed by two additional focusing steps: differentiation and appropriate resource allocation, as will be seen in the Pareto-based focusing methodology.

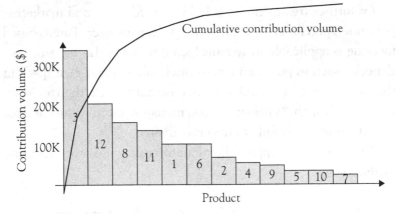

Figure 3.2 Pareto product contribution volume analysis

Building a Pareto Diagram

1. List all sources of a phenomenon. For each source list its corresponding contribution to the phenomenon in the relevant measure (financial, frequency, response time, downtime, and so on). See Table 3.1.

2. Rank all sources in descending order from the source with the largest contribution to the source with the smallest contribution (see Table 3.2).

3. Draw a histogram of the sources where the vertical axis depicts the contribution to the phenomenon, and the height of the bar for each source is proportional to the contribution of that source (see Figure 3.2).

The Pareto-Based Focusing Methodology

Managers use the Pareto rule in all areas of life, sometimes intuitively, and sometimes methodically. The Pareto rule is effective and efficient in the presence of resource constraints (also known as *scarce resources* or *bottlenecks*). As we shall see in Chapter 4, managers frequently are the bottlenecks in their systems, but the Pareto rule can help managers pick the most important issues to focus on for further treatment. This holds true for sales and marketing personnel, purchasers, and any other scarce resource. Pareto-based focusing is applicable in systems facing resource shortages or bottlenecks, such as purchasing personnel, salespeople, shelf space in the supermarket, or capital. If there is no bottleneck, then all issues can be dealt with. Without a focus, managers often waste valuable time devoting their full attention to all areas.

To effectively apply the Pareto rule, use the focusing methodology:

- *Classification*: Classify the sources of the phenomenon.

- *Differentiation*: Apply a differential policy to the different classes of sources.

- *Resource allocation*: Assign resources according to the policies defined earlier.

Example 1: Applying the Focusing Methodology in Purchasing

In company X, the personnel in the purchasing department have become a system bottleneck. They do not have the time to successfully negotiate with all suppliers. Using the Pareto-based focusing methodology, they can improve their performance in the following way:

- *Classification*: Purchasers must classify suppliers using ABC classification:

  —Group A suppliers are those 20 percent of all suppliers that account for 80 percent of the dollar value of all purchases.

  —Group B suppliers are those 30 percent of all suppliers that account for 10 percent of the total value of all purchases.

—Group C suppliers are those 50 percent of all suppliers that account for only 10 percent of purchase value.

- *Differentiation:* A differential policy must be set for each group of suppliers:

  —Group A suppliers—Carry out comprehensive negotiations at the beginning of the year, and detailed negotiations on each of the largest purchase orders throughout the year.

  —Group B suppliers—Do periodic comparative price follow-ups for the most significant items purchased.

  —Group C suppliers—Conduct annual negotiations on price discounts.

- *Resource allocation:*

  —Group A—Most purchasers' resources should be devoted to negotiations with this group.

  —Group B—Few resources should be invested in dealing with this group.

  —Group C—Suppliers should occasionally be evaluated.

Note: The classification of suppliers or items by monetary volume is essential for effective management. However, it may not always be sufficient to focus on monetary value alone. Other criteria may need to be considered to classify the criticality of items, such as lead time from order of item until delivery, delivery dates of items that could delay production, single source items, or shortages in items. The purchasing and technical departments should classify items using Pareto classification according to item criticality (see Livne and Ronen, 1990).

Example 2: Applying the Focusing Methodology in Sales

A subsidiary of a multinational company in the information technology (IT) industry sells systems and provides support and services. The main bottleneck for this company is its salespeople. The Pareto focusing steps implemented by this company are as follows:

- *Classification:* Customers are classified according to their contribution to profit, as A, B, or C customers. Later, the company decided to integrate the three groups into two:

  —Group A—15 percent of the customers that account for 80 percent of the sales contribution. These are large accounts such as industrial companies, banks and financial services companies, service companies, government agencies. These customers were designated as Named Accounts (NA).

  —Group B—The rest of the customers, designated as General Business (GB) customers.

- *Differentiation:* Apply a different policy for each group.

  —Group A (NA) was handled by the company's sales and marketing people.

  —Group B (GB) was handled by business partners and small distributors that specialized in selling to small companies. It was agreed that the business partners and the small distributors would share the contribution with the company and in return become an approved supplier and receive company training and support.

- *Resource allocation:*

  —Group A (NA)—Received most of the company's resources.

—Group B (GB)—A special unit was established to coordinate with the business partners, train them, and support them when required.

The Focusing Table and Matrix

The focusing table and matrix are methods that expand the Pareto analysis and include the effort or cost as well as the benefits involved in dealing with each factor.

The method has two stages:

1. Building the focusing table (also known as the *easy-important* table)
2. Building the focusing matrix

Example: The Focusing Table

A marketing and promotions team was considering its focus on potential customers. The dilemma was that all customers had growth potential, but due to the limited numbers of qualified marketing personnel, it was not possible to handle them all.

For each customer, an estimate was compiled including the extra contribution volume stemming from the additional sales, as well as the effort invested by the marketing people—the company's bottleneck. This analysis was based on past experience by the marketing managers, who estimated the expected sales volume and the time needed to get the relevant contracts signed (in other words, expectancy of the sales contribution and time needed).

The team built a focusing table in which each customer was given an importance score—ranging from 1 (small contribution) to 5 (large contribution)—according to their sales contribution. Each customer was also given an ease of handling score by the marketing people—ranging from 1 (more marketing resources needed) to 5 (less marketing resources needed), as shown in Table 3.3.

Table 3.3 Example of use of focusing table

Number	Clients	Importance	Ease of Acquiring
1	A	5	3
2	B	3	3
3	C	5	5
4	D	3	5
5	E	4	5

Note: The focusing table is an approximation of specific contributions. This is discussed in detail in Chapter 5. It is better to classify by specific contribution if those measures can be adequately quantified.

Generating the Focusing Matrix

Once the focusing table is complete, the focusing matrix is generated as shown in Figure 3.3 Preferred clients are near the upper right corner of the matrix. Client C is dominant over all others because he is the most important and the easiest to handle (*qua* marketing efforts). There is no dominance relationship between client A and E, and the decision makers can exercise priorities. The decision makers must choose the clients to focus on, and the focusing matrix is an effective tool for making this decision.

The focusing matrix can be very useful for the following situations:

- Choosing among products for development

- Choosing among products for marketing and market penetration

- Choosing among activities in the process of organizational improvement

- Assisting in the process of specification tapering in development processes

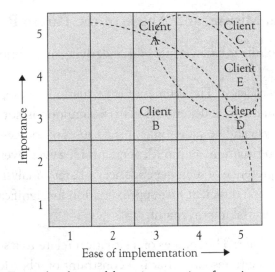

Figure 3.3 Example of use of focusing matrix—focusing on clients

Guidelines for Using the Focusing Table and Matrix

• Make a list of subjects to work with (8–12 subjects) and arrange them in a focusing table like Table 3.3 using number, subject, importance, and ease of acquiring as data elements.

• Arrange subjects in a focusing matrix by importance and ease of treatment, as shown in Figure 3.3.

• Choose subjects for immediate attention. Preference is for subjects in the upper right-hand corner of the matrix, who are both important and easy to treat.

It may be wise to choose subjects who are difficult to treat but whose value is very big because they help improve the system. Or it might be wiser to consider subjects that are easy to treat with little contribution, just to demonstrate quick results. The eventual choice of subjects is a portfolio choice problem.

The Use, Misuse, and Abuse of the Pareto Rule

The Pareto rule is based on several underlying assumptions:

- *Independence:* The sources of the situation investigated are mutually independent. This assumption is not always valid because some of the causes or sources of a given situation are interdependent. However, even in the presence of such dependence, a Pareto analysis is a good and sufficient first approximation for significant managerial improvement.

- *Constraint:* The sources of a situation relate to a scarce resource (a resource that is a constraint or a bottleneck). The rationale behind the Pareto rule is the inability to deal with all problems because of a constrained resource. Thus, when a resource is a system constraint (see Chapter 4), one must decide what will or will not be done. Naturally, the focus should be on what is most essential for the organization. Hence, Pareto analysis is only relevant in situations where resource shortages such as budget, bottleneck time, and so on, do exist.

- *Importance:* The severity of the phenomenon is a measure of importance. This is not true in many situations. For example, let us consider the erroneous Pareto analysis of the sources for failures according to the frequency of their occurrences. In effect, there are failures with low incidence but with severe consequences in the damage they cause, and there are frequent failures with negligible damage. Thus, it is recommended to use Pareto analysis where the relevant benefits or damages for the organization are noted at the vertical axis. This is called an *outcome-based Pareto analysis:* benefits or harms.

- *Equal treatment costs:* The effort or costs of treating each source of a situation is equal. It is not true that the efforts and costs needed to deal with a specific factor are the same. There could be a source of importance that can de dealt with easily and with low costs. Hence, it is better to use the focusing table (easy-important) described earlier in this chapter. The focusing table is actually a two-dimensional Pareto analysis that considers both the importance and the difficulty of treating each problem source.

- *Use of relevant parameters:* The choice of issues for treatment is done using correct judgment and will improve system performance. This assumption states that dealing with each situation requires using measures that are relevant for achieving organizational goals. However, this is not always the case. For example, there are insurance companies that base their decisions on income from premiums (production) and not on contribution or profit. A market analysis or an insurance agent evaluation based on this nonrelevant production parameter could result in failure and severe consequences for the insurance company.

Solutions to Failures of Pareto Rule Implementation
- Pareto analysis should be performed only for situations related to scarce resources (see Chapter 4).

- The situation should be measured by parameters correlated with organizational goals such as contribution or profit.

- When the efforts or costs needed to treat different sources of a situation are not equal, it is wise to resort to using a focusing table and matrix.

Summary

Pareto analysis is a highly useful tool for managers in every area. A manager who does not employ the Pareto rule does not fully utilize its potential. The focusing methodology is an effective tool in today's complex management world. The methodology *focuses* the manager on what is important and essential, and transforms the decision-making environment into a simpler and clearer one.

Use of the focusing methodology requires a high level of management, especially during the *differentiation* stage. This stage requires making a variety of simultaneous policy decisions on various levels and the ability to classify various situations for each policy.

Using the Pareto rule and focusing methodology can greatly assist in managerial decision-making processes. It is a tool that differentiates between the important and the more important and emphasizes focusing on the most important issues. A Pareto analysis using the focusing methodology focuses decision makers on a few areas that require most of their attention. Focusing on Group A items or the upper right-hand corner of the focusing matrix encourages an effective use of management time.

Part II

New Approaches in Management

4

Managing the System by Its Constraints

Management by constraints is an innovative and very effective approach developed by Goldratt (Goldratt and Cox, 1988). We consider it a managerial breakthrough that has brought about significant improvements in organizations worldwide in the past two decades. The seven focusing steps of management by constraints are based on the conceptual foundation of operations research methods such as linear programming (Ronen and Starr, 1990). The methodology of management by constraints is typical for the satisficer approach (Chapter 2). It provides satisfactory solutions that bring about significant and rather rapid improvements in organizational performance.

Management by constraints is based on a seven-step process:

1. Determine the system's goal.
2. Establish global performance measures.
3. Identify the system constraint.
4. Decide how to exploit the constraint and break dummy and policy constraints.
5. Subordinate the rest of the system to the above decision (the constraint).
6. Elevate and break the constraint.
7. If a constraint was broken return to step 3. Do not let inertia become the system constraint.

43

Step 1—Determine the System's Goal

The goal of the organization is of the utmost importance and should guide every decision and action in the organization. Once the goal has been determined, every person in the organization must evaluate the congruence of every decision or action with this goal. Unfortunately, not enough attention is devoted to this important area. A goal is something we aspire to but can never achieve, for example, achieving maximal value, having zero accidents or zero hospital-based infections.

The goal of a business organization should be to increase shareholders' value. Maximal cash flow or maximum profit over time might be considered an approximation of the real goal of a business organization. Simply stated, "making more money today as well as in the future" (Goldratt and Cox, 1988). It is clear that such a goal can sustain itself over time only if the interests of workers, suppliers, customers, and the community are taken into consideration.

In not-for-profit organizations, the goal is usually determined by the organization's mission. In such organizations, the goal might include achieving the maximum in some performance measure that is dependent on a scarce resource (e.g., budget). For example, the goal of a public health care organization is to maximize the quality of medical services provided to its customers subject to budgetary constraints. Some not-for-profit organizations may have multiple goals or complex goals. For example, the goals of a highway patrol department are to prevent accidents and improve traffic flow. The process of defining the goal(s) in not-for-profit organizations is extremely important even if it may take a long time.

A maintenance department in a large public organization handled electronic equipment maintenance for the whole organization. The department's perceived goal was to repair as many nonfunctional (broken) units as possible in a minimal amount of time. During a discussion with the organization's management, the department's goal was redefined to maintain a predetermined level of available equipment units in stock. As a result, it turned out that about one-third of the work done in the past was unnecessary since the repaired equipment was not needed at all or that there was similar equipment available to perform the same tasks.

While determining the goal of any suborganization, it is important to ensure congruence of this goal with that of the whole organization. The absence of such congruence can easily lead to suboptimization.

The role of a development department in a large technological organization was defined as "maintaining technological innovative leadership." As a result, the department developed state-of-the-art technological products, but unfortunately the market reaction was not favorable. The goal of the department was changed to "developing leading technological solutions according to market needs, as defined by the market, and to gain maximum cash flow durably." Quite rapidly, the organization's business performance was significantly improved.

Step 2—Establish Global Performance Measures

To evaluate the managerial activity of an organization and determine if that activity helps the organization achieve its goal, we must identify global performance measures that are compatible with the goal. Organizational performance measures are a guiding compass that points in the direction of the goal. Relevant measures for a business organization are the *value of the company* (defined as the present value of cash flow) and the measure of *economic value added* (EVA) as described in Chapter 18. Sometimes it is difficult to see the relation between mid-level managerial decisions and measures of cash flow or value enhancement. Thus, there is a need for additional measures.

There is no single perfect performance measure that can be improved to help an organization achieve its goal. However, we can define six basic performance measures with each measure addressing a different dimension of organizational performance. These six performance measures are:

1. **T**—Throughput
2. **OE**—Operating Expenses
3. **I**—Inventory
4. **LT**—Lead Time
5. **Q**—Quality
6. **DDP**—Due-Date Performance

These measures are used for managerial control, for rewarding executives and workers, and for supporting decision-making processes. Chapter 13 continues the discussion on this topic.

Defining organizational objectives utilizes organizational performance measures. Organizational objectives are quantitative objectives defined in terms of relevant performance measures. As opposed to goals, objectives should be defined in a manner that makes them achievable.

Step 3—Identify the System Constraint

Constraint: *Any element or factor that prevents an organization from achieving a higher level of performance with respect to its goal.*

The philosophy of management by constraints is based on identifying the causes that prevent the system from achieving its goal.

The concept behind this approach is unique; there is no search for factors that can assist in improving system performance, but rather, a search for factors that restrict system performance. The relevant questions are: What stops the system? What prevents the system from achieving the goal? Every system has a constraint. There is always something that prevents it from achieving the goal. If there were no constraints, the system would achieve perfect performance.

Experience shows that a system has a small number of constraints—a few factors that prevent it from achieving its goal.

There are four types of constraints in a managerial system:

1. Resource constraint

2. Market constraint

3. Policy constraint

4. Dummy constraint

Resource Constraint

A *resource constraint* (or bottleneck) is a resource that is so heavily loaded that it cannot perform all of its assigned tasks. This is the resource that constrains the performance of the entire system.

Because this constraint is a *system constraint*, the system cannot meet its goal. If the capacity of the constraining resource was larger, then it would be possible to increase system throughput and improve goal achievement.

Figure 4.1 presents generic examples for various managerial systems. The framework of a *1–2–3 process* shows a variety of work processes.

In the process depicted in Figure 4.2, every unit must be processed at each of the three departments, beginning in department 1

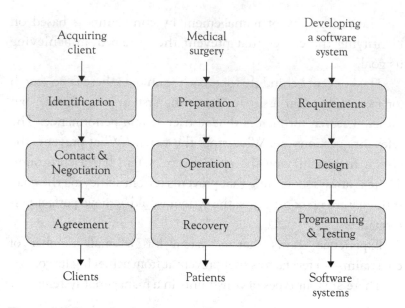

Figure 4.1 Examples for system processes

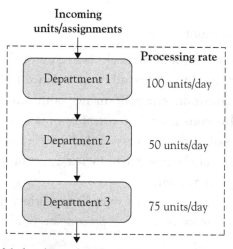

Figure 4.2 A system with a resource constraint

and ending in department 3. Department 2 is the resource that is the system constraint as it can process only 50 units per day while the other departments can produce 100 to 75 units per day. The market demand is for 300 units per day. Department 2 is the resource that dictates the throughput of the whole system to be, at most, 50 units per day. Departments 1 and 3, even though they cannot provide for the full daily demand, are not factors that constrain the system throughput and should not be treated as bottlenecks.

In Figure 4.2 we say:

- The system has a resource constraint.

- Department 2 is the system's bottleneck.

If we increase the daily capacity of departments 1 and 3, the throughput (capacity) of the whole system does not change. On the other hand, increasing the throughput of department 2 will increase system throughput. The bottleneck, department 2, dictates the throughput for the whole system and should be treated as the organizational "goose that lays golden eggs." A lost hour in the bottleneck is a lost hour for the entire system (Goldratt and Cox, 1988). We should consider the bottleneck as the "money printing machine" of the organization: The greater the use of the money printing machine, the higher the throughput of the whole system.

Bottlenecks exist in all areas of life:

- In an operating room of one hospital, the surgeon is the bottleneck; in another hospital, it is the anesthetist; and in a third hospital, the bottleneck is the operating room itself.

- In a highway system, intersections are bottlenecks.

- In a supermarket, a bottleneck could be a cashier or shelf space.

- In an insurance claims office, the bottleneck is lawyers who have to approve every settlement.

- In an airport during peak times, the runway is a bottleneck.

- In a high-tech company, the team leaders are the bottleneck; in another company, the system engineers are the bottleneck.

We can identify several situations with organizational bottlenecks.

Shortage of a Critical Resource

A resource constraint (also referred to as bottleneck or *internal constraint*) could be a specific employee, a group of employees, or an equipment shortage. For example: an experienced microwave engineer in research and development (R&D), a team leader of software engineers, a heat treatment thermal oven, a skilled surgeon in a hospital, a busy intersection in the city, or a modem in a communications network could all be a possible bottleneck.

Relieving a bottleneck simply by adding resources is not recommended as a general solution as it may require extensive capital or long training periods if the bottleneck is a highly skilled professional.

Permanent Bottlenecks

There are situations where *permanent bottlenecks* exist:

- *Sales and marketing personnel* are bottlenecks in their systems. The demand for salespeople is driven by leads reaching their desks from potential customers, from meetings in trade shows, and from customer lists. The effective demand is virtually infinite relative to the available salesforce and, as such, they are permanent bottlenecks (Pass and Ronen, 2003).

- *Research and development personnel* have an infinite demand for their abilities, talent, and services. This demand stems from customer orders, from ideas of R&D personnel themselves, from ideas of the salesforce, and from continual requests for changes and improvements. This turns them into permanent bottlenecks.

- An *expensive resource* can be a permanent bottleneck. The production line (FAB) in a semiconductor plant and the shelf space in a supermarket in the center of a city can be permanent bottlenecks. Physicians who have expertise and knowledge that is rare and unique very quickly become permanent bottlenecks in hospitals due to the demands placed on them, likewise for senior partners in law firms or in accounting firms.

Peak Time Resource Constraints

As opposed to a situation with a constant shortage of a critical resource over time, peak time resource constraints are characterized by shortages during certain time intervals. During the rest of the time, these resources are not system bottlenecks (Ronen and others, 2001). Some examples of this situation are found in hospital emergency departments where personnel must treat many accident victims at the same time; at tables in a restaurant at peak times; at the color printing machine at a soft drinks can manufacturer during the summer; at a tax preparation firm during tax season. In these work environments, there are resources that operate at excess capacity most of the time and as a shortage during peak times. System managers must exercise two types of policies: one for times of excess capacity, and the other for peak demand. Good management of such situations requires, among other things, differential pricing of goods and services according to different demand periods. Peak time management is discussed in detail in Chapter 6.

Seasonality

Some examples of peak time management relate to seasonality where different seasons exhibit different demand patterns. This is a special case of peak time management. Seasonality calls for different managerial policies for on and off-season (such as different pricing for different seasons).

Discrete Events of Resource Constraints

Even firms with excess capacities occasionally face a shortage of a critical resource due to unforeseen circumstance such as natural disasters, equipment breakdown, or labor disputes.

The situations described previously demonstrate the need to develop a decision-making methodology for an environment with resource constraints, whether continuous or temporary.

A constraint must be clearly defined. A shortage of high-quality, skilled personnel does not define a constraint in a high-tech company. The definition must be more specific. For example, we should specify if the bottleneck is made up of system engineers, team leaders, microwave experts, and so on.

A *control test* to identify the constraint is a test of "more or less." We must answer the questions: If we could increase the throughput of the resource identified as the bottleneck, would the throughput of the whole system increase? If we reduce the throughput of this resource, will the system throughput decrease? If the answers are yes, then this resource is indeed a system bottleneck.

Market Constraint

Market constraint: *Arises in a situation where the market demand is less than the output capacity of each resource. Thus, market demand is the constraint that prevents the system from achieving its goal.*

Market constraint usually includes an excess capacity of production or services, or a situation where the supply exceeds the demand. This raises the need to increase demand.

In the situation depicted in Figure 4.2, market demand changed from 300 units to 25 units (shown in Figure 4.3). The market constrains the system and prevents it from achieving its goal. Each one of the three resources has an excess capacity. This situation can be referred to as a market constraint, excess capacity, or external constraint. To validate that we have correctly identified the market as the system constraint, we must apply the control test: If market demand increases, will it increase system throughput? If the answer is yes (as it is in the case presented here), then the market is indeed the system constraint.

Most industrial and service organizations today face a situation where the market is the constraint, mainly because of global competition. Only a fraction of organizations can afford to be in a situation where an internal constraint forces it to turn away demand due to lack of resources. This is discussed in Chapter 18.

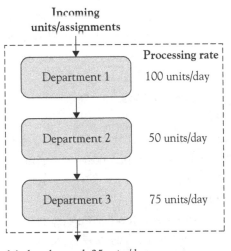

Figure 4.3 A system with a market constraint

Policy Constraint

Policy constraint: Adopting an inappropriate policy that limits system performance and may also push in a direction that is against organizational goals. This is also known as policy failure.

In situations of policy constraint, the inappropriate policy prevents the system from achieving its goal and thus becomes a system constraint. Every organization should set policy in important areas. Sometimes, a policy that may have been appropriate in previous years may become a policy constraint when changes occur in the business environment. In other situations, a local view may cause policy constraints that drive the system toward suboptimization.

In an effort to contain costs, a CEO of a high-tech company decided to forbid any overtime work for *all* employees in *all* departments (bottlenecks as well as nonbottlenecks). This constrained the number of products that could be sold to the market, and customers were obliged to buy products from competitors. This decision was obviously a policy constraint that worked against the company's goals.

⊶⦁⫷⦁⊷

The purchasing department of a large organization gave the instruction: "Do not process any purchase orders between the 25th and the end of the month." This policy was intended to improve cash flow. The policy may be reasonable when purchasing items with a heavy monetary value (Type A in Pareto). However, if we are dealing with less expensive materials, or office supplies, the delay in purchasing may harm the organization because it may delay delivery of products or services to the clients.

Further examples of policy constraints:

- Setting the price of products or services in the *cost-plus* approach—adding a fixed profit margin to the actual cost of the product or service. This policy constraint leads to throughput loss: in some cases, the organization is unable to sell because the prices determined by the market and the competition are lower than the cost-plus prices; in other cases, the cost-plus prices are lower than those of competitors or the prices that the customers are willing to pay.

- A very common policy constraint is the use of local performance measures, or measures that are not congruent with the organizational goal (see Chapter 13). Measuring people, units, or processes using inappropriate measures leads to bad decisions and is a detriment to achieving goals (e.g., measuring salespersons by the number of units sold rather than by the products' profit to contribution).

- Premiums and norms that depend only on quantity processed is a policy constraint. This can lead management to increase production without considering quality, and could create an incentive to create outputs for which there is no demand.

- An inappropriate usage of the traditional costing routines may lead to bad decisions and throughput loss. This important issue is the topic of Chapter 15.

- Continuing to invest in a failing project just because large amounts have already been invested in it is a policy failure (the sunk cost effect).

- Across-the-board personnel cuts of 10 percent is a policy constraint that may be counterproductive for the organization.

Any policy that is applied across the board throughout an organization may be a policy constraint. What is right for one department may not be right for another. There is a need for differential management.

To ascertain that we have correctly identified a policy constraint as a system constraint, we apply a control test: If we could break the policy constraint, could it increase throughput and improve the value of the firms? If the answer is yes, then there is a policy constraint that is a system constraint.

Dummy Constraint

Dummy constraint: *A situation where the system bottleneck is a cheap resource relative to other resources in the system.*

This is a situation where system throughput is constrained because of a resource whose cost is marginal.

A hospital operating room (OR) used for coronary angiographies was not managing to keep its schedule of procedures. A careful analysis showed that all the needed resources were available—surgeons, radiologists, nurses, surgical kits, and so on. Even though OR staff were available, there were times that the OR was not utilized. The unused time resulted from waiting for the cleaning person to clean the OR between procedures. The problem arose because management wanted to reduce cleaning costs. Initially there were two cleaners during every shift: one was in the OR and the other in the intensive care rooms. A workflow analysis showed that labor utilization of each cleaner was only 40 percent. This was very disturbing to management and they laid off one cleaner, leaving the second responsible for both the OR and the intensive care rooms. When cleaning was needed in the OR, the cleaner was occasionally busy in the intensive care rooms and vice versa. A very inexpensive resource, the cleaning person, became a system constraint, resulting in reduced OR productivity and throughput.

In an industrial company, the lack of sufficient of inexpensive containers to store the bottleneck machine's output blocked the bottleneck machine thereby blocking the system's throughput.

In a high-tech company, a shortage of personnel with Printed Circuit Board (PCB) layout skills was a major cause for delays in development projects. A PCB layout person is a relatively inexpensive resource compared to the hardware developers who depend on his or her services. Due to that shortage, the company was behind schedule and had to pay severe penalties.

A shortage in phone lines, fax machines, copier paper, printers, digital thermometers, and blood pressure monitors are all types of dummy constraints. These are relatively inexpensive resources compared to the cost of other resources and compared to the potential damage of decreased throughput.

To determine that a dummy constraint is indeed a system constraint, we must apply the control test: If we could break the dummy constraint, could it increase throughput and enhance company value? If the answer is yes, then the dummy constraint is indeed a system constraint.

Tools for Identifying Constraints

A constraint can be identified in several ways:

- *Ask the field people.* The workers in the field know the work, and using their experience and intuition, they are often able to pinpoint the real bottleneck.

- *Tour the work area.* This helps identify the bottleneck that is usually the place where patients, materials, or paperwork pile up.

- *Ask the evening cleaning crew.* They frequently know where the inventory or paperwork is piled.

Several tools to describe constraints that are discussed later in this chapter include:

- Process flow diagram

- Time analysis

- Load analysis

- Cost-utilization diagram

Process Flow Diagram

A process flow diagram is a basic flowchart that describes the work flow in the system (Figure 4.4). It depicts the steps of the process and the decision nodes. To facilitate bottleneck identification, simplify the process flow diagram (8 to 12 steps) to reflect only the main work process and ignore marginal ones and exceptions.

Each work step should include two time parameters:

1. *Net time:* Actual processing time of the step.
2. *Gross time:* Includes processing time and waiting time.

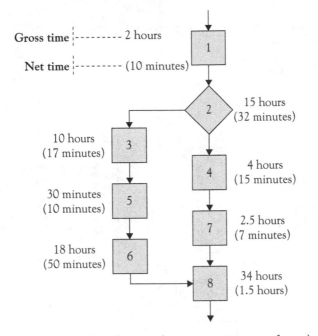

Figure 4.4 A process flow diagram (net time is in parentheses)

The basic process flow diagram can be expanded into a two-dimensional diagram that presents the various units in the organization that perform various tasks (Figure 4.5)

The process flow diagram may also improve communication within the organization. It is a simple visual aid that helps people understand work flow. The process of drawing the flow diagram in itself provides new insights into the existing work process, which may have been routine for many years. While drawing a process flow diagram, workers can identify the system bottleneck and even identify flaws in the existing process.

Time Analysis

Analyzing the gross time of a typical entity (patient, record, product, customer, batch, and so on) enables identification of the station where the entity spent the longest time. This station could

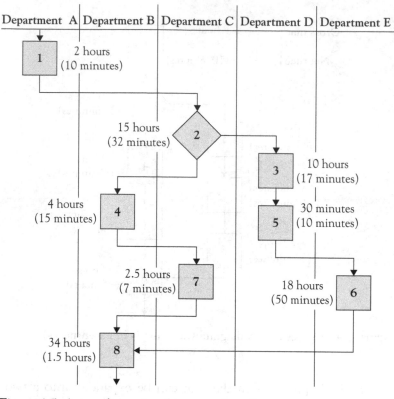

Figure 4.5 A two-dimensional process flow diagram

be a system constraint. Waiting in queue before the constraint usually accounts for the longest time interval. For example, step 8 in Figure 4.5 has the longest (gross) duration of 34 hours, and is thus a suspect for being the system constraint.

Load Analysis (Capacity Utilization)

Load analysis is a simple and clear tool for identifying the system bottleneck, which may be the most heavily utilized resource in the system.

To determine the load on resources in the system during the time of analysis, several data must be examined:

- Total number of labor hours during the time period analyzed

- The overall planned work—number of units we plan to work on (provide service, produce, plan, etc.) with a specification of quantities by type of customer, product, development task, or service

- A table describing the effort in labor hours that each resource is required to invest in each product, customer, development, and so on

A manufacturing company received many orders for certain products, and the question is whether the company can produce the entire order. The plant is working 190 hours per month. The orders for next month consists of 100 units of product type A, 50 of type B, 25 of type C, and 200 of type D. The plant consists of 4 production stations. Table 4.1 shows the number of labor hours required for the processing of each product type at each station.

In the load analysis table (Table 4.2) multiply the planned quantity by the labor hours of the resource per unit for each product and each resource. As a second step, calculate the load by adding all the labor hours invested by the resource in the different products and dividing by the total number of labor hours per month—190.

Table 4.1 Labor hours per unit per station

| Product | Labor Hours per Product | | | |
	Station 1	Station 2	Station 3	Station 4
A	0.6	0.15	0.73	—
B	0.35	0.72	1.18	0.5
C	1.6	—	1.36	2.56
D	0.2	0.06	0.44	0.41

Table 4.2 Load analysis

Product	Planned Quantity	Station 1	Station 2	Station 3	Station 4
A	100	$100 \times 0.6 = 60$	$100 \times 0.15 = 15$	$100 \times 0.73 = 73$	—
B	50	$50 \times 0.35 = 17$	$50 \times 0.72 = 36$	$50 \times 1.18 = 59$	$50 \times 0.5 = 25$
C	25	$25 \times 1.6 = 40$	—	$25 \times 1.36 = 34$	$25 \times 2.56 = 64$
D	200	$200 \times 0.2 = 40$	$200 \times 0.06 = 12$	$200 \times 0.44 = 88$	$200 \times 0.41 = 82$
Total hours		157	63	254	171
Load		83%	33%	134%	90%

The load analysis shows that station 3 cannot perform all its tasks to meet market demand. It is the most heavily utilized station and is therefore the system constraint.

The Cost-Utilization Diagram

A cost-utilization (CUT) diagram of a system is a simple graphic tool first developed for analyzing computer systems (Borovitz and Ein-Dor, 1977) and later adapted for analysis of system constraints (Ronen and Spector, 1992).

A CUT diagram is a bar graph (histogram) where every bar represents a resource. The height of the bar represents the resource utilization (load) between 0 percent to 100 percent. The width of each bar represents the relative cost of the resource. The relative costs of the resources can be:

- Based on the marginal cost of each resource—the cost associated with adding one unit of the resource. This could be adding one employee to a workstation or adding a machine. The recommended approach for using a CUT diagram may be:

  —Based on the total cost of each resource.

  —Based on the amortization of each resource.

  —Based on a cost ratio derived from subjective assessments of the people preparing the diagram. This represents the subjective view of the relative cost or relative scarcity of the resource.

Note: The order of bars on the horizontal axis is of no importance. In a sequential process we can arrange the bars according to the sequence of resources in the process.

To understand the value of a CUT diagram examine the process depicted in Figure 4.6. Consider the load and resource cost of the various departments (Table 4.3).

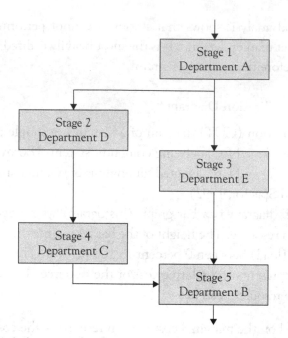

Figure 4.6 An example of a system and its work process

The CUT diagram in Figure 4.7 uses the data from Table 4.3. It shows that the bottleneck is department E, with no capacity problems in any of the other four departments.

Figure 4.7 depicts a situation where an expensive bottleneck is the only resource operating at full utilization. Such situations arise in operating rooms where the surgeon or the anesthetist is a bottleneck while other resources are only partially utilized, in

Table 4.3 Load analysis with a bottleneck

Resource	Load (%)	Cost of Resource ($K)
Department A	55	100
Department B	80	50
Department C	45	40
Department D	65	100
Department E	100	280

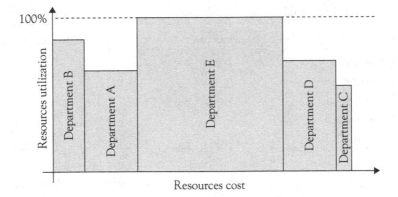

Figure 4.7 A CUT diagram for a system with a resource constraint

an airline where all the planes are fully utilized and the crews only partially, in a mechanical manufacturing company where the expensive CNC machine is fully utilized and other machinery is not, or in a local supermarket where the shelves are utilized fully.

In this situation, the following points need attention:

- Management must decide if the organizational constraint should be an internal resource constraint or, whether strategically and economically, it should operate at excess capacity.

- When a system has excess capacity in nonbottleneck components, management should consider selling or renting out this excess capacity in an external market. For example, if a surgeon is the bottleneck in the OR of a hospital and as a result the OR is underutilized, it may be worthwhile to rent out the OR time to external surgeons. Alternatively, an effort could be made to elevate this constraint by hiring an additional surgeon.

- You must evaluate the selling price of services or products that use bottleneck resources.

Table 4.4 Load analysis in a system with a market constraint

Resource	Load (%)	Cost of Resource ($K)
Department A	65	10
Department B	80	17
Department C	45	15
Department D	70	15
Department E	55	28

Figure 4.6 also presents the process of another system. However, in the second system, the load of the resources as well as their costs are different. Table 4.4 presents this new data. The CUT diagram for Table 4.4 is presented in Figure 4.8.

The CUT diagram shows that the system has market demands that are lower than the capacity of each of its resources. The system has a market constraint and is at excess capacity. The throughput is 80 percent of the potential throughput of the component with the highest utilization.

The following points deserve to be discussed:

- Management must decide whether the constraint should be external (market) while considering the excess capacity.

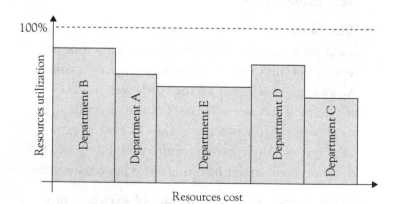

Figure 4.8 CUT diagram for a system with a market constraint

- Management must analyze whether the market constraint is temporary or permanent, and identify the reasons for its existence (internal sources such as quality, price, response time, or external factors like competitors, demographic or regulatory changes, or changes in customer tastes and preferences).

- Management should consider the option of taking on additional work, while making sure this does not create a bottleneck. The planning phase requires reserving a capacity to protect the process throughput from fluctuations (see Chapter 14).

Consider a third example whose process is also described in Figure 4.6. The load and cost figures are presented in Table 4.5. The CUT diagram presented in Figure 4.9 illustrates the system's problem. The system throughput is constrained by a very cheap resource. A small investment may be needed to increase capacity in Department E, leading to increased system throughput. This is a dummy constraint.

Here are some uses of the CUT diagram for decision-making problems:

- *Investment decisions:* The CUT diagram serves as a tool for investment decisions that relate to one or more components of the process. We should assure

Table 4.5 Load analysis for a system with a dummy constraint

Resource	Load (%)	Cost of Resource ($K)
Department A	65	200
Department B	75	350
Department C	40	380
Department D	70	590
Department E	100	10

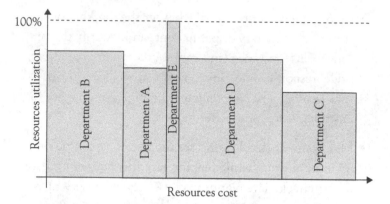

Figure 4.9 CUT diagram for a system with a dummy constraint

that the additional throughput achieved by breaking the constraint is worth the investment. Frequently, if we double the resource of the bottleneck, we do not always double the system throughput because the bottleneck may have shifted to another resource or step, and the gains in throughput are only marginal.

We should analyze the impact of the new capacity on the entire system. This assists the decision maker in deciding whether to also invest in another department, which may now become the new bottleneck.

• *Make or buy decisions:* This tool is also useful in assessing the impact of a decision to provide a new service or produce a new product on the overall load of the system. The new load forms the basis for a make or buy decision. This tool is also useful for choosing the products or services to be delegated to subcontactors.

The CUT diagram also assists managers in making decisions about stopping a service or production of a certain product and strategic decisions on price policy and its impact on operational loads (see details in Chapter 16).

Routine Use of CUT Diagrams
- Construct a table that compiles the various resources, the load percentages, and their costs.

- Draw a histogram in which every resource has a bar where height represents load and width represents cost. Draw the 100 percent load line.

- Identify any problems that emerge in the diagram (dummy constraints, large excess capacity, and so on).

- Decide how to rectify the problems.

Summary

Management by constraints is a management theory that focuses on the system's constraints, which are the factors that limit and constrain system performance. Constraints can be categorized into four types: resource constraints (bottlenecks), market constraints (excess capacity), policy constraints, and dummy constraints.

The most common constraint in the competitive business environment is the market constraint. However, there are many instances where resource constraints (bottlenecks) prevent the system from achieving its goal. There are always bottlenecks in research and development, sales and marketing. Therefore, we refer to these as permanent bottlenecks. Expensive resources or temporary loads during peak times cause resource constraints in the system. Dummy constraints are very inexpensive bottlenecks and must be quickly eliminated. Policy constraints result from policies and rules set by the organization (usually in the past) that hinder performance.

Identifying bottlenecks can be achieved by visiting the work areas, interviewing people, or by using process flow diagrams, load analysis, and CUT diagrams.

5

Management by Constraints in a Bottleneck Environment

This chapter focuses on situations where system throughput is limited because of a resource constraint (bottleneck). In these situations, you must focus on the constraining resource and manage it efficiently and effectively. Any improvement that adds effective capacity to the constraint, adds throughput to the whole organization.

Step 4—Decide How to Exploit the Constraint and Break Dummy and Policy Constraints

In a situation of resource shortage (human or material), the inclination is to solve the resource shortage by seeking additional personnel for service, sales, development, or production, or by acquiring additional equipment.

The step of exploiting and utilizing the constraint means we can *do much more* with what we already have. That is, extract significant additional output by focused management of bottleneck resources. The decision about whether to increase resources should be postponed until after full exploitation of the improvement potential of the current resource constraints.

Improvement through exploitation can be achieved relatively fast, and therefore, it is the most realistic improvement for the short term. Experience has shown that in every system it is possible to

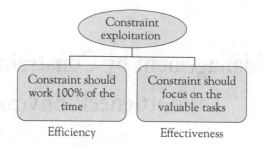

Figure 5.1 Exploiting and utilizing the resource

extract more by better system management and focus on existing constraints. Exploitation is performed on two dimensions: efficiency and effectiveness (see Figure 5.1). At the same time, we must break policy and dummy constraints:

- *Efficiency:* Increase bottleneck utilization as close as possible to 100 percent.

- *Effectiveness:* Because the bottleneck cannot supply the entire demand, decide on the most effective product or service mix for the bottleneck.

Efficiency—Increasing Constraint Utilization

The bottleneck determines system throughput. We must make sure that it operates at the maximum possible utilization—as close as possible to 100 percent. An hour of bottleneck utilization is an hour of work for the entire system. An hour lost in the bottleneck is an hour lost for the entire system (Goldratt and Cox, 2004).

Experience gained in working with hundreds of organizations shows that we can significantly *increase* bottleneck throughput in sales, marketing, development, and operations *without adding resources* through better focused management of resources (Mabin and Balderstone, 2000).

For the bottleneck to work more efficiently, one should:

- Increase bottleneck utilization capacity to as close as possible to 100 percent.

- Reduce bottleneck ineffective (garbage) time.

Increasing Bottleneck Utilization

Increasing bottleneck utilization can be achieved by measuring idle times and analyzing these times using the Pareto focusing methodology.

In an industrial company, a bottleneck in operations was an expensive machine. Measurement of idle time revealed that the machine was idle 32 percent of the time. Idle times were handled as follows:

- *Problem classification:* A Pareto classification of the problems revealed that 20 percent of problems (type A problems) account for 80 percent of idle time. These problems are:

  —Maintenance problems.

  —Shortages in materials to be processed at the bottleneck.

  —Concurrent lunch breaks of all bottleneck employees.

- *Differential policy:* Management decided to focus only on type A problems. Other sources of idle time will be monitored occasionally to verify that they do not cause more idle time than in the past.

- *Allocation of improvement resources:* Most resources will be devoted to type A problems.

(continued)

Management took the following steps using existing resources:

- Lunch breaks were staggered across three hours so the bottleneck could operate at full capacity during lunchtime.

- Maintenance problems were monitored and preventive maintenance was undertaken. The maintenance department was instructed to give the bottleneck machine top priority.

- Lack of material in front of the bottleneck machine was resolved by the DBR scheduling system (see later in this chapter).

The operating rooms (ORs) in a public hospital were idle 42 percent of the time causing a bottleneck. The two main causes for idle times were (1) waiting for the cleaning crew (dummy constraint) and (2) cancelled operations by the anesthetist who discovered that patients had not undergone all required tests (i.e., arrived with incomplete kits, see Chapter 12). Idle time of the ORs drastically decreased when another cleaning crew was designated for the OR area, and when a preoperative clinic made sure that a complete kit was attained about one week before the scheduled surgery for each patient.

Reducing Ineffective Time (Garbage Time)

Garbage time: *The time when a bottleneck is devoted to activities that do not add value to the customer, the service, or the product, or when the bottleneck is devoted to activities it should not perform. This is an ineffective use of the bottleneck resource. The garbage plant is similarly defined and includes wasted materials and all other expenses.*

In a high-tech company, the senior team leader in the development department, who was a bottleneck, was busy about one day a week supporting staff in their use of word processing software and electronic spreadsheets.

In a large insurance company, the bottleneck was the underwriter. Analysis showed that a significant portion of her time was spent looking for files, filing documents, and photocopying forms. Analysis of the ineffective (garbage) time and implementing simple solutions led to significant increase in throughput.

The sales personnel of a large multinational company estimated that 50 percent of their time was ineffective. This was similar to assessments in other firms. They applied the focusing methodology as follows:

- *Classifying garbage time causes:* The various causes were classified into A, B, C groups. Group A consisted of 20 percent of the causes and accounted for 80 percent of the garbage time. Group A included the following:

  1. Working with an incomplete kit (see Chapter 12). The salesforce approached customers without full knowledge and information about their customers' needs, thus requiring frequent repeat visits. The information was occasionally available in the firm but did not reach the sales department.

  2. False identification of the decision maker in the customer's organization.

  3. Dealing with administrative and logistic problems of the customer (e.g., shipments, missing items, inquiries).

(*continued*)

> • *Differential policy:* The firm decided to treat only Group A causes of garbage time and leave the smaller causes for later treatment.
>
> • *Resource allocation:* The majority of management resources were devoted to decreasing these Group A problems.
>
> By applying the focusing methodology, the garbage time of the salesforce was reduced from 50 percent to 40 percent, which is equivalent to increasing the salesforce by 20 percent. The profit also increased as a result.

Effectiveness

Due to the fact that the bottleneck cannot supply the entire demand, one must decide on the product or service mix, or the project, or customers on whom the bottleneck will work.

Strategic gating: A *process of prioritization that defines the value of the different tasks, products, services, projects, or customers for the organization and decides by priority which ones will be carried out, and which ones will be dropped.*

> In a large communication company, the research and development (R&D) department was working on four innovative products simultaneously, each being a potential breakthrough in its area. Estimating the load in the development department indicated that the timetables dictated by the market would allow the development of only two products. A strategic gating decision was made to halt

the development of two of the four products. This decision eventually resulted in a competitive time to market for one of the devices, enhancing the value of the company.

***

In a large downtown supermarket, there are 15,000 stock keeping units (SKUs). The supermarket's bottleneck is shelf space. The purchaser for this supermarket is swamped with suppliers knocking on her door, representing 150,000 relevant SKUs. She needs strategic prioritization to choose those products that would increase profits. Every product has a potential profit, but a shortage of shelf space requires prioritization that excludes some products altogether.

***

In developing new products in the R&D department, there is a need for further screening of the requested features and specifications, in order to effectively use the developmental resources and get to the market on time.

***

The salespeople in a technological organization were debating about which potential customers to focus on. While going through a strategic gating process, they decided to focus on the North American market and put most of their efforts there. It was decided not to approach the European market at that time.

***

(*continued*)

A manufacturing company produced a wide range of products. The company's bottleneck was an expensive manufacturing line that the company did not plan to expand. The marketing people conducted a strategic gating process in order to choose the preferred products that the bottlenecked line would produce. They discontinued about 10 percent of the products assessed as less valuable and took them out of the company's catalog.

Prioritization Methods—Strategic Gating

There are several methods for prioritization:

1. *Pareto diagram*: A Pareto diagram can be drawn for the potential profit contribution to the system or for any other relevant parameter. This is a simple and fast method but it does not take into account the bottleneck time needed for each activity.

2. *Focusing table (easy-important) and focusing matrix*: Potential tasks or projects are listed in a focusing table. For every task, list the importance (expected contribution to profit, value-enhancing capability, or expected effect on company goals) on a scale of 1 to 5. Then, list the ease of achieving each task (use of bottleneck time) on a scale of 1 to 5. The various tasks are mapped on a focusing matrix, which helps prioritize the preferred tasks.

    Importance and ease of implementation should be measured on objective dimensions: value enhancement or profit. Ease of implementation can be measured, for example, by work hours needed by the bottleneck resource.

The information technology (IT) department of a large telecommunication company was the source of a bottleneck for many activities. Each department wanted numerous, specific IT applications to be developed. Management needed to prioritize these projects. Project ease of implementation was measured by the number of person-hours required by the bottleneck resource to complete the project tasks. Project importance was measured by expected profits to be realized in the next three years by implementing these applications. As a result of this prioritization, 750 projects were chosen out of the 1,500 that had been waiting for months in the IT department and the department response time decreased dramatically.

The sales department in a company that sells services and IT solutions has classified its customers using a focusing matrix. Thus, the salespeople, who were the company's bottleneck, only invested their time and sales efforts on the most valuable and profitable customers.

3. *Specific contribution:* To rank the most valuable products, jobs, or customers, focus on specific contributions.

> Specific contribution (*the contribution per unit of a bot-tleneck resource*) *of a product, task, service, or customer: The expected contribution divided by the time investment of the bottleneck resource.*

In a strategic gating process, calculate the specific contribution for every product, service, task, or customer. Then choose the combination of the items with the highest specific contribution up to the constraint capacity. Analyzing specific contributions can help the sales departments in their decisions about which customers deserve to be the focus of scarce sales resources. The marketing and development departments can use specific contribution in new product development decisions.

Note: the use of specific contribution is the correct and complete process for prioritization (Geri and Ronen, 2005). Using a focusing table (easy-important) offers a good approximation when it is difficult to quantify parameters. In a situation where the focusing table and matrix are constructed by parameters such as contribution on the one hand, and work hours on the other, graphic representations helps in visualizing calculated specific contributions. Many organizations prefer to perform strategic gating at the level of a focusing table and focusing matrix because the graphic representation makes it easier to decide.

Example 1: An R&D department of an electronic firm was considering the four projects presented in Table 5.1.

Prioritization according to specific contribution is

1. Project 2
2. Project 4
3. Project 1
4. Project 3

Example 2: In large supermarkets, shelf space can be a resource constraint. Product prioritization should consider specific contribution per shelf length in order to maximize overall profits.

Table 5.1 Imaging projects

Project	Contribution ($K)	Development Effort (Person-Years)	Specific Contribution ($K per Person-Year)
1	56	0.5	112
2	2,470	1	2,470
3	345	5	69
4	1,250	2	612.5

Example 3: In a private hospital that specializes in providing surgical services where external surgeons bring in external patients, the operating rooms were the system bottleneck. For several years it was believed that gynecological surgical procedures were the most profitable for the hospital. A specific contribution analysis was performed and operations were ranked in a Pareto diagram in descending order by specific contribution per hour of operating room utilization (Figure 5.2). The specific contributions by rank as shown in Figure 5.2 are vascular surgery, neurosurgery, orthopedics, ENT, urology, and finally, gynecology. This graph helped hospital staff to determine the types of operations to focus on by priority. Eighteen months after these findings, OR utilization increased by 17 percent and hospital profits almost tripled.

The Mirabilis Effect

Any strategic gating decision can be a difficult one for decision makers. A decision about what to focus on and what to produce always carries with it the complimentary decision of what to give up.

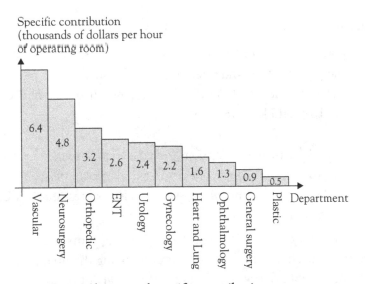

Figure 5.2 Pareto diagram of specific contribution

Because gating decisions are made in conditions of uncertainty, there is always doubt about whether the expected contributions and efforts have been assessed correctly. Additionally, there is some fear that the product rejected through prioritization could turn out to be another success story like Mirabilis. Mirabilis was a small Israeli high-tech firm that developed the ICQ software that was sold to AOL for over $400 million. This product should have been assessed a higher expected contribution resulting in a higher specific contribution. The fact that a product is not assessed at a higher value during the decision-making process indicates the presence of other products that seem to have higher success probabilities.

Firms need managerial maturity to realize that the rules of physics cannot be bent and that there is no system that can perform *all* desired tasks. If management does not prioritize the tasks, the employees will act according to their priorities without regard to global considerations for the benefit of the organization. In situations of indecision, the development of services or products will be delayed or the focus is not on the right customers.

Global Decision-Making Methodology

Analyzing specific contribution is only one part of tactical and strategic prioritization and screening of tasks, services, or products. The global decision-making (GDM) process (discussed further in Chapter 16) includes three steps:

1. *Make global economic decisions from the CEO's perspective.* In this process, evaluate the decision from a global perspective by looking at the whole system. This process may utilize specific contribution.

2. *Make strategic considerations.* Consider long-term and other strategic considerations, only after assessing the financial implications of priority changes brought about by the decisions made in the previous step.

When one or more of the alternatives in the prioritization process has indirect marketing implications or broader strategic implications, expand the analysis of expected contributions and prepare a mini business plan for each alternative.

3. *Change local performance measures (if needed)*. Local performance measures may occasionally prevent a correct prioritization process. For example, prioritizing customers by the local performance measure of sales volume introduces erratic priorities; therefore, the performance measure should be changed to contribution volume.

Breaking Policy and Dummy Constraints

Bottlenecks must be exploited efficiently and effectively. Dummy and policy constraints must be broken. The dummy constraint of the cleaning person in the OR can be immediately remedied by hiring additional personnel. It does not take an economist to perform a cost-benefit analysis to justify this solution.

Dealing with policy constraints is a bit more difficult. For example, elimination of overtime work (which usually occurs at the end of the quarter or at the end of a year) can be solved by a policy that differentiates between work centers that are bottlenecks and other work centers. This allows the manager to manage a petty cash account of the overtime budget for the bottlenecks.

Step 5—Subordinate the Rest of the System to the Previous Decision (the Constraint)

Once we focus on the constraint (bottleneck) and improve its management, we need to create a policy for managing and operating noncritical resources. The remaining resources should *serve and assist* the bottleneck. The noncritical resources should be available to assist when needed. For example, in a group dental practice, dentists are system constraints. The other workers (hygienists, assistants, secretary) should all assist the dentists.

Noncritical resources must be available to assist system constraints, especially in peak times. For example, in peak tourist seasons, the runways of an airport are a bottleneck. All other workers and managers must contribute their share to efficiently exploit the runway times for fast and safe takeoffs and landings.

Henry Ford offered customers the Model T Ford "in any color the customer wants, as long as it is black." Henry Ford's policy resulted from subordination to the assembly line constraint that could not keep up with market demand. This was a resource constraint. To maximize throughput, it was important for Ford not to change colors during production. This policy assured maximum profit and value for Ford by subordinating the whole system (including customers) to production.

Henry Ford's failure was that he stuck to his policy even when new competitors entered the market; then the resource constraint became a market constraint resulting in a steep drop in sales and market share. The right step would have been to realize that there was now a market constraint and subordinate the system to this constraint. Competition and customers' needs should have driven Ford to produce a variety of cars: different styles, colors, or amenities.

In knowledge-based organizations, it is common to find subordination to *technology* rather than to *market*. The development of a new product is occasionally based on a brilliant technological idea without identification of a target customer or market.

In a hospital operating room (OR), the bottleneck could be the anesthetists, the nurses, or the OR capacity itself. Management must identify the bottleneck and subordinate all others to serve and assist the bottleneck to ensure it functions efficiently.

Additional examples:

- In maintenance, priority should be given to the bottleneck. When the bottleneck fails, the relevant maintenance people should drop all other tasks and assist in fixing the bottleneck because it stops all system output.

- Releasing tasks for service or development should be scheduled according to the bottleneck pace.

- If efficient use of a bottleneck calls for batches of 100 units at a time, then all departments should subordinate to this constraint even if they prefer to prepare larger batches.

- Technical support people who assist the presale process should coordinate and subordinate their timetables to those of the senior salespeople, who are the organization's bottleneck.

Subordination Mechanisms

Subordinating noncritical resources to an organizational constraint can be achieved using the following mechanisms:

- Tactical gating
- Drum-Buffer-Rope (DBR)

Tactical Gating

To ensure maximum system performance, the constraint must work efficiently and effectively. Subordinating the rest of the system to the constraint is achieved via a mechanism of releasing tasks into the system. This is the tactical gating mechanism. Tactical gating means the controlled release of tasks (jobs) to the system. To assure efficient operation of the bottleneck, the tactical gating mechanism should employ the following policy:

1. All tasks should be released for work in the *right batch size* (see Chapter 11).

2. Only tasks screened by the strategic gating process should be released for workup.

3. All tasks should be released only through the body or person in charge of the gating (the gater). A task that has not been released by the gater should not be processed.

4. All tasks (in development, medical service, production) should enter the system with a *complete kit* (see Chapter 12).

5. All tasks should enter according to an appropriate *scheduling mechanism*, for example the DBR.

Drum-Buffer-Rope

The DBR mechanism presented in Figure 5.3 is a scheduling mechanism for entering tasks into the system (Goldratt and Cox, 2004; Schragenheim and Ronen, 1990). It is appropriate for production, R&D, service industries, and health care systems.

Drum   The drum provides the rhythm for the flow of tasks through the system. The system constraint determines the rate at which tasks should enter the system and flow through it. In the presence of a resource constraint, the drum is the *work rate of the bottleneck*. In the case of a market constraint, the *rate of market demand* dictates the pace for the whole system. Thus, the rate of inserting tasks

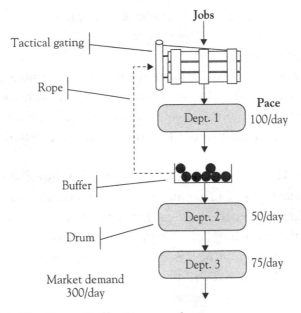

Figure 5.3 The Drum-Buffer-Rope mechanism

into the system is governed by the constraint and not by noncritical resources (see Chapter 9).

Buffer   A controlled quantity of tasks that accumulates before the bottleneck to assure it is fully utilized. The buffer serves to protect the system against fluctuations that arise from malfunctions and delays in the chain feeding the bottleneck. Such fluctuations can be caused by:

- Worker absenteeism
- Technical problems and human errors in the service or production process
- Low quality of information or materials
- No-shows of patients to the clinic or hospital
- Delays in the supply of raw materials and components

The buffer protects the bottleneck output from various fluctuations by assuring continuity of its operation. (See Chapter 14 for a discussion on fluctuations.)

The size of the buffer is measured in terms of bottleneck hours. To determine buffer size, we must examine the various fluctuations and time to correct them. For example, if 95 percent of fluctuations are handled within four hours, this time determines the buffer size.

Note: There is also an overflow buffer. In situations where there is a physical flow of materials, such as in production or logistics, malfunctions may occur in steps that come after the bottleneck. To protect the bottleneck throughput in such situations, additional storage capacity must be arranged for the outcome of the bottleneck in order to provide for a continuity of work. This storage capacity is the overflow buffer.

Rope   This is a *logical rope* that transfers information on the situation in the buffer to the tactical gating mechanism, which coordinates the release of tasks into the system. When the number of tasks in the buffer becomes smaller, additional tasks are released into the system:

- *DBR in an orthodontics clinic.* The orthodontists and clerical staff of the clinic schedule patient appointments so that the orthodontists (the bottleneck) are utilized and are not idle. They create a buffer of about a 15-minute wait for each orthodontist (about two patients waiting). If the buffer were larger, patients would complain about the excessive waiting. In this clinic, each orthodontist (the constraint) works in three parallel rooms. While he or she is seeing a patient in one room, the two other rooms serve as buffers where patients are waiting to be seen. In addition to the two buffer rooms, two additional patients are waiting in the waiting area. This only involves a 15-minute wait time on average for patients, but assures a high capacity utilization of the orthodontists.

To reduce potential fluctuations in patient arrivals, the clinic staff calls the patients the day before the scheduled appointment to confirm the appointment.

- *DBR in development.* DBR in development is designed so that assignments (activities, jobs) are released systematically. Each development person should have a buffer of assignments (about four to six working weeks). If some activity is stuck in the system (such as an incomplete kit caused by a specification change), the development person can continue with another activity. The gator releases the next assignment only if the developer has completed his previous assignments. See Chapters 10 and 21 for more details.

- *DBR in airports.* In airports, the runway infrastructure is a bottleneck. To assure that runways operate close to 100 percent capacity, arriving planes use the waiting circles above the airport, which serve as buffers. The buffer size depends on safety considerations. When the buffer is full, approaching aircraft are instructed to slow down their approach; circle in wider circles; or in extreme situations, are diverted to other airports. The control tower is responsible for gating. When a plane lands, it is immediately directed to a side road to allow another plane to land and another plane to enter the buffer.

- *DBR in sales.* In a multinational firm, every salesperson was in charge of 40 existing customers and 100 new potential customers. The company shifted to DBR scheduling of sales personnel. Today, they operate in a focused manner where the buffer is defined by a 10 + 10 approach: Every salesperson is in charge of managing and preserving 10 existing customers and 10 potential new customers.

Step 6—Elevate and Break the Constraint

The previous five steps of management by constraints dealt with increasing the output of a given system without making any changes in the system itself. Making *structural changes* in the system can *increase the effective capacity* of the bottleneck and increase the throughput of the whole system.

Elevating and breaking the constraint can be achieved in two ways:

1. Elevate by using capital investment
2. Elevate without investment through the use of an offloading mechanism

Elevate by Using Capital Investment

An effective increase in the capacity of the constraint through the acquisition of additional resources can be achieved in one of the following ways:

- Recruiting additional staff

- Purchasing additional equipment

- Working additional shifts

- Working overtime

- Hiring subcontractors

- Outsourcing

- Recruiting distributors and value-added retailers (VARs) for the salesforce

In the court system, judges can be a bottleneck. To elevate the constraints, paralegals may assist judges in routine activities.

A large insurance company was involved in numerous litigations over claims. The company attorneys became a bottleneck, so it started using the services of outside law firms.

Elevate without Investment through the Use of an Offloading Mechanism

Offload: *Relieving the load from the bottleneck by transferring some of the workload to noncritical resources.*

The offload process involves transfer of work from the constraint to noncritical resources that have excess capacity. From the system's perspective, it does not matter if these resources perform the task of the bottleneck at a slower pace than the bottleneck does. The important fact is that they contribute to the overall output. In some cases, the offload is achieved using structured processes that need lesser expertise.

In a large life insurance company, the underwriter had to check and approve every purchase request for life insurance policies. She was the bottleneck and caused delays that eventually led to the cancellation of some requests. She approved applications, made decisions about whether to sell proposed life insurance, and

(*continued*)

determined premiums. Her level of expertise was second to none. She was a scarce resource.

By training clerks and other employees to do some of her tasks, offloading was achieved. About 25 percent of the requests were rather standard and their approval process was structured and straightforward. Even though each case required a short processing time by the underwriter, offloading these cases to others released 15 percent of her time. This resulted in shorter response time for request approval and increased system output (Eden and Ronen, 1993).

In one plant of a large multinational company whose sales exceeded $1 billion per year, the packaging department was the cause of a bottleneck during peak time. To solve the problem, a second-hand packaging machine was purchased for a relatively low price. The second machine works parallel to the main machine for three weeks a year, and serves as an offload mechanism.

Additional examples:

- A dental hygienist relieves the dentist by performing some of the tasks.

- In a supermarket during peak times, the number of registers is a bottleneck. Adding packers at each register offloads some of the cashiers' work to a less expensive resource.

- In universities, teaching assistants and research assistants serve as an offload mechanism for the expensive resource of professors and senior researchers.

Step 7—If a Constraint Was Broken Return to Step 3. Do Not Let Inertia Become the System Constraint

If a constraint is broken, return to the step of identifying the new system constraint and not letting inertia become the system constraint. There is always a constraint (bottleneck) in a system. The task is to identify constraints, manage them, break them, and face a new constraint when it appears. By moving from constraint to constraint, system output increases. Figure 5.4 describes the improvement process in the surgical department of a hospital.

In routine processes, constraints do not change frequently and are rather stable. In one-time processes (projects, sales campaigns, and so on), constraints change rapidly and bottlenecks can move from one place to another.

Managerial inertia can be detrimental to organizational performance. An organization accustomed to a constraint being in one place, may occasionally behave as if the constraint was still there, even though improvement steps have already broken this constraint and moved it elsewhere.

In the previously mentioned example of Henry Ford, the resource constraint at the assembly line was broken, and the

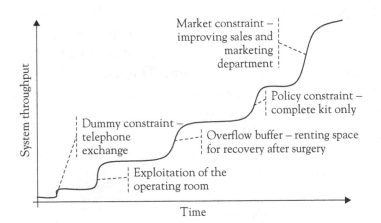

Figure 5.4 Continuous improvement in a surgical department

constraint became a market constraint. However, out of inertia, Ford's managers continued to focus on the efficient use of internal resources and did not view the market as the system constraint.

Curse of the Blessing

Using the techniques described in this book—such as management by constraints—may result in a rapid increase in throughput and a significant decrease in response times to customers, as well as an improvement in quality.

As a result of these improvements, an organization usually becomes more attractive to its customers and the demand for its services or products increases. Incautious management may lead a company to accepting commitments beyond its new effective capacity. This could lead to delays, operational difficulties, and cause a severe blow to a recently enhanced reputation. This is the *curse of the blessing*. When an organization achieves significant improvement, it must remain careful about increasing its commitments and always proceed gradually.

Summary

Management by constraints is the most advanced management theory today. It includes focusing steps that significantly increase system throughput within a short time by focusing on bottlenecks and other constraints. This methodology allows for significant improvement in areas such as, sales, marketing, service, R&D, and production in a relatively short time frame while using existing resources. The next chapter elaborates on this theory of constraints and how to use it when the market is the system constraint.

6

Managing by Constraints When the Market Is the Constraint

A system always has a constraint. In the previous chapter we discussed situations involving scarce resources where the constraints were these resources. There are many situations of excess operational capacity where the market becomes a system constraint. Proper use of the management by constraints methodology in these situations yields improvements in throughput, profits, and the value of the firm.

The steps of management by constraints in a system where the market is the constraint are the same as those where resources are constraints (Pass and Ronen, 2003):

- Determine the system's goal.

- Establish global performance measures.

- Identify the system constraint.

- Decide how to exploit the constraint and break dummy and policy constraints.

- Subordinate the system to the above decision (the constraint).

- Elevate and break the constraint.

- If a constraint was broken return to step 3. Do not let inertia become the system constraint.

Steps 1 through 3, where the goal and performance measures are defined and the system bottleneck is identified, are common to both resource and market constraints. The essence of steps 4 through 6 in both situations is similar, but the methods and tools for handling market constraints are different from those that are appropriate for a resource constraint. Here too, step 4 (exploiting the constraint) can be implemented immediately. Step 5 is implemented in the intermediate term. Step 6 requires introducing more substantial changes to the system and is therefore a step aimed at the medium to long term.

Treating a *market constraint* is more difficult than treating a resource constraint. Managing an internal bottleneck offers management more control of what is happening in the inner circles of the organization, while some of the factors involved in handling market constraints are beyond the control of management.

Most organizations are faced with a market constraint. In today's fierce, global competition, it is wise to have excess capacity (or protective capacity) in production and service resources. Firms usually cannot afford a situation where the marketing and salesforce succeed in obtaining orders, while the operational factor is the constraint that prevents or delays the fulfillment of those orders.

Managing a market constraint is key for the success of many firms and businesses. The approaches presented in this chapter should be valuable tools for accomplishing this.

Step 4—Decide How to Exploit the Constraint and Break Policy and Dummy Constraints

Exploiting a market constraint means exploiting the existing market and the existing sales ability more efficiently and effectively. In other words, doing more using the existing resources. This exploitation can be achieved through efficient operation of marketing and sales strategy effectiveness, while breaking policy and dummy constraints

Figure 6.1 Exploiting a market constraint

(see Figure 6.1). This implies the need to strike the existing market and achieve maximum profit from existing and potential customers and products using existing personnel.

Marketing and Sales Efficiency

Exploiting Marketing and Sales Personnel

Marketing and sales personnel are usually permanent bottlenecks. As such, we must exploit them and utilize their time:

- Salesforce garbage time must be reduced. Sales personnel are frequently busy dealing with logistical problems, time-consuming efforts to follow up on orders, and so on. The time spent on these tasks must be reduced.

- Sales and marketing operations should be *structured* with stable and simple processes. There are many cases where marketing and sales processes are not congruent with organizational needs or the market. The introduction of a new service or product may suffer from incomplete and disorderly marketing and from the fact that information does not reach all relevant parties. There are many examples in which customers are the ones who update the cashiers about various promotions.

Improving Response to Market Needs

- *Reduce response times in price bids, sales, and marketing.* The contribution of sales to profits can be improved by shortening response times of preparing tenders, along with other marketing and sales processes. Despite the common claim that every customer is different, or every product is unique, there is room for improving work processes to be uniform for every similar class of customers. The process of Request for Quotations (RFQ) for customers, especially in response to bids, must be structured, simple, and clear.

- *Shorten the Time to Market (TTM) of services and products.* A shorter TTM of new products and services enables a company to reach customers faster than the competition, and allows customers to realize better prices. Operational efficiency may enhance sales. Submitting bids with fast quoted lead times for a product or service, often makes the organization more attractive to customers and could increase its sales profits.

- *Improve service or product quality.* Improvement in the service or production processes may increase the perceived value of the firm's products or services and could increase sales profits.

- *Reduce costs.* Operational efficiency, by the sales and marketing personnel as well as the operational bodies, can improve response times, quality, and system output.

The objective is to achieve, with existing resources and current costs, higher output, higher contributions, improved cash flow, and value enhancement for the firm. However, one must also evaluate the cost reduction. A careful cost analysis and decisions on cost containment in the right places can significantly improve cash flow. Cost savings can sometimes permit price reduction, which may improve a company's competitiveness. Chapter 17 discusses this further when we compare the *throughput world* to the *cost world*.

Marketing Strategy Effectiveness

The previous chapter introduced the concept of strategic gating to screen and prioritize customers or products based on their specific contribution or their positioning on the focusing matrix (easy-important). Even when an organization is at excess capacity and facing a market constraint, the sales and marketing personnel are the source of a permanent bottleneck. The potential demand for their services always exceeds their resources. There are always more potential customers, marketing initiatives, sales to existing customers, and offerings of new services or products than the sales and marketing personnel have time available. This screening procedure is, therefore, extremely important and enables companies to focus on products, services, or customers that make the highest specific contributions, increasing organizational performance and value.

As a result, we can state:

- Do not abandon sales of services or products to customers or markets where sales personnel are minimally involved, even if the contribution volume is not large. For example, repeat sales to existing customers should not be rejected, because most of the relevant marketing and sales efforts have already been completed. These are usually considered sales with a high specific contribution because they only require short investments of time by sales or marketing personnel.

- For sales of services or products, or for customers who require substantial investments of time, we need to perform a prioritization process of the strategic gating. The prioritization should be based on the ratio between the expected contribution of the sales and the amount of time needed by the sales and marketing personnel (the bottleneck) in order to reach these sales. Table 6.1 presents the calculation of the specific contributions of the various customers relative to the sales effort involved.

A salesperson should first approach the customer with the highest specific contribution. The top choice in this example is Company 2. The salesperson may then focus on Company 1, and so on, until he fills up 100 percent of his time. This analysis must also consider strategic considerations (see the three stage model in Chapter 16).

Strategic gating should also be performed on the variety of services and products sold by the organization. Experience shows

Table 6.1 The specific contribution of customers relative to the sales effort

Customer	Contribution to Profit ($)	Sales Effort (days)	Specific Contribution ($ per day)
Company 1	2,345,000	120	19,500
Company 2	5,600,000	30	186,700
Company 3	575,000	80	7,200
Company 4	12,650,000	500	2,500

that by focusing on a smaller number of services and products, it is possible to achieve a higher volume of contributions. Occasionally, it may be advisable to consider ceasing sales of services and products whose total contribution volume is negligible. Cessation of sales can be done in two ways:

1. Discontinue offering them to the market.

2. If there is concern that the market will not react positively to cessation of sales, then *raise* the price of the product. If there is no demand at the new price, the product will fade away. However, if demand persists, then the higher price will increase profits. This situation may reveal that the previous price was too low. There are many cases where raising the price did not diminish demand, but rather increased it.

Note: It is common to think that stopping sales of certain products or of a product line may decrease sales of the entire line. Every situation must be examined specifically. With proper planning it is usually possible to increase profits.

Using Excellence in Response Times and Quality as a Strategic Leverage

Japanese firms have captured the world market in cars and home electronics through the quality of the products. Their operational excellence, which enabled high quality with low production costs, fast response times, and low inventories, established a strategic advantage in the eyes of the customer who is willing to pay a premium for *made in Japan*.

Superb operational ability must not rely on low costs and competitive operating expenses. The challenge is to bring the excellence in quality and operations to establish a strategic advantage for the organization.

> The computer manufacturer Dell has achieved fast response times and low inventory costs through efficient operations and logistics management. As a result, it captured a large market share of personal computers and servers.
>
> The Sony Corporation has been able to charge its customers a substantial premium for the perceived quality of its products in comparison to the competition's.

Prioritizing in Bid/No-Bid Processes

In companies where the majority of sales are completed through participation in bids, there must be an important step of deciding whether to respond to a bid. This process is known as bid/no-bid (or go/no-go). The bids should be evaluated according to their compatibility with the company strategy, the chances of winning, and the potential contribution to profits. Tenders that do not meet the criteria should be answered with a no-bid, thus preventing unnecessary effort by the permanent bottlenecks of the system (marketing and sales personnel, technical experts). A policy where an organization responds positively (bid) to every request becomes a policy constraint (see also Chapter 20).

Breaking Policy and Dummy Constraints

In order to increase the contribution volume of sales, we must identify policy and dummy constraints that interfere with the organization's efforts to cope with the market:

- *Avoid the blind use of traditional cost accounting.* As we shall see in Chapter 15, the blind use of classical pricing can harm the organization. There are organizations where the selling price is built on cost+. The desire to *always* have the selling price above the costs (including indirect costs) may lead to erroneous decisions and loss of business opportunities.

- *Avoid giving up small customer orders.* There is no reason to reject small customers or small orders that do not take up much time of the sales and marketing bottlenecks.

- *Avoid selling only complete sets (assortments).* Certain industries (e.g., shoes and clothing) tend to sell to stores in complete sets only. These sets have a predetermined assortment of styles and sizes. However, preparing a specified, nonstandard, assortment according to the needs of a specific store does not take up much bottleneck time, so there is no reason not to sell what the customer wants. It is wise to continuously study demand patterns in order to update the composition of standard sets to the actual market demand.

- *Avoid selling a complete product line or nothing.* There are companies with a policy of selling customers an entire basket of services or products, or nothing at all. In many case, selling a partial basket can yield nice profits.

- *Avoid rewarding sales personnel by sales volume.* This is one of the most common incentives or rewards in sales; however, it encourages the salesforce to maximize sales volume but not necessarily the total contribution to profits. There is a need to shift to a reward and measurement system so that profit or contribution volume plays the major role.

- *Avoid rewarding salespeople regardless of returns or cancellations.* This policy encourages salespeople to sign as many contracts with customers as possible without checking

their real need and their ability to pay. This policy
constraint can be rectified by rewarding the salesforce
by *actual* contribution volume (subtracting returns
and cancellation) and only after payments have been
received.

- *Avoid dummy constraints*. For example, lack of a fax
  machine or other communication mode for sales
  personnel.

Breaking policy and dummy constraints like those discussed
previously is an important factor in increasing an organization's
profits.

Step 5—Subordinate the Rest of the System to the Previous Decision (the Constraint)

There is an obvious advantage for organizations that meet customers' needs better than the competition. In a situation with a market
constraint, the organization must *subordinate the whole system to the
market,* meaning that every member of the organization must subordinate himself to the market and its needs. Some dimensions of
subordination are:

- *Customization to customer demands and needs*. In a
  competitive market there is a need to customize services and products to the various needs of customers.
  Customization is important and especially worthwhile
  when it does not require development or marketing
  resources, but only efforts from operational entities
  that are not bottlenecks. When customization requires
  some development, strategic gating should help decision makers decide how to best utilize the constrained
  development resources.

A producer of telecommunication equipment decided to exert a differential customization policy. It designed new products according to the requirements of it's A customers. The requests of its B customers were incorporated into a road map for future versions of standard products. C customers would be able to buy only existing standard products.

- *Fast response to customer needs.* To beat the competition, adjust to the due date required by the customer and subordinate the whole system to the market timetable.

- *Direct link to the end customer.* Establishing a direct link with the end customer is especially important in those cases where the organization uses external distributors to sell its services and products. The organization must then establish a permanent communications process to determine the needs of the distributors and end customers. It is worthwhile to make an effort to establish a connection with the end customers by bypassing the hurdles of the distribution channels and agents. For example, if a hospital or clinic has referrals from HMOs or other insurance companies, the hospital should establish a direct link with the insured to fully understand their needs.

- *Adjusting the organizational structure to customer types or customer needs.* To better serve the market, make sure that the organizational structure is compatible with customer needs. Occasionally, the organizational structure is based on a geographical segmentation or is geared toward achieving operational efficiency. It may be better to redesign the structure to reflect different customer types. For example, a business/organizational

structure with divisions for different customers: gov-
ernmental customers, large customers, Small Office
Home Office (SOHO) customers, or household customers where each division provides all services to its
customers.

- *Subordinating technology to market needs.* High-tech
  organizations have a constant conflict between marketing and development departments. Many technological
  organizations were built on technological know-how
  and development breakthroughs. In such situations,
  development may occasionally dictate organizational
  road maps (see also Chapter 21). Development and
  technology must be subordinated to the market via marketing personnel. Defining services and products should
  be done in harmony between marketing and development, but subordination should always be to the market.

- *Market segmentation and product differentiation.* In case
  of excess capacity, an organization can meet specific
  demands of different market segments by product and
  price differentiation. This allows channeling of excess
  operational capacity toward generating additional
  profits (Goldratt, 1990). It is essential to assure the
  cooperation and goodwill of operations staff, as this
  segmentation causes additional managerial complexity
  for them (see Chapter 16).

Step 6—Elevate and Break the Constraint

In this step, examine how to increase the contribution from sales
or services by creating *added value* to existing customers, introducing new products or services, approaching new markets, identifying
new customers, combining marketing with new sales channels, and
strategic cooperation.

This step requires establishing a *focused strategy*. Occasionally, in situations with a market constraint, organizations may be tempted to shoot in all directions, cast a wide net and wait until the fish are caught. Such a policy can waste the sales and marketing bottleneck. In contrast, a focused policy that targets the main objectives and focuses efforts on these targets usually yields better outcomes.

To elevate and break the market constraint:

1. *Establish a focused strategy.* A focused strategy is necessary for increasing profit. For details, see Chapter 18.
2. *Enter a new product or market.* Mergers and acquisitions of firms that have appropriate products or markets is a relatively fast way to gain throughput.
3. *Add marketing and sales channels.* Examples of adding marketing and sales channels might include new distributors, selling to private labels, Original Equipment Manufacturer (OEM), Value-Added Reseller (VAR), or entering the world of e-business.
4. *Practice market segmentation and product differentiation.* Every market segment has different needs and requirements. Products and services must be adapted according to targeted segments.
5. *Stretch the brand.* Stretching the brand implies taking advantage of the success of one brand to create a family of related or similar products to sell under the same brand.
6. *Create added value for the customer.* In this category we can include product features that add perceived value to the customer, such as, creating a package of complementary services and products, managing the customer's facilities, shifting to outsourcing of customer activities, managing inventory for the customer, building customer loyalty (customer clubs) or Customer Relationships Management (CRM).
7. *Build cooperation and strategic alliances.*

Step 7—If a Constraint Was Broken, Return to Step 3. Do Not Let Inertia Become the System Constraint

If the constraint is broken, look for the next constraint and manage the system accordingly. In some situations a resource constrained system loses some demand and becomes a system with excess capacity (i.e., a market constraint). The reverse is also true: a market-constrained system serving the customers with short lead time and excellent quality may increase its demand and become a bottleneck.

For example, a company with a market constraint (excess capacity in operations) improved its response time by targeting its products and services to a specific group of customers, thereby gaining a significant increase in throughput and sales. The constraint was turned into a resource constraint and the company focused on the internal bottleneck.

Managing Marketing and Sales

Focusing on Most Valuable Customers (MVCs) as a Value Driver

Investing in marketing and sales efforts to existing and potential customers leads to increase in throughput. To make the best use of their scarce time, marketing and sales personnel should focus on existing and potential customers with high specific contributions. These customers are *Most Valuable Customers* (MVCs).

MVCs are type A customers in the Pareto analysis of the organization—about 20 percent of customers (existing and potential) that contribute 80 percent of contribution volume.

> In a multinational company, salespeople handled 40 existing customers and about 100 potential customers. The firm adopted a policy of focused management and shifted to a 10 + 10 approach: every salesperson now handles sales and retention for 10 existing customers and tries to approach 10 new customers. This new approach resulted in an immediate increase in throughput.

Such focusing enables better response to the needs of MVCs by:

- Establishing tight personal contacts with influential people in the customer organization.

- Collecting and analyzing data about the customer and relevant markets.

- Providing special service to MVCs in all units of the organization (red-carpet or VIP treatment).

- Analyzing the needs of MVCs and identifying channels for providing more *value to the customer.*

- Determining customer policy.

- Employing risk management vis-à-vis the customer.

- Applying structured management of meetings with the customer.

- Using structured management of contracts with the customer.

It is nearly impossible to give such VIP treatment to all customers, but if salespeople focus on MVCs, the result should be increase in profits.

Peak Management

The application of the management by constraints theory may help reduce the effect of peak-time loads. Appropriate management of such systems requires differential policies for peak and dip periods, such as differential pricing of products or services during different times. The reduction of temporary loads during peak times can be achieved using the following steps (Ronen and others, 2001):

1. *Stretching peak times:* This allows work to be spread over a longer period. For example, to overcome the load created at

busy intersections during peak hours, earlier work start times were established at one company, while opening times for nearby schools were delayed (see also Chapter 11).

2. *Capacity planning.* Usually, planning capacities is based on average loads, which can result in excess capacity during slow periods and resource constraints during peak periods. Good planning should provide for adequate service and performance at all times. Strategic decisions about capacity planning should reduce or even prevent excessive peak-time loads. Examples of situations that benefit from this kind of planning are staffing in fast food restaurants, planning the number of tellers in a bank, or the number of cashiers in a busy supermarket. Planning should provide the infrastructure for peak times and a mechanism for adjusting the level of labor to the load.

3. *Transferring load to low load periods.* An appropriate pricing or reward policy can divert some of the demand to low load periods. Some examples that demonstrate this idea are the pricing policies of airlines and phone companies.

4. *Using temporary help.* Peak times are characterized by the lack of production or service resources during certain distinct periods. Using temporary help can remedy these situations. Tax firms hire temporary help during tax season; restaurants hire temporary help during lunch breaks; and in some movie theaters, ushers and cashiers assist the snack-bar employees during peak times.

In a work environment with obvious peak times, some resources operate at excess capacity most of the time and at a shortage of capacity during peak times. As a result, management must handle two types of policies: one for times of excess capacity and one for times of shortages. In hospital emergency departments (EDs) there are sometimes large variations in patient arrival rates between day and night. These EDs have excess capacity (day ED) on the one hand, and a resource constraints (night ED) on the other hand, and should be managed accordingly.

Where Should the Constraint Be Located?

The location of the system constraint is an important strategic issue. Until now, we have considered situations with a given system and the goals to improve that system. In order to strategically place the constraint, we must consider three strategic questions about the resources of the organization:

1. Where should the constraint be located?
2. Where is the constraint located now?
3. How can we transfer the constraint to the proper place?

The first question, "Where should the constraint be located?" can be broken down into two parts:

1. Does the constraint have to be internal (resource constraint) or external (market constraint)?
2. If the constraint is a resource constraint, then which resource has to be the constraint?

The advantages of placing the constraint in the system as an internal bottleneck are obvious—savings in resources, control over demand, and control over the system. These advantages translate into the ability to sort and screen orders, customers, services, and products and into better control of planning and implementation. In this case, the cost of the system and the cost of operating it are relatively low. However, the firm may miss out on business opportunities due to the lack of capacity, and this may allow competitors to enter the market which poses a threat to the organization in the long run. Choosing a resource constraint is most appropriate for firms with critical and expensive resources, or capacity that is difficult to increase. Management should decide wether to have a market constraint or a resource constraint.

If the chosen constraint is a resource constraint, then it should be the most critical or most expensive resource in the system.

In most cases in today's competitive market, the resource constraint should not be located in operations. Operations can usually be expanded or subcontracted. Whenever the production process is a standard one, operations should not be a system constraint. The head of operations in a business firm should make operations *transparent* to decision makers, that is, he should see to it that the needed quantities are produced on the predetermined timetables and at the required quality. Operations may then contribute its share to strategy and to the success of the firm. Realizing good and effective operations and achieving transparency is a difficult mission. On top of it, operations' resources should have protective, and even excess, capacity. Through accumulated experience, managers at production plants in Japan have realized this, and they are designing their production lines with an excess capacity of about 30 percent. It is clear that protective capacity is just one way to create transparent operations. The appropriate use of the managerial approaches described in earlier chapters is a necessary condition for achieving a situation where operations is not a system constraint.

Choosing to have a market constraint means that the organization decided to carry excess capacity. Usually, an organization with excess capacity should not give up on orders or on possibilities for increasing output. Excess capacity can also help the firm deal with occasional demands, large contracts, and exploit market opportunities.

Choosing a market constraint carries a higher price tag because of the investment in resources. A market constraint is more appropriate for organizations where resource costs are not high.

Additionally, an organization must examine whether research and development, or marketing and sales are actually permanent bottlenecks. In situations where these departments are not bottlenecks, the causes should be examined at strategic and tactical levels.

Summary

Sales and marketing personnel are permanent bottlenecks. To increase their output we must make them more efficient and effective. Efficiency can be achieved by reducing the noneffective time of the salesforce. Effectiveness can be achieved by focusing on most valuable customers through strategic gating. The seven steps of management by constraints, in addition to product differentiation and market segmentation, can increase the contribution of sales and enhance the value of the organization.

7

Focused Current Reality Tree

A current reality tree (CRT) is a focusing tool based on logical thinking (Dettmer, 1998; Goldratt, 1994). This tool is used to identify *core problems* in an organization. The underlying assumption is that each organization has a few core problems, with most other problems being symptoms of those core problems. If we solve the core problems, then many of the other problems will be solved as well.

The objectives of this tool:

- Identify the core problems of the organization, the system, or the subsystem.

- Deepen the understanding that every system has a *small* number of core problems, which are the cause of *most* problems.

- Establish communication channels among managers in an organization.

When a patient goes to his doctor for a check-up and complains about various symptoms (headaches, perspiration, high fever), a good doctor tries to find the patient's core problems and treat them.

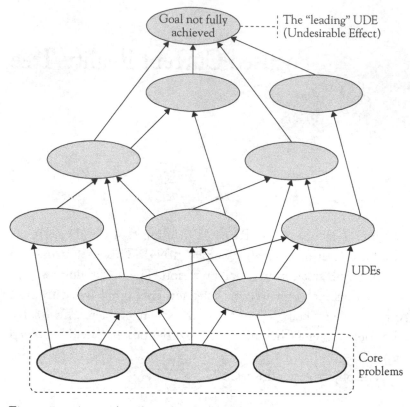

Figure 7.1 A template for a focused Current Reality Tree

Focused current reality tree (fCRT): *A graphic manage-rial tool that helps identify the core problems of a system or organization.*

An fCRT displays a logical tree showing cause-effect relations among problems of an organization (see Figure 7.1).

Principles of a Focused Current Reality Tree

An fCRT can be constructed by a single manager or by a team. Because the tool is subjective, and because organizational problems look different from different perspectives, it is better to have the fCRT constructed by a team of managers and workers. Occasionally, an fCRT may be constructed by an outside consulting group that has been called in to diagnose the organization's problems.

Information Sources

The information sources for constructing an fCRT are:

- Personal knowledge of managers and workers

- Interviews with managers and workers

- Site visits at the firm or organization

- Balance sheets, marketing reports, operations reports, and other organizational reports

- Interviews with customers and suppliers

Undesirable Effects

For a phenomenon to be considered an undesirable effect (UDE) and to be included in the fCRT, three conditions must be satisfied:

1. The phenomenon must *exist.*
2. The phenomenon must be *undesirable.*
3. The phenomenon must be *under our control or influence*

The third condition is especially important. A statement like "the exchange rate of the dollar versus the euro is too high" does not enter the analysis as a UDE—we have no control over the currency exchange rate. However, "lack of protection against currency risks" might be considered as a UDE.

Additionally, there are phenomena beyond our control, but we can influence them. "Many customers leave the company" is a legitimate UDE. Competition can affect desertion, but we have a strong *influence* on customer desertion.

Undesirable effects should always be written as *negative* statements.

Leading Undesirable Effect

A list of UDEs should always include the *leading UDE*, which states that we are not achieving our goal. In business organizations, the leading UDE could be expressed as: "The value of the firm is not sufficiently enhanced" or "Goal is not fully achieved." All UDEs in an fCRT should relate to the leading UDE. A UDE is a particular issue that contributes to the leading UDE of not achieving the goal.

For the analysis using the fCRT to be simple and fast, we should limit our focus to 8 to 14 UDEs.

Brainstorming, interviewing, and the examination of documents and reports may help suggest UDEs for your list. Reduce the number of UDEs by:

- Aggregating similar UDEs under one broad category

- Deleting UDEs that are less important relative to others on the list

Logical Relations of Undesirable Effects

Cause-effect relation between UDEs can be depicted by an arrow leading from the UDE that is the *cause* to the UDE that is the *effect* (Figure 7.2). An example of a cause-effect relation is presented in Figure 7.3.

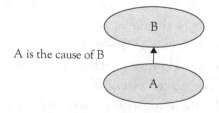

A is the cause of B

Figure 7.2 Cause-effect relation between UDEs

Figure 7.3 Example: Cause-effect relation between UDEs

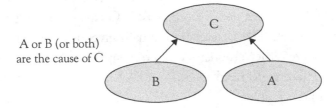

Figure 7.4 Logical relation of extensive OR

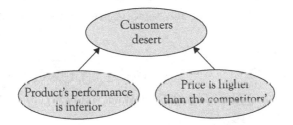

Figure 7.5 Example: An extensive OR logical relation

An *extensive OR relation* is presented in Figure 7.4. When an extensive OR relationship exists, and when *both* UDE A *and* UDE B exist, then the effect is much more severe than in a situation where only one of them would be the cause for UDE C.

When our prices are higher than competitors' prices, customers desert us. When the performance of our products is inferior, customers desert. If both UDEs (high price *and* poor performance) occur at the same time, even more customers desert the system (Figure 7.5).

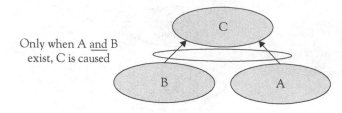

Only when A <u>and</u> B
exist, C is caused

Figure 7.6 Logical AND relation

An AND relation, as presented in Figure 7.6, is relevant in situations only when A and B both exist – C exists. The advantage in identifying AND logical relations usually gives us enough information to solve either problem A or problem B, and to avoid problem C. There is no need to deal with both A and B. Figure 7.7 presents an example.

The contribution volume drops as a result of combining two UDEs simultaneously: the contribution per unit drops, and the number of units sold does not increase. Sometimes, dealing with one of these UDEs is enough to solve the problem of decreasing contribution volume.

A *loop relation*—UDE A is the cause of UDE B. UDE B is the cause of UDE C, and UDE C is the cause of UDE A—is depicted in Figure 7.8. An example of a loop relation is presented in Figure 7.9.

Inferences

Inferences are explanations or conclusions and insights that are not included in the list of UDEs. These are usually logical relations

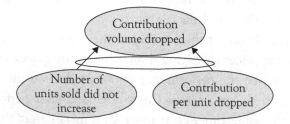

Figure 7.7 Example: An AND logical relation

A is the reason for B,
B is the reason for C, and
C is the reason for A

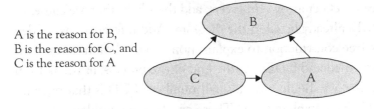

Figure 7.8 Logical loop relation

Figure 7.9 Example: Loop relation

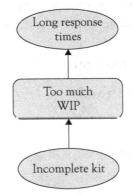

Figure 7.10 Example: Inference

that explain nontrivial relations among UDEs. These relations are
drawn as rectangles (see Figure 7.10).

Constructing a Focused Current Reality Tree

Construction of an fCRT begins with the leading UDE. Then
position all UDEs that have been identified as direct causes of the
leading UDE underneath the leading UDE. These should be linked

with cause-effect arrows. In layers, add the UDEs that are causes of the UDEs already listed in the diagram. Add inferences as needed during tree construction to explain nontrivial relations among insights learned and UDEs. At the end of the process, at the bottom of the tree, we should have a small number of UDEs that have no other UDEs to explain them. These are the core problems.

Core Problems

The number of core problems is usually small, around one to three. If you end up with a larger number of UDEs at the bottom of the tree, try to think of factors or issues that could be causing them. These extra UDEs should be listed under the previous ones and connected to them by causal links. This should lead you to the real core problems. Core problems can be either UDEs or inferences (conclusions of the team constructing the fCRT).

Examples of core problems in organizations:

- "Management is too centralized."

- "Lack of a clear strategy."

- "Unstructured processes."

- "Inappropriate performance measures."

- "Lack of focus."

- "The company is driven by technological thinking rather than by business thinking."

- "There is a gap between professional and managerial abilities."

Orthogonal control is an independent check regarding the identification of core problems. After the core problems have been identified, we must ask the question: "If we solve the core problems, does the leading UDE change significantly?"

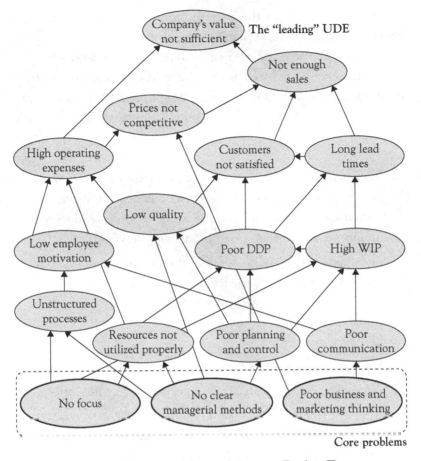

Figure 7.11 Example: Typical focused Current Reality Tree

For example, one core problem identified in an fCRT was lack of focus. Does solving this problem significantly enhance the value of the firm? If the answer is yes, then this is a core problem that must be dealt with. If not, the tree should be reexamined. Figure 7.11 presents a typical fCRT.

Advantages and Disadvantages of the fCRT

In positive terms, the fCRT is a simple tool that helps management identify and focus on core problems. It encourages better communication within the organization and enables distinction between a symptom (UDE) and a core problem.

Negatively, the fCRT is a subjective tool. However, this disadvantage can be reduced when the fCRT is constructed by a team, especially if the team is interdisciplinary. Orthogonal control also helps diminish this disadvantage. Routine use of the fCRT involves:

1. Collecting information about the problems in the organization by using personal knowledge of managers, interviews with managers and workers, site visits, reports and documents, and interviews with customers and suppliers.

2. Articulating the leading UDE of the organization. In a business organization, the leading UDE may be "value of the organization is not sufficiently enhanced." In other organizations, refer to the organizational goal and state the leading UDE accordingly.

3. Listing the main UDEs (usually 8 to 14 of them).

4. Arranging the UDEs in cause-effect relations where the leading UDE is at the top.

5. Identifying the core problems of the organization or unit (not more than three).

6. Applying orthogonal control. Ask yourself, "Does solving each of the identified core problems significantly improve the leading UDE?"

7. Making a list of action items that deal with the core problems. Use a focusing table and matrix.

Summary

An fCRT is a simple tool for detecting core problems in organizations. The use of this tool helps organizations identify their own small number of core problems and realize that solving these core problems would enhance the value of their organization. The fCRT also serves as a communication tool within the organization. Because this is a subjective tool, it is recommended that the fCRT be constructed by interdisciplinary teams.

8

Resolving Managerial Conflicts

Webster's dictionary defines conflict as "a prolonged struggle; a trial of strength; strong disagreement." In this chapter, we focus on those managerial conflicts where opposing alternatives have a *common goal.*

Conflict: *A clash between two alternative actions with a common goal.*

Common managerial conflicts:

- Decentralization versus centralization. Example: Decentralization of marketing and sales to various divisions versus centralization of marketing and sales to the company's headquarters.

- Focusing on a large variety of services or products versus focusing on a limited number.

- Maintaining large inventories versus maintaining small inventories.

- Developing a generic product in the future versus developing a specific product now because of requests by customers.

- Implementing a project structure versus implementing a matrix structure.

Use the steps to deal with managerial conflicts:

1. Describe the conflict with a conflict resolution diagram (CRD) (Goldratt, 1994).
2. Challenge the assumptions of the CRD with the following approaches:

   —Differentiation

   —Globalization

   —Breaking assumptions
3. Create actions for implementation based on the challenged assumptions.

One company is considering offering a broad line of services and products versus offering a limited variety. Both alternatives have their own advantages. Offering a large variety could improve throughput and enhance the company's value. Offering only a limited variety may allow the company to focus, specialize, and reduce costs. Both alternatives create value for the company, and the common goal is, of course, value enhancement.

A conflict is sometimes handled by searching for a compromise using various optimization techniques. Figure 8.1. summarizes approaches that may be used to deal with conflicts. In the previous example, an optimization tool may suggest an exact optimal solution—offering, for example, exactly 346 stock keeping units (SKUs). Using such a solution could cause the company to lose the advantage it might gain through diversification with a large variety and the focusing and quality achieved with a small variety.

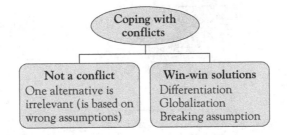

Figure 8.1 Resolving conflicts

The suggested methodology solves conflicts in one of two ways:

1. Generates a solution that preserves most of the advantages and reduces the disadvantages of each alternative. This is a win-win approach, which can be achieved through differentiation, globalization, and by breaking assumptions. Identifying such situations is not assured, but experience shows us that it is usually possible.
2. Presents one alternative as irrelevant or based on wrong assumptions. This converts the situation into one without any real conflict.

Figure 8.1 summarizes the approaches used to resolve conflicts.

Three-Step Methodology

Describe the Conflict with a Conflict Resolution Diagram

The CRD is an important communication tool used to present conflicts and to try to resolve them (Figure 8.2). The following elements appear in the CRD:

- The goal of the system or subsystem

- The two alternatives that create the conflict

- The assumptions about advantages of each alternative, or the need for each, based on the system's goal

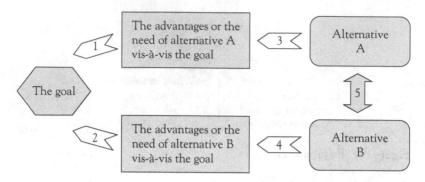

Figure 8.2 Conflict resolution diagram

The various elements are logically linked: Arrows 1, 2, 3, and 4 represent conditional relations, while arrow 5 depicts the alleged impossibility of simultaneously satisfying both alternatives.

Assumptions in the CRD are:

Assumption 1: The advantages of alternative A contribute toward achieving the goal.

Assumption 2: The advantages of alternative B contribute toward achieving the goal.

Assumption 3: Action based on alternative A brings advantages toward achieving the goal.

Assumption 4: Action based on alternative B brings advantages toward achieving the goal.

Assumption 5: Alternatives A and B *cannot* be acted on simultaneously.

Figure 8.3 presents the CRD from the products/services variety example.

Challenge the Assumptions of the Conflict Resolution Diagram

We now discuss conflict resolution using one or more of the following tools:

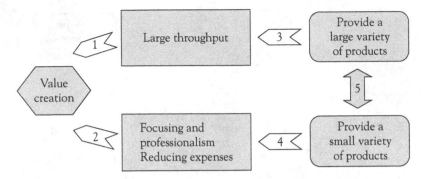

Figure 8.3 Conflict resolution diagram for product variety

- Differentiation

- Globalization

- Breaking of assumptions

Differentiation

An illustration of the conflict resolution of the previous product variety example using a differentiation mechanism follows.

A Pareto analysis of the various products shows that 20 percent of the products account for 80 percent of the company's contribution to profits. According to policy, the customers are offered the entire variety of products. However, the products of group A in the Pareto analysis are provided by the company *itself*, while group B and C products are provided through a *subcontractor*.

Globalization

A large public organization needs to renew part of its fleet of cars. The conflict is whether to buy less expensive cars, or more expensive and reliable ones. The CRD for this example is presented in Figure 8.4.

When we look at car purchases from a global perspective, we should assess the life cycle cost (LCC) of the fleet. This is an

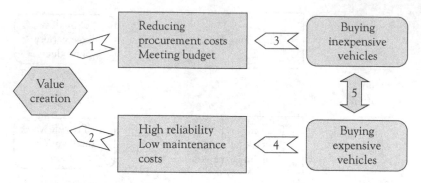

Figure 8.4 Example: A car fleet CRD

expansion of the system (globalization) across time. Analysis shows that from the LCC perspective, buying the expensive cars actually saves money. Because of high maintenance costs, fuel costs, and the high mileage these cars are expected to drive, the purchase price is only a small part of the LCC. The budget constraint problem is also resolved by spreading payments out over a period of several years. In this example, the alternative of buying inexpensive cars is proven to be irrelevant since it is obviously inferior, so there is no conflict.

Breaking Assumptions

Mechanisms for *breaking assumptions* offer a way to check the assumptions that exist in every CRD:

Assumption 1: Advantages of alternative A contribute to the goal.

Assumption 2: Advantages of alternative B contribute to the goal.

Assumption 3: Choosing alternative A brings out the advantages noted.

Assumption 4: Choosing alternative B brings out the advantages noted.

Assumption 5: It is *not* possible to act concurrently according to both alternatives A and B.

The development department of a software company is creating a special version of an existing product for a specific customer. Two questions discussed in a heated conflict during a customer-management meeting were: "Should we start development imme-diately?" or "Should we first spend time to define the project in an orderly and structured manner?" This conflict is presented in (Figure 8.5).

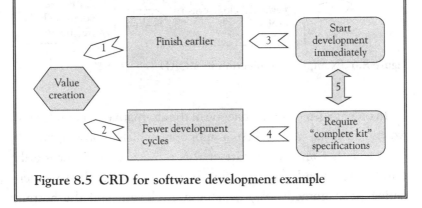

Figure 8.5 CRD for software development example

Assumptions at the basis of this conflict are:

1. An early completion of the project enhances the value of the firm.
2. Development in fewer cycles enhances the value of the firm.
3. If we start the project earlier, we finish it earlier.
4. If we provide orderly definitions for requested changes and the differentiation requirements of the customer, then development can be conducted using fewer development cycles.
5. It is not possible to start the development immediately and provide complete definitions in a structured manner at the same time.

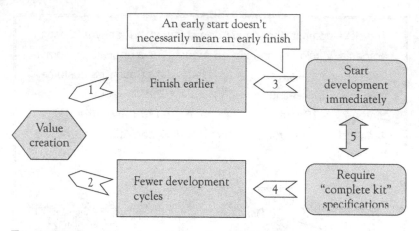

Figure 8.6 Example: An injection in a CRD

In order to demonstrate that one of the alternatives is not relevant, we try to break the weakest assumption, which is assumption 3. It is clear that an earlier start of this project doesn't necessarily translate to an earlier completion. If this is the case, the top alternative (start immediately) is actually irrelevant and the bottom one should be chosen.

Resolving a conflict by breaking an assumption is called *injection*. The injection added to the CRD is shown in Figure 8.6.

Create Actions for Implementation Based on the Challenged Assumptions

Using the focusing table and the focusing matrix, create an action plan to resolve the conflict.

Steps to follow in the routine use of the conflict resolution approach include:

1. Define the goal of the system or subsystem.
2. Display the conflict in a CRD.
3. Try to resolve the conflict by differentiation, globalization, or by breaking assumptions.

4. When breaking assumptions, add injection(s) to the CRD.
5. Make a list of action items that resolve the conflict. Make use of the focusing table and matrix.

Summary

Managerial conflicts stem from seemingly contradictory action alternatives that share common objective functions. Many conflicts can be resolved either through reaching win-win solutions or by concluding that one alternative is irrelevant.

Conflict resolution can be achieved by displaying the conflict on a CRD and analysis of the CRD using differentiation, globalization, and assumption breaking.

9

The Efficiencies Syndrome

In previous chapters, we've seen that bottlenecks, critical resources of the organization, must be exploited and that other resources must be subordinated to the constraint.

Experience has taught us that the management of noncritical resources of an organization is usually associated with a painful policy failure (a policy constraint) known as the *efficiencies syndrome* (see Goldratt and Cox, 2004). This situation is common among managers and workers in all types of organizations (service, industry, health, development, and not-for-profit organizations).

Efficiencies syndrome: *A situation where there is a desire to operate noncritical resources more than is needed, while emphasizing the utilization of inputs rather than focusing on outputs.*

The *efficiencies syndrome* is illustrated by the *1–2–3 process* in Figure 9.1. Under current conditions, the output of this 1–2–3 process is 50 units per day, and the (capacity) utilization of the resources of the three departments is 50 percent, 100 percent, and 67 percent, respectively.

What happens if we measure the system by average resource utilization? The average utilization is 72 percent. To increase the average utilization, workers in department 1 are trying to reach

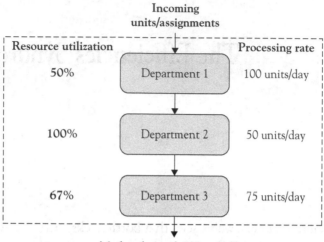

Market demand: 300 units/day

Figure 9.1 A 1–2–3 process and department utilization

100 percent maximum resource utilization. As a result, average utilization increases to 90 percent. The workers in department 3 are also trying to increase utilization to 100 percent, but they are limited by what department 2 (the bottleneck) supplies to them.

Even though the measure of average resource utilization has increased, the system output has not. However, exploiting the other resources may result in undesirable effects on the system:

- People work harder without increasing effective output.

- Control over what is important deteriorates.

- The quality of decisions decreases.

- The amount of work in process increases.

- Resources (personnel, materials, and equipment) are wasted.

- Expenditures are increased.

- Output is decreased.

- Working harder with less output may lead to a loss of confidence in management.

Sometimes, the efficiencies syndrome may result in:

- Workers who must work or at least look like they are working because Western culture views an idle person as lazy

- Fear of being transferred or laid off

- Lack of a global vision and a belief that fully utilizing resources contributes to achieving goals

- Lack of distinction between critical resources (bottle-necks) and noncritical resources

- Feeling that purchasing equipment or hiring personnel must be justified

- Measuring systems by inputs (as is reflected in local premiums and norms)

- Measuring systems by resource utilization

- Desire to look important and busy

A newly hired engineer in a high-tech company needs another computer. Management declined the request because the utilization of the other computers was low and it was assumed that several operators could share a computer. Because the request was declined, one of the engineers spent time writing an application to duplicate files, just to increase the utilization of the existing computers in the hope of justifying the need for another one.

A worker in another firm told the following story: "In the morning we throw the garbage from the garbage cans onto the floor and

(continued)

start sweeping the floor so that when the boss arrives he sees that we are busy."

A large organization experienced the *neon effect*. All workers were eager to demonstrate that they worked late. The office neon lights stay on until the late hours of the evening (even when workers are not there). The number of hours that the offices were lighted was a measure of workers' diligence and their importance to the system. In this organization, it was known that some of the managers called their subordinates' offices at very late hours, without any necessity, just so the subordinates knew that the boss might be looking for them late in the day.

In a not-for-profit organization, all meetings begin at 10:00 p.m. because before that everybody is busy. . .

In a high-tech organization, management decided to evaluate the capacity utilization of newly purchased equipment. They generated comparative data on the utilization of similar machines in various departments. As a result, workers kept the engines of the machines running even during setup, eventually resulting in serious damage to some machines.

In a new start-up firm, all employees work from early in the morning until late at night because this is customary in similar companies.

The efficiencies syndrome is responsible for *stretching time* and for the *drawer effect* where workers make sure they have some work to do during times of trouble (when they have to justify their existence).

> In a large maintenance center, technicians leave some pieces of problem equipment undiagnosed to use as an "alibi" during days when they don't have other repairs to do.

Dealing with the Efficiencies Syndrome

Failures of the efficiencies syndrome are clear and may provide examples of *system chaos*. These phenomenon do not exist with individuals outside of business: People do not judge their car use by its utilization, but rather by its effectiveness. People do not expect their computers to be processing bits and bytes all the time.

We must shift our focus to throughput and learn to live with the fact that noncritical resources may be idle some of the time, especially if we want to achieve fast response times.

What should workers do during idle times? Here are some suggestions:

- Flexible training and self-learning

- Activities for process improvement and quality management

- Shift workers to help at bottlenecks

- Shift work from the bottleneck departments to less busy departments

- Preventive maintenance

From a global perspective, a product or service line does not have to be balanced in terms of its capacity. Most lines contain different resources, some expensive and some inexpensive. It is not expected that the capacity utilization of the clerical or cleaning staff in a clinic will be the same as the capacity utilization of expensive resources like physicians and nurses. It is inconceivable that a lower-paid worker will be a bottleneck and will bring the whole system to a halt. Hence, line balancing does not stand the test of reality. Because of fluctuations, there is an extra motivation to create *excess capacity* in some resources, as is discussed further in Chapter 14.

The existence of excess capacity in the system, which is positive for the system and its throughput, could produce failures if the system people contract an efficiencies syndrome. This could lead to nonbottleneck resources becoming system constraints. A good manager should be able to deal with an efficiencies syndrome and find appropriate solutions. This syndrome is not easy to deal with. It requires a common language and a common approach for managers and employees.

Summary

The efficiencies syndrome causes human resources and equipment to work more than is necessary. This syndrome is fueled by managerial and cultural factors. The desire to show that you are busy, taking a local perspective and inappropriate measurement, all work to enhance this syndrome. Resolving the syndrome requires a change in organizational thinking, which is not easy to implement.

10

Evils of Long Response Times

Long response times for service, for production, and for development processes are a major concern in today's management world. In this chapter, we examine the relationship between response time and the amount of work in process (WIP), so that we may find ways to shorten these times.

Types of Inventories

The management of physical inventories (hardware, components, materials, documents, or files) and nonphysical and human inventories (pieces of software, business information to be processed, patients in the hospital or waiting for tests, or customers waiting in a bank) plays an important role in the management of business systems, operational systems, health care systems, and not-for-profit systems. Three types of inventories are shown in Figure 10.1.

Raw materials (RM): *Items that have not yet been handled: materials, components, information, or tasks before they enter the system to be processed.*

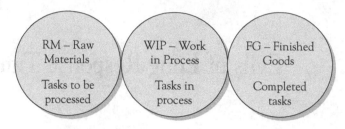

Figure 10.1 Types of inventories

Work in process (WIP): *Items in process: intermediate products or tasks that have entered the system for processing. The processing on these items has not yet been completed.*

Examples of work in process (WIP):

- Software and hardware that are still in development

- Items on an assembly line

- Purchase orders in the negotiating process or in the approval stage

- Receipts handled in the accounting department

- Business information that is being processed

- Patients being treated in the emergency room

- Systems waiting for assembly and calibration at the integration department

- Equipment and instruments being repaired in the maintenance department

- Legal files waiting for a verdict or for a hearing

Finished goods (FG): *Completed items: products, information, and tasks that have been processed completely.*

This chapter focuses only on WIP. Methods for managing WIP are different from those for managing raw materials or finished goods. Applying tools used for WIP management to other inventory types can harm the organization.

Work in Process

Figure 10.2 presents two organizations, A and B. The organizations are similar and perform identical functions. This example can be applied to many types of organizations.

Both organizations operate in the same market and have similar resources and capabilities. The entry pace of units (tasks, jobs) in each organization is 20 units per hour, and the departure pace is also 20 units per hour. The difference between the two organizations is the amount of WIP: Organization A has 60 units present in the system, while Organization B has 20 units

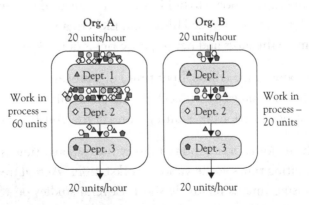

Figure 10.2 The high WIP organization versus the low WIP organization

in the system. These numbers include units being processed in each department as well as units still waiting for processing in each department. Ignore for a moment the reasons that cause the difference in the amount of WIP between the two organizations, and focus on the question: "Does the higher level of WIP in Organization A improve or harm this organization's performance?"

Relationship between Response Time and Work in Process Level

High levels of WIP lead to long response times, and the average response time of the system is proportional to the WIP level. As shown in Figure 10.2, the average time spent processing a unit in Organization A is three hours, compared to one hour in Organization B. The number of units waiting in Organization A is 60 compared to 20 in Organization B. On average, the throughput time (time from entry until departure) of a unit entering Organization A is three hours (60/20 = 3) while throughput time in Organization B is only one hour (20/20 = 1).

Average response time of the process equals the WIP divided by the system throughput pace. This is Little's formula of queuing theory and can be shown to hold true for any queue discipline (e.g., FIFO, LIFO, and so on; see Hillier and Lieberman, 2002).

Examine the gross and net response times of the system:

Gross response time (throughput time) of a process
  = Processing times (net times) of individual units (or customers)
    in various stations + Waiting times of the unit (or customer)

In the majority of situations, most of the response time is caused by the waiting times at the various workstations. Actual treatment or processing time is relatively short. Several studies on response times in various service and industry organizations have shown that the net processing time is only 5 percent to 10 percent of the total response time. Our personal experience shows that, in many cases, *work time is no more than 1 percent of the total response time.* Several examples demonstrate this surprising ratio:

- A purchase request for an item, from the request initiation until the delivery to the supplier, takes several days (gross time). The actual time spent on the request by the purchasing people at various workstations barely exceeds one hour.

- The process of approving a loan or a mortgage takes several days, while the actual net time spent on the forms is no longer than two hours.

- The response time of a subcontractor for the assembly of electronic boards—from receiving the components to shipment—is on average one to two weeks. The net touch-labor time at the various stages of the process is about one to two hours.

- The average gross time for a patient in a hospital emergency room is about four hours. The total net treatment time is only a few minutes.

The Evils of WIP and Long Response Time

Evils of work in process: *Undesirable consequences of high levels of WIP; the damage to organizational performance caused by high levels of WIP.*

Evils of a long response time: *Undesirable consequences resulting from a long response time; the damage to the performance of the organization caused by its long response time.*

The response time of a process is proportional to the amount of WIP. If we reduce the amount of WIP, the response time is reduced. Because response time is proportional to the amount of WIP, the evils of a long response time are actually identical to the evils of WIP.

Reduction in Throughput   Windows of opportunity for new services or products are only open for short time periods. An organization with fast response times (to submitting proposals, development, production, or arranging business plans) can take advantage of these opportunities. When organizations act quickly to bring out new services or products and commit for short response times, they are able to command higher prices. Companies with innovative products that reach the market ahead of the competition can usually "skim the cream" from the market. Also, being first to market enables organizations to capture a significant market share, making it difficult for competitors to penetrate the market.

High Operating Expenses   Accumulation of WIP and long response times lead to high operating expenses (inventory carrying costs, maintenance, and control) and additional finance expenses.

Diminished Quality   The longer the response time and the longer work stays at WIP status, the more the quality diminishes. There are two reasons that account for this:

1. Materials delayed during the process are left unprotected and vulnerable to environmental, physical, mechanical, and other damages. In service units or information technology departments, the quality of decisions and the quality of treatment diminishes because of the amount of time that has passed. This is especially true if there are many changes of treating hands.

2. Longer response times mean that it takes longer for feedback about mistakes to arrive at the responsible station. Since the responsible station is not getting immediate feedback, it continues to produce defective products or services.

Examples include the following:

- The quality of an insurance claim decision or a court decision diminishes when a claim is handled by many people or many judges.

- The longer a patient spends in the hospital or in a clinic, the more he or she is exposed to the possibility of contracting infections.

- A claims case receives inferior treatment in court the longer it stays as WIP. This is because nonrelevant documents begin to pile up, and the hands treating the case may change.

Diminished Control   When WIP piles up, workers may realize degrees of freedom in selecting preferred work tasks. As a result, managerial control and the ability of management to dictate priorities may diminish. Reducing the amount of WIP allows better and more effective control.

Diminished Flexibility to Market and Technological Changes   Long response times and accumulating WIP make it difficult to introduce changes in services or products. Such changes are needed when market preferences change or when engineering changes need to be made. Occasionally, there is a need to trash the entire WIP, especially if there is pressure to introduce a new product to the market immediately. In other situations, where costs have accumulated due to high levels of WIP, there is a temptation to wait to make the needed changes until most of the inventory has been consumed. This could result in missing a window of opportunity.

Diminished Cash Flow   A company needs return capital to finance WIP. Companies with slow response times and large inventories may face a crisis caused by unfavorable cash flow. They are usually required to pay for raw materials within a short time, and payments may be received rather late due to the long response time.

Diminished Motivation   Managers and workers who operate in an environment with large volumes of WIP and long response times experience frustration resulting from work pressure and frequent shifting from task to task. When they are continuously faced with a desired throughput that is not achievable and frustration about timetables that cannot be met, workers and managers experience diminished motivation.

Missed Deadlines   Accumulation of WIP and long response times diminish the organization's ability to meet deadlines and adhere to established timetables.

Lack of Customer Satisfaction   Inferior quality services, treatments, or products that are constantly delivered late create customer dissatisfaction, which may also lead to customer desertion.

Diminished Forecasting Capability   Forecasting is important to organizations in planning human resources, raw materials inventory, developing marketing and sales channels, and cash flow. The ability to forecast is a function of the forecasting horizon. The relationship between the validity of forecasts and the forecasting horizon is presented in Figure 10.3 (Goldratt and Fox, 1986).

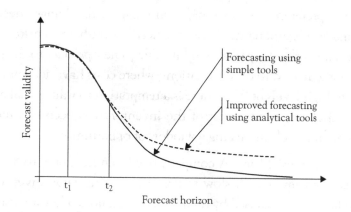

Figure 10.3 The effect of the forecasting horizon on the forecasting validity

Improving forecasting ability through use of analytical and marketing tools can assist organizations. By reducing system response times, companies can significantly improve forecasting ability. If the system response time is t_2 (days or weeks) then we must forecast the market demand at that time. If the response time is reduced to t_1, the market demand forecasting quality should improve drastically. One way to reduce response times is by reducing the amount of WIP.

Diminished Throughput   High levels of WIP cause system inefficiency, which diminishes throughput. Work that comes in and out of a bottleneck can make the bottleneck inefficient. Jobs that enter the bottleneck at inappropriate times because of lack of control, also diminish system throughput.

A company specializing in the production of advanced electronic systems won an international contract worth millions of dollars. Performance in the firm was poor with delays in delivering orders, high production costs, quality problems (including large numbers of rejects), and other managerial undesirable effects (Coman, Koller, and Ronen, 1996). The company tried to remedy the situation by introducing technological changes, to no avail. They also considered introducing a sophisticated information system. A careful analysis of the situation revealed a large amount of WIP, resulting in very long response times. Some components were damaged because of the high level of WIP—when components suffered lengthy exposures to oxygen and humidity in the air, component and equipment failure occurred. Once the firm reduced the amount of WIP and response times, they started to produce with high throughput and near zero failure rates to the full satisfaction of customers.

(*continued*)

In an insurance company, the response time for generating policies was about six weeks from the time the customer signed the application form until the policy went into effect. During this long time period, many potential customers cancelled their applications. Additionally, many files piled up in the office causing the employees to feel pressured, which resulted in mistakes in policy preparation and in the approval process. Some of these mistakes were a result of files being handled by many people over the course of several weeks. The reduction of WIP and the resulting reduction in response time yielded higher quality, which caused the number of cancelled requests to drop dramatically. This enabled management to focus on the more important issues of the firm—those relating to marketing (Eden and Ronen, 1993).

In an agency providing temporary manpower, the process of assigning workers to employers was very lengthy. As a result, many potential workers simply disappeared from the scene when they managed to find assignments on their own or through other agencies. This type of situation is sometimes referred to as *evaporating inventory.* Shortening the processing response time greatly improved the situation.

In a software development department, programmers and computer scientists were assigned a large number of tasks. Each software developer was responsible for about 20 to 40 tasks. The staff (software engineers, programmers, and technical engineers) usually started work on one task and then moved on to other urgent tasks without completing the first one. As a result, WIP was high and the average response time on all tasks was relatively long. The employees wasted a great deal of time reworking tasks that had already been partially processed. The process was not controlled properly, and due dates on all projects were not met. Reducing the level of WIP led to a reduction in the response time and an improvement in quality and throughput.

Causes of Excess Work in Process

Several policy constraints are responsible for the accumulation of WIP above the level that is required for efficient operation of the system. These include:

- *The efficiencies syndrome.* Because of this syndrome, which causes additional (unnecessary) work for non-critical resources, there is an excessive buildup of work in process.

- *Viewing inventory as assets.* Looking at an organization from the narrow perspective of financial accounting can encourage management to mistakenly increase inventory in order to show larger assets on the balance sheet (Geri and Ronen, 2005). Negative effects resulting from an organization's excessive WIP outweigh the possible negative accounting exposure effects of showing smaller inventories.

- *Ignorance.* Misunderstanding the negative effects of WIP and not being aware of methods to reduce it, result in excessive WIP.

Summary

Long response times and high levels of WIP are responsible for diminished work quality and customer dissatisfaction. Throughput,

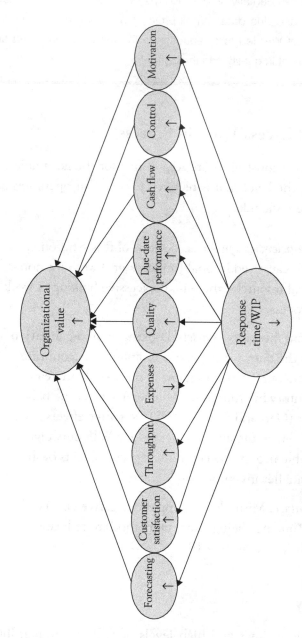

Figure 10.4 The impact of reducing WIP on organizational function and value

control, and cash flow could also be impacted. Also, maintaining excessive inventories and working through excessive response times may cause additional expenses.

Shortening response time and reducing WIP levels can work as leverages for significant improvements in organizational performance and value enhancement. Figure 10.4 offers a summary. Methods to reduce the volume of WIP and shorten response time are discussed in Chapter 11.

11

Reducing Response Times

Short response times have strategic and tactical importance. They serve as strategic value drivers for an organization.

At the strategic level, short response times provide an organization with the flexibility to move from one product to another, from one service to another, with the ability to react quickly to customer requests, and to manage rapid market changes. In a changing market, with its inherent uncertainty, a flexible organization can adapt itself quickly to changes in the environment and increase its chances of survival and success.

At the tactical level (as we have seen in the previous chapter), fast response times enable companies to function with low levels of work in process (WIP), thereby reducing costs and increasing throughput.

Methods for Reducing Response Times and Work in Process

Reducing response times and reducing the amount of WIP can be achieved by various methods, including:

- Strategic gating

- Tactical gating

- Working with a complete kit

- Managing bottlenecks

- Using the just-in-time (JIT) method

- Measurement and control

- Implementing the drum-buffer-rope (DBR) mechanism

- Practicing quality improvement and reduction of the garbage plant

- Avoiding bad multitasking (BMT)

- Using concurrent engineering (CE)

- Implementing group technology (GT)

- Working in parallel rather than serially

Strategic Gating

Strategic gating is a managerial tool that screens out tasks that should not reach the system and therefore, should not consume the scarce time of the bottleneck. Organizations that routinely apply strategic gating, especially in areas of research and development, and marketing and sales, reduce workloads by up to 25 percent, which reduces the response time for the important tasks. The time to market is also reduced, which, in turn, contributes to competitiveness.

Tactical Gating

Tactical gating is the controlled release of tasks into the system and is appropriate for all organizations. After passing the strategic gating, screening tasks are subject to the tactical gating mechanism (Pass and Ronen, 2003). The rules of tactical gating are:

- Release only tasks with a complete kit.

- Release tasks in small and appropriate batches.

- Assure that all tasks are released by one source (the gater) that is responsible for the tactical gating.
  The timing of task release is determined by the bottleneck capacity, while maintaining an appropriate buffer in front of the bottleneck (e.g., the DBR mechanism).

These rules are discussed in detail later in this chapter.

Working with a Complete Kit

Working with a complete kit is an important principle in reducing response times. This principle and ways to implement it are discussed in Chapter 12.

Managing Bottlenecks

Managing bottlenecks according to the management by constraints approach yields higher throughput on the one hand, and a reduction of response time on the other.

Using the Just-in-Time (JIT) Method

The just-in-time (JIT) method is of utmost importance in reducing response times. It emerged from industrial plants in Japan and has also been utilized successfully in service organizations and health care organizations. About 70 percent of the success attributable to JIT is based on universal concepts and techniques that do not relate to Japanese culture; these concepts and techniques have been applied successfully in Japan, the United States, and Europe. The remaining 30 percent contribution is culture dependent and is not addressed in this book.

JIT is a method that stands on its own and can be applied as is. However, experience clearly demonstrates that the application outcomes are better when JIT is combined with other managerial approaches, such as management by constraints, managing for quality, the complete kit concept, and others.

The JIT method can be summarized by three basic and simple rules:

Rule I: Work only as needed in terms of time, quantity, and specifications.

Rule II: Work in small, appropriate, and smart batches.

Rule III: Avoid waste and activities that do not add value to the organization.

Rule I of the Just-in-Time Method

This rule implies that a product or service should not be delivered earlier or later than the target time, you should not produce more than or less than the required quantity, and a product should not be under- or overdesigned regarding its specifications. We can identify two types of managerial deviations from Rule I of JIT:

1. Shortage Deviation   If, for example, demand is 10 units and the actual supply is only 8, then this is a serious deviation that interferes with supply to customers, interferes with cash flow, and damages the company's reputation. However, such a deviation can be dealt with through the use of the organization's routine control mechanisms, as well as natural mechanisms of the organization that may close the gap:

- The worker himself, knowing he is not able to meet demand, meets the shortage within a short time.

- The worker's superior monitors the demanded quantities and makes sure the deviation is corrected.

- Sales and marketing managers work to close the gap if others have not done so.

- The financial manager points out situations with cash flow gaps.

- The customer approaches management with a request
  to correct the deviation.

In other words, the organizational mechanisms work to close the gap.

2. *Surplus Deviation*   If, for example, demand is 10 units, but 12 units have been provided, then this deviation is not usually handled in the short term by the routine mechanisms of the organization and does not naturally generate feedback for workers and managers. Correction mechanisms are not triggered because of the following:

- The worker feels like he or she is overachieving.

- Managers sometimes do not care about the surplus
  because they are busy putting out fires elsewhere in the
  organization.

- Sales and marketing personnel have no knowledge
  about such a surplus.

- The financial manager deals with this situation at the
  end of the year, or at best, at the end of a quarter. At
  that time, the accountants become involved and try to
  write down inventories.

- Customers may be totally unaware of surpluses.

Surplus deviations are not routinely dealt with even though they are harmful:

- If the resource is a bottleneck, then generating a surplus
  of 2 units (20 percent) wastes the resource 20 percent of
  the time. The entire system loses 20 percent of its real
  throughput.

- Generating the surplus required using materials and components beyond those planned for inhibits their use for other products.

- WIP is increased.

- Creates unneeded finished goods inventory.

In summary, being early may be as bad as being late. Similarly, overproduction may be as bad as underproduction. The effect of *double stealing* bottleneck time and materials causes bad planning and delays in supply. In addition, the increased WIP inventory brings up all the evils described in the previous chapter. The bottom line of Rule I of JIT is that a surplus deviation is as bad as a shortage deviation.

Implementing Rule I of JIT   For research and development (R&D) processes, Rule I of JIT mainly refers to work that is *just in spec*. Namely, all work should be done within the requirements or specifications of the task. Products and services should be developed according to the requirements or specifications without deviation. Although deviation from specifications is very common in R&D, workers should refrain from it. Deviation from requirements and specifications has two manifestations: *overspecification* and *overdesign*.

Overspecification: *Defining product or service specifications beyond the actual needs of the customer or the market.*

Overdesign: *Designing and developing products or services beyond what is required by the specifications and/or the requirements of the customer or the market.*

This phenomenon of overspecification and overdesign usually originates during the interaction of R&D and marketing staff members. Marketing staff members face pressure to bring a product to the market as quickly as possible, when they may not be fully acquainted with the customer or market requirements. Therefore, marketing quite often deliberately defines excessive development requirements in order to *leave all options open*. There is also a hidden understanding that some of the requirements will be downgraded eventually because the marketing requirements are difficult (sometimes even impossible) to attain.

In some cases, the developers, especially the inexperienced ones, have a strong technology drive, which leads them to try to develop products that are at the forefront of technology (state of the art). Yet, in other situations, developers want to create options for future extensions of the products (growth potential). As a result, there is a silent conspiracy of shared interest by marketing and R&D to introduce overspecification and overdesign into the development of new products.

Another manifestation of overspecification in development is the issue of *tight tolerances*. Tight tolerances do not guarantee the achievement of a better product or service. Time pressures on R&D and the difficulty in attaining excessive tolerances sometimes lead to delays and extra costs. In cases where the delay is too large, the decision to waive tolerances is taken at a lower level. Thus, overspecification may actually lead to underspecification.

Based on our work with dozens of R&D organizations and departments worldwide, more than 25 percent of development efforts are invested in issues and activities that don't add value, contradict Rule I of JIT, and may be considered *garbage time*. Additional issues related to development management are introduced in Chapter 22.

The implementation of Rule I of JIT is also very useful and important for equipment maintenance, which should be completed only as needed.

> In a large maintenance organization, one-third of labor hours
> were devoted to repairing equipment that was not in demand at
> the time of repair or equipment that was not used (because of the
>
> *(continued)*

> introduction of a new generation of equipment or of having a sur-
> plus of given equipment). As a result, the organization was late
> with many of the urgently needed repairs. Working in the spirit of
> Rule I of JIT resulted in a reduction of unnecessary repairs. This
> reduced the backlog and improved the company's ability to meet
> deadlines.

Violating Rule I of JIT   Figure 11.1 demonstrates what happens
when Rule I of JIT is violated: The 1–2–3 production process has
a demand of 10 units per month for each of three products: A, B,
and C.

It is clear that demand can be met with current resources.
Occasionally, the production manager wants to work with batches
of 20 units of every product. The motivation is to save set-up

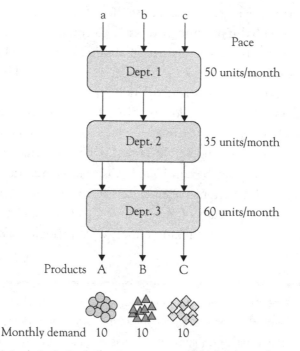

Figure 11.1 A 1–2–3 production system with three products

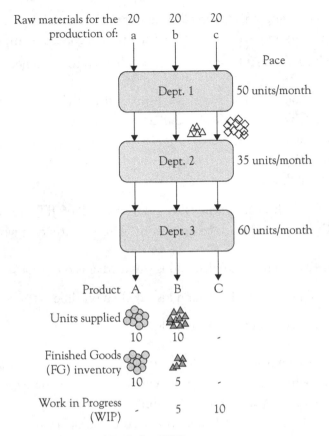

Figure 11.2 Violation of Rule I of JIT

times, to save paperwork, or to be able to measure performance by quantity (a very common policy constraint). The resulting process is presented in Figure 11.2. Twenty units of product A were put into production. They went through the following three-stage process:

First, 10 units were delivered to customers and 10 units were stacked in finished goods inventory.

Second, the 20-unit batch of product B became stuck in department 2 and the batch was split: Five units were left as WIP inventory, and 15 units finished all three processing stages. Ten of those were delivered to the customers and five were left over in finished goods inventory.

Third, product C units were not delivered to customers.

The company produced 35 units rather than 30. However, product C was not produced at all and not supplied to customers. If the firm had followed Rule I of JIT, every product would have been produced in quantities of 10 units and delivery to customers would have been flawless.

The 40–20–40 Phenomenon   Ignoring Rule I of JIT creates the *40–20–40 phenomenon* in organizations. This is a situation where:

- 40 percent of the demand is supplied ahead of time

- 20 percent of the demand is supplied on time

- 40 percent of the demand is supplied late

Observing Rule I of JIT *balances the line*: Demand that was previously delivered late will be delivered on time at the expense of the demand that was previously fulfilled *too early*.

The 40–20–40 phenomenon is also common in research and development. Because of a lack of clear prioritization or as a result of priorities determined by pressure from different parties, managers of resource groups conduct a *high percentage* of their tasks (e.g., software, hardware, electronic design, analysis) *ahead of time*. Balancing the line by determining adequate priorities, results in a significant improvement in the R&D function. The 40–20–40 phenomenon sometimes comes into play when products contain unnecessary parameters or tolerances that are too tight, while necessary parameters are not developed due to time limits.

The following example demonstrates what might happen if we violate Rule I of JIT: A surgeon wants to start operating at 10:00 A.M., but tells the operating room (OR) staff that he wants everything to be ready at 9:30 A.M., the OR staff request that the patient arrive at the hospital at 9:00 A.M., and the nursing staff on the ward summon an orderly to transport the patient at 8:00 A.M. Should they work according to Rule I of JIT, the patient would be transferred to the OR close to 9:30 or so.

Rule II of JIT

A batch (lot) refers to a situation where several units are processed sequentially one after another. Common batch types are:

- Working (production) batches
- Transfer batches

Working batch: *The number of units (or labor hours) that are worked continuously at a workstation. The amount of work between one setup and the next.*

In service or production processes, a working batch reflects a group of units processed at a work center in between two setups. The determination of batch size is one of the important questions to ask when planning a service or production. In development projects, batch size is actually the size of a work package. Splitting the project into appropriate work packages and activities is a major factor in the effective management of projects.

Batch size may vary along the process of material or information flow. For example, in a production process:

- The purchase batch for total production—10,000 units
- The shipment batch from the materials' supplier— 1,000 units
- Batch size when inspecting a shipment—500 units

- Production (working) batch—100 units

- Transfer batch between workstations—50 units

- Batch size for delivery to customer—250 units

Transfer batch: *Number of units, number of work hours, or the frequency of work transfer between one workstation and another.*

An example of a transfer batch in health care could be: how frequently a consultant-specialist visits the emergency department or how frequently blood specimens are transferred from the ward to the lab. Transfer batches are a key issue in service organizations.

The size of a transfer batch does not have to match the work batch (Goldratt and Fox, 1986). The transfer batch can be bigger than, smaller than, or equal to the work batch. In general, it is advisable to *make the transfer batches as small as possible*, provided this does not interfere with the process and does not cost more. Figures 11.3 and 11.4 illustrate the effects of transfer batch size. Both figures have the same production (working) batches of 25 units with different transfer batch size.

In the work regime shown in Figure 11.3, 25 units of the batch are transferred from station 1 to station 2 after the whole batch has been processed by station 1. Once it is fully processed in station 2, the batch is then transferred to station 3. After being processed in station 3, the batch is sent to the customer. The system response time under this regime is long—t_1. In addition, there is concern that the bottleneck (station 2) may be idle while waiting for the batch at station 1 to be finished.

In Figure 11.4 the working batch remains 25 units, but the transfer batch has now been cut down to five units. Once five units have been processed at a given station, they are transferred to the

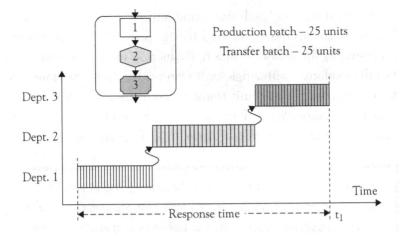

Figure 11.3 Response time of a 1–2–3 system with a transfer batch of 25 units

next workstation. The obvious result is that response time has been dramatically reduced from t_1 to the shorter t_3. To fully exploit this improvement, we have to create willingness on the part of customers to accept partial shipments. Thus, the first units can be sent to the customer after a very short time period—t_2. In many situations, customers are happy to receive some units, with the rest to follow shortly thereafter.

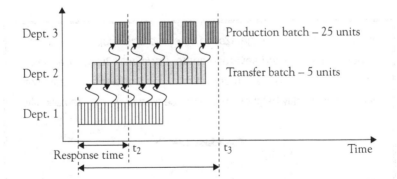

Figure 11.4 Response time of a 1–2–3 system with a transfer batch size of 5 units

An ideal transfer batch size is one unit. With one-unit transfer batches, each unit is transferred to the next station, after being processed by the previous station. Reduction in response time can be fully exploited with single-unit transfer batches. The downside to implementing a one-unit transfer batch size includes the additional conveyance needed, the added effort, and the annoyance in dealing with many transfers of single units from station to station.

> In the emergency room of a large hospital, some patients have their blood drawn for various tests. In the past, the staff waited until several specimens were on the tray before having someone transfer them to the lab. The transfer batch was one hour (the average number of samples in an hour), causing an average wait of half an hour per specimen. Today, each blood sample is transferred to the lab immediately. The shorter response time of test results yielded a shorter patient stay in the emergency room and led to quicker diagnosis and treatment.

In production and maintenance processes, the transfer batch is usually measured in units. In service organizations, the transfer batch is usually measured in terms of the *frequency of transfer*— every one hour, every two days, and so on.

> In a large logistical organization, the average response time for repairing parts lasted several months. Parts were transferred from station to station once a month. When the transfer batches were reduced to weekly batches, the response time dropped dramatically.
>
> In a large manufacturing company, response time was reduced by a factor of 10 simply by reducing the size of the transfer batch.

> Transfer batches had been determined by the size of transfer contain-
> ers. When the large containers were replaced by smaller ones, the fre-
> quency of transfers increased and response times were shortened.
>
> ❦
>
> The 7-Eleven store chain in Tokyo delivers goods to thousands of
> its stores every two hours. This means better use of the limited and
> expensive shelf space for the stores.

Working (Production) Batches   A new setup is initiated only when
the work on the current batch is completed and workers are ready
to move on to the next batch.

It may be helpful to examine the impact of shifting from large
working batches to smaller ones. Figure 11.5 offers an example
of working with large batches, while Figure 11.6 shows those
large batches after they are split into four smaller working batches.

The idea of working with small working batches is one major contribution Japan made to the world of management. Reducing batch
size brings about a miraculous proportional reduction in response time

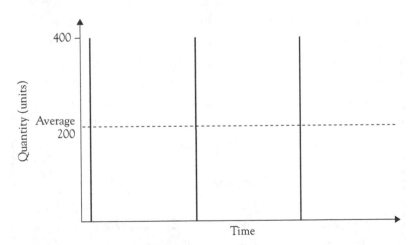

Figure 11.5 Working with large working batches

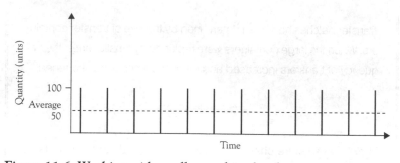

Figure 11.6 Working with smaller working batches

and the amount of work in process. Figures 11.5 and 11.6 show that a shift from monthly batches to weekly ones reduced the amount of WIP from 200 units to 50 units, with system response time most likely reduced as well. The reduction of the working batch size yields two positive outcomes: (1) reduction of WIP and response times, and (2) better adherence to timetables and improvement in quality and service to the customer. Experience has shown that the benefits from applying Rule II of JIT are immediate.

In a billing department of a large credit card company, preparing bills and mailing them was done once a month. At the end of the month employees experienced peak activity, and the pressure generated problems and mistakes. To overcome this problem, workflow was altered so that the tasks were divided into three times a month. The new work schedule helped overcome the majority of billing errors and cut down on the number of resources needed to generate and send out the bills. It also substantially cut the number of customer complaints to the call center.

In a hospital lab, the staff used to wait for a full tray to fill up before starting the autoanalyzer. Reducing the size of the working batch and operating the analyzer more frequently cut down the response time of returning results drastically, which in turn resulted in better patient care. The cost of extra reagents was negligible.

In a high-tech company, systems were manufactured in six-month supply batches. Engineers discovered malfunctions that required changes in the electronic boards when they were assembling the first units. The firm moved to production of smaller batches with a two-week supply horizon. The cycle time was drastically reduced, as were the number of rejects resulting from changes and repairs.

In a development department of a high-tech company, it was common to split projects into large work packages, with each package consisting of six months' worth of work. Reducing the work packages to four to six weeks' worth of work, cut response time significantly.

In a printed circuit board manufacturing company, lot size was reduced by half. As a result, lead time was immediately reduced by 50 percent.

Rule II of JIT recommends working with *small*, *appropriate*, and *smart* batches:

- *Small batches*. Usually smaller than those used presently. In our experience, if most organizations worked with smaller batches, they could reduce response times and improve other performance measures.

- *Appropriate batches*. Batch sizes that are congruent with the supply rate expected by the customer.

- *Smart batches*. Using common sense in consideration of the special needs of the organization.

In a department that manufactures printed circuit boards in a large high-tech company: one unit of each board was needed for the assembly of the system prototype. Based on the experience of the developers, three units of each board were ordered. This took into account the long lead time needed to produce the extra units and the expectation of some changes. The controller was rounding the invoice up to 5 units, and the production person was producing batches of 10 units.

Smart batches imply that common sense should enter into the considerations in determining batch size.

During the production of a prototype, company management decided that printed circuit boards would be produced in no more than three-unit batches in order to reduce the surplus cost caused by working excessively large batches. This decision was successfully implemented and the system's response time was significantly improved. One day an argument arose: A certain prototype required four identical boards. Because the batch ordered exceeded the allowed three-unit board limit for one prototype, the order was rejected by the manufacturing department.

Effects of reducing batch size (both working batches and transfer batches) are immediate, are relatively easy to implement, and have a major impact on reducing system response times.

Strategic Importance of Reducing Response Times and Working with Small Batches

Working with small batches allows firms to produce a *large variety* of products, while achieving shorter response times. Smaller batches also mean better customization of products, higher quality products, and faster delivery times.

Working with big batches implies longer response times. This in turn requires organizations to carry a larger finished goods inventory, tying down capital and increasing costs. The higher costs result from high-inventory carrying costs and the need to occasionally sell unneeded inventory at low prices.

The following concerns prevent us from working with small batches:

- Fear of increasing the number of setups

- Economies of scale thinking

- Fear of more complex control

- Fear of increasing cost per unit

Fear of Increasing the Number of Setups

Set-up time is a nonproductive time. During setup, you cannot produce or provide service. Because the setup process was traditionally long and complex, there has been a tendency to avoid setups as much as possible, leading to working with larger batches.

The modern approach is to refrain from long and disorderly setups. Experience demonstrates that set-up times can be reduced by large percentages without large investments (Shingo, 1996).

Reducing setup time by 50 percent allows a similar reduction in the working batch size while maintaining the same ratio between productive time (working on the batch) and nonproductive time (setup). This achieves all the benefits of working with small working batches—short response time, flexible response to different customers, better quality—without additional costs.

> In a can manufacturing company, the color printing machine was the bottleneck. The employees reduced set-up time to a minimum. In addition, came up with an idea about how to continue production during the machine's set-up time—bypass the color printing machine and produce blank cans that do not require color printing and that are in demand by small beverage manufacturers.

The framework of management by constraints shows that additional setups in resources that are not bottlenecks do not cost money. For example, Table 11.1 presents the relation between the capacity utilization and the reduction of 50 percent in the batch size in a work center with 60 percent capacity utilization.

As long as the resource is not a bottleneck, working with small batches affects the capacity utilization of this resource only moderately, and the resource remains a nonbottleneck.

Economies of Scale Thinking

People are used to the concept of economies of scale where large quantities imply savings. However, economies of scale may not always be relevant and must be considered in specific situations. When batches are processed in a system with excess capacity, economies of scale are not important. On the contrary, working with

Table 11.1 The effect of batch size on the load of noncritical resources

	Large Batch (%)	Small Batch—Half the Large Batch (%)
Percentage of productive work	50	50
Percentage of set-up time	10	20
Total capacity utilization	60	70

large batches increases response time and more evils of WIP. This is a drawback, not a benefit of economies of scale.

When a workstation is a bottleneck, set-up time should be *shortened* as much as possible. In addition, you should analyze whether a specific situation would benefit from the utilization of *larger* batches in the bottleneck station compared to other stations (Goldratt and Cox, 2004).

Fear of More Complex Control

Working with small batches and splitting a batch into several smaller transfer batches seemingly leads to more complex control issues. There is no doubt that shifting to smaller working batches and transfer batches leads to handling more batches. However, the shorter times for each batch create a situation where the number of batches in the system at any given time is *smaller* rather than bigger. Hence follow-up and control are easier (Karp and Ronen, 1992). Moreover, working with smaller batches, along with the use of strategic and tactical gating, complete kits, and so on, clears the system of work congestion and tasks in process, so that the control process becomes even simpler.

Increasing Cost per Unit   A worker or manager who works in a system using the classical costing approach (see details in Chapter 15) for control and decision making may resist shifting to working with smaller batches out of fear that this may negatively affect the cost per unit measure.

For example, in a nonbottleneck station, set-up time is one hour and the processing time of one unit is one quarter of an hour, the cost per unit in a batch of 100 is:

$$T(100) = (1 + 1/4 \times 100)/100 = 0.26 \text{ hours/unit}$$

Shifting the batch size to 10 increases the cost per unit to:

$$T(10) = (1 + 1/4 \times 10)/10 = 0.35 \text{ hours/unit}$$

This measurement of cost per unit is a local view that causes suboptimization, especially in a station that is not a bottleneck. A global-system view requires consideration of the total benefits versus the harms of working with large batches, including the evils of WIP.

Rule III of JIT

Waste is any activity, process, or use of capital that does not contribute added value to the organization, the customer, the process, or the product. Examples of waste:

- Overproduction

- Waiting times

- Extra conveyance

- Processing rejects

- Surplus stock

- Poor quality

- Extra space

- Capital surplus

- Overrequirements, overspecification, and overdesign of the product or service

- Unnecessary steps and processes

Rule III of JIT is a general principle: Waste can be dealt with through the Pareto rule, the focusing matrix, or through the principles of management by constraints.

Measurement and Control

Measurement, follow-up, and control of lead times and levels of WIP generate rapid improvement in these parameters, and helps create an environment that maintains improvement efforts. Measurement, even if not supported by other methods, brings about significant improvement. This method is discussed in greater detail in Chapter 13.

Implementing the Drum-Buffer-Rope Mechanism

The DBR mechanism schedules the controlled release of tasks into the process, thus limiting the amount of WIP. Timing is determined by the capacity of the constraint with the maintenance of a buffer ahead of it. Implementing DBR in marketing, sales, production, development, and service systems leads to a significant reduction of the work process.

Quality Improvement and Reduction of the Garbage Plant

The poor quality of processes in sales, marketing, development, production, or service results in the increase of lead times and the amount of WIP because of rework and retreatment. Approaches for process quality improvement and process control mechanisms are presented in Chapter 17.

Avoiding Bad Multitasking

The phenomenon of bad multitasking (BMT) is common in all areas of management, and is especially prominent in development processes (Goldratt, 1997). This is the phenomenon of jumping back and forth between many open tasks that are waiting to be processed. The results of BMT are:

- Decrease in throughput

- Longer response times for finishing tasks

- Late deliveries

- Reduced work quality

- Increased WIP, including all its evils

To demonstrate the negative effect of BMT, we analyze a situation in which an engineer develops software modules for three projects that are managed by three different project managers. The development of each module is expected to take two weeks. The first module must be ready in two weeks, the second in four weeks, and the third in six weeks. Things happen somewhat differently as can be seen in Figure 11.7.

The software development engineer begins work on the project-1 module. At first, he sets everything up mentally: he submerges himself into the problem, he works to understand it, he collects the necessary data by asking questions, then he arranges the work environment. After finishing the setup, he begins the actual work on the module for project 1.

About one week into the project, the engineer bumps into the manager for project 2 who is surprised to hear that work has not yet begun on the module for her project. After yielding to the pressure she applies, the engineer *stops* working on project 1 and starts working on project 2.

First, he starts with the mental setup for project 2 and works to fully understand the problem. Then he continues working on the module for project 2. The same story repeats itself after several days when he coincidentally meets the manager of project 3 in the cafeteria. She too is surprised that *her* project has received a low priority and that work on it has not yet begun. After pressure is exerted by the manager of project 3, the engineer stops working on project 2 and shifts to project 3, again having to go through a mental setup. Now the project 1 manager exerts pressure because he feels his project is already late. So, the developer stops working on project 3 and returns to project 1. However, he must redo the mental setup because time has passed and he has already forgotten some things.

At the end, none of the modules were delivered on time. Furthermore, due to the additional mental setup times while switching

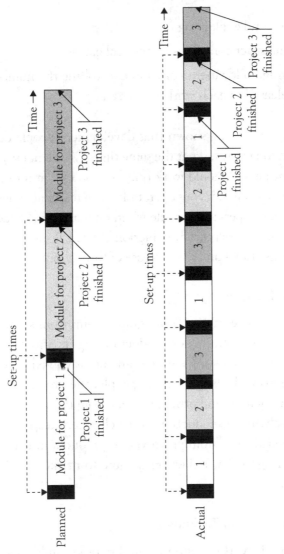

Figure 11.7 The negative effect of BMT

between projects, valuable time was lost at the bottleneck, and the quality of work suffered.

Reducing BMT can be done using the following steps:

1. Teaching and explaining
2. Applying strict control using tactical gating
3. Measuring, following-up on, and controlling the number of tasks released to each worker

Field experience has shown that development people occasionally work on too many tasks at the same time. We are not saying that development people should work only on one task at a time; however, two to four simultaneous open tasks are a reasonable number to ensure that developers are not idle when one task is held back (e.g., waiting for data). A significant reduction of BMT leads to the reduction of response times and the increase of throughput and quality.

Concurrent Engineering

Concurrent engineering (CE) integrates teams from several disciplines to work on a project or product during its entire life cycle. Product designers share information and are involved in decisions and discussions with the marketing people, the production teams, procurement, quality, and other partners, from the very beginning. This approach enables reduction of development response time—the time needed to go from prototype to production. It is possible to achieve a significant reduction in time to market, as shown in Chapter 21.

Implementing Group Technology

Group technology (GT) groups similar tasks under specialized work groups. A hospital emergency department can be improved by being separated into surgical, internal medicine, pediatric, and gynecological ED's. Within each specialized ED, the variance between patients is small. Each specialized group can thus offer more professional, structured, and uniform medical diagnoses and treatments because each employs the relevant specialists.

Group technology also exists in production processes. Work teams are assembled to be responsible for the *entire product*, not just one production step. Insurance companies form work teams to specialize in specific markets and defined clients.

The classical approach in operations management creates *functionally* specialized teams, so that customers or products move between teams (Figure 11.8). In a GT approach, integrative teams provide the entire process needed by the customers or products in one place (Figure 11.9).

Figures 11.8 and 11.9 illustrate how a complex workflow under the functional structure becomes rather simple under the GT method. In addition, the GT method generates a *collective responsibility and accountability of the group* to the customers or the products of the group. The GT method yields faster response times, reduction in WIP, and increased output (Burbridge, 1968). Most cases do not require added resources to achieve improved performance.

A full GT (100 percent) arrangement is rarely achieved. There are usually some common resources shared by several groups. For example, wave-soldering machines in the electronics industry can be shared by all groups.

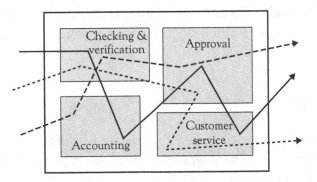

Figure 11.8 A claims department arrangement by functional structure

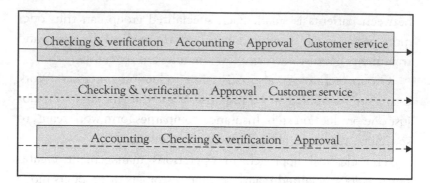

Figure 11.9 A claims department arrangement using the GT method by services or customers

Experience has shown that the GT method succeeds under the following conditions:

- The work volume justifies a specialized group for a long time horizon.

- The resources shared by the various teams are not bottlenecks.

- There is motivation and team spirit.

Working in Parallel Rather Than Serially

Performing tasks in parallel rather than serially helps to reduce response times considerably. This is especially true for project response times (detailed in Chapter 20).

Summary

Reducing response times is a strategic and tactical objective for the organization. This chapter discussed several methods to help reduce response times.

The significant contribution of JIT to management may be realized by focusing on short response times and viewing WIP as a *burden*, not as an *asset*. The JIT method turns attention to the evils caused by WIP inventories. Another JIT technique worth noting—the use of small working batches and transfer batches—may help shorten set-up times.

Reducing response times by focusing, using management by constraints, changing performance measures, using the complete kit concept, and embracing a global view of enhancing the value of the firm can yield significant improvements in the performance of an organization.

12

The Complete Kit Concept

The Complete Kit concept (Ronen, 1992) is one of the simplest and most effective tools available for managers. The Complete Kit has been successfully implemented in various industries, service organizations, research and development (R&D) departments, health care systems, and not-for-profit organizations.

Complete Kit: *The set of items needed to complete a given task (e.g., information, drawings, materials, components, documents, tools).*

Aspects of the Complete Kit

According to the Compete Kit concept, you should start working on a task only when all components necessary for its completion are on hand. This leads to better response times, better quality, increase in throughput, and lower costs.

Three hundred different components are required to assemble each unit of a specific printed circuit board (PCB). One internal customer from the assembly department has ordered 50 PCB units. The requested delivery time is, as usual, yesterday. So far, the

(continued)

purchasing department has managed to acquire 298 components of the 300 components necessary for assembling the PCBs.

Because of the pressure to supply the PCBs on time, management suggests that the workers begin assembling the 50 boards with the 298 available components, and add the remaining two components later, when they arrive. This suggestion seems reasonable, especially since purchasing has informed management that the two missing components are on their way to the factory (by air freight).

In the end, 50 PCBs have been assembled with only 298 out of the required 300 components. The order is stalled in process waiting for the two remaining components. The production of PCBs for other systems has been stopped because of this urgent order, and assembly of different systems is behind schedule. As a result, these systems will not be delivered to customers on time. The missing components arrived two weeks later. Because of the pressure to complete the assembly of the PCBs, management approved the use of a quicker manual assembly procedure. Eventually, the 50 completed PCBs fail the final quality test because one of the two components that were manually assembled was assembled erroneously.

An image-processing department in a company's development division is a source of pride for a company thanks to its technological capabilities and the advanced products it has developed. This department's products have been integrated into the company systems and are an important promotional tool. The department, especially its scientists and engineers, are the company's bottleneck, and the project managers are competing for their valuable time.

In the past, hallway conversations resulted in some of the most successful developments, although product specifications were actually only general principles. In these cases, people who requested the development would later approach the department and ask to make some changes because their intentions had changed. An average of six to seven developmental cycles were required for every algorithm that was developed in the department. This was not a result of technological difficulties because 70 percent of the algorithms were based on existing common algorithms that had been previously developed in the department. The extra developmental cycles were usually due to the lack of definitions and specifications. The department personnel would start to develop an algorithm (even a common one) using an incomplete kit (missing information about specifications and definitions). This information was actually available within the company and only required some clarification and formulation.

Working with a Complete Kit leads to better and faster results in production, maintenance, engineering, development, marketing, sales, purchasing, logistics, and other managerial processes. The Complete Kit concept is based on common sense, is clear and easy to implement, and offers results that can be seen within a short period of time.

The Complete Kit concept does not mean that all of the necessary parts (in case of production) or all of the necessary information (in case of development) needs to be ready and available before beginning the entire endeavor. For example, a radar system manufactured for international airports is composed of three parts—antenna, transmitter, and receiver. The receiver is also composed of different components. A Complete Kit is defined for each subassembly. On the most basic level, assembling a printed circuit board (PCB) should begin with a Complete Kit of all PCB components. On the module (or subsystem) level, the assembly should only be started when all of its necessary parts are available.

There are two types of kits: The InKit and the OutKit.

InKit: *The Complete Kit required before the start of the job in order to be able to complete the job.*

According to the Complete Kit concept, the completeness of the kit is important because it allows workers to begin a task and complete it without stoppages that may stem from missing materials, information, or tools.

OutKit: *The Complete Kit of outcomes/outputs that a task should supply to succeeding tasks or clients.*

We can only say that a task has been completed when the OutKit defined for the task has also been completed. Within a single process, the OutKit of one stage becomes part of the InKit of succeeding stages. The contents of the OutKit for a task must also be included in the InKit list for this task.

Evils of Working with an Incomplete Kit

Working with an incomplete kit can lead to an accumulation of work in process (WIP). It is impossible to complete a task with missing information, materials, or components. Beginning a task with an incomplete kit causes delays during the process and increases the levels of WIP.

The problems of working with an incomplete kit include:

- Poor quality and more rework.

- Longer response time.

- Decline in throughput.

- Higher operating expenses.

- Missed deadlines.

- Less control over the process—controlling the system becomes very complex. In addition to the difficulties of controlling more WIP, the lists of missing components of each product that is still in process must also be managed and controlled. Also, workers have to create a book of rules, which states how to deal with each specific case of a missing item in the kit.

- Decline in cash flow and an increase in demand for working capital.

- Decline in staff motivation.

- Less willingness to put effort into ensuring the arrival of the missing kit items—if working with an incomplete kit is legitimate then why bother to ensure a complete kit.

What Prevents People from Using a Complete Kit?

Although it creates many problems, managers and employees continue to work with incomplete kits for various reasons, including:

- *The efficiencies syndrome.* The desire to utilize resources as much as possible. Following the fallacious notion that staff should be busy all the time causes managers to have employees working on incomplete kits just so that they are not idle. Additionally, it also means more WIP, less throughput, and more operating expenses.

- *The illusion of saving time.* One managerial misconception is that an early start on an assignment always leads to an early completion. In situations where work is begun with an incomplete kit, the opposite is actually true. Starting with an incomplete kit creates more WIP, which leads to longer response times. Working with a

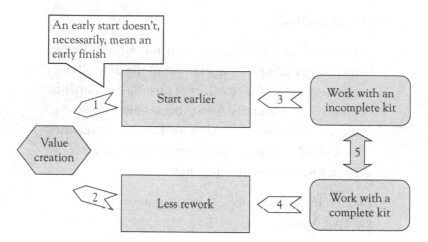

Figure 12.1 Working with a Complete Kit versus an incomplete kit

Complete Kit versus working with an incomplete kit can be seen in Figure 12.1.

According to one assumption, early starts lead to an early completion and to more throughput. Breaking this assumption leaves us with another alternative: working only with a Complete Kit. Employees have a number of reasons for continuing to work with incomplete kits:

- *Pressure for immediate response*. The customer who places an order is usually applying pressure for an immediate response. Just to satisfy the customer, work is started with an incomplete kit (i.e., we are already working on it).

- *Anxiety to show goodwill on the part of the staff*. As a result of management pressure, employees do not want to be the ones delaying the process. So they express their goodwill by working with incomplete kits.

- *Inappropriate planning of assembly levels*. In production, there is a tendency to decrease the number of assembly levels as a result of logistics based on subcontractors. This leads to an increase in the contents of the Complete Kit needed for each level, an increase in the difficulty of completing the kit, and an increase in pressure to start work with an incomplete kit.

- *Because of uncertainty in research and development (R&D), it is assumed that it is not possible to define complete specifications.* Working with an incomplete kit in R&D is sometimes done ideologically, because it is assumed that there is a large uncertainty and no need to fully define the specifications.

Specific Implementations of the Complete Kit Concept

In Production

In production, the Complete Kit is composed of two major components:

1. Materials or parts
2. Information—drawings, specifications, requirements, and so on

There are three rules to follow to assist in implementing the Complete Kit concept in production:

1. Do not start producing, processing, or assembling without a Complete Kit.
2. Appoint a gater—a person to be responsible for the completeness of the kits. The gater should be responsible for:
   - Releasing tasks to the system only with Complete Kits.
   - Releasing tasks only when needed according to the planned timetable and DBR mechanism.

- Releasing tasks to the system in appropriate batches according to the needed deliveries and in compliance with the JIT II rule (the small batch concept).

- Releasing tasks according to the consumption of the buffer in front of the bottleneck. In case of an unexpected increase in buffer size, release of tasks to the system is stopped, and a debriefing takes place to determine the causes of the increase.

3. If the sum of processing and assembling times exceeds 50 percent of the total lead time, breaking the assembly into subassemblies with appropriate kits must be considered.

The following example demonstrates this: The lead time of a certain process is four weeks, while the processing time is three weeks. The work includes two actions: (1) A manual assembly process and electronic wiring, which is the main part of the job; and (2) a short process of adding a connector to the wiring.

In many cases, the connector is not available and the purchasing process is long. Starting work on the wiring before the arrival of the connector helps workers meet deadlines. The work process should therefore be defined as having two independent assembly levels: one is wiring, and the other is attaching the connector. Wiring should be done according to the specifications listed in its Complete Kit and we have three weeks to get the connector, which is part of the Complete Kit for the second level.

In Development

In development processes, a Complete Kit mostly includes information—specifications, definitions, and requirements—and some hardware.

Development projects are classified according to the project uncertainty into A, B, C, and D projects (see Chapter 21).

A and B projects are projects with low technological uncertainty, while projects C and D have high technological uncertainty.

Projects A and B are projects where the system performances are within a familiar performance domain. Since the technological uncertainty is very low, a Complete Kit of specifications and requirements can be defined. In almost every organization that deals with development, experience has shown that A and B projects (as well as subprojects with an A and B character within C and D projects) make up more than 70 percent of the effort invested in the development process. In such projects and subprojects, work should only start with Complete Kits.

There is usually a great deal of uncertainty in C and D projects. In such cases, the Mandatory Kit concept should be applied.

Mandatory Kit: *The minimal information needed to begin a project or a task.*

In C and D projects, the minimal information needed to begin a project should be defined by the customer who placed the order and the person executing it. The same holds true for tasks in C and D projects.

The Complete Kit concept in R&D is described in Figure 12.2. The conflict can be solved using differentiation:

- In C and D projects: A Mandatory Kit should be used.

- In A and B projects: A Complete Kit should be used.

In Knowledge-Based Labor

In purchasing systems, bookkeeping, insurance, banking, the court system, law firms, accounting firms, and in health care systems, the

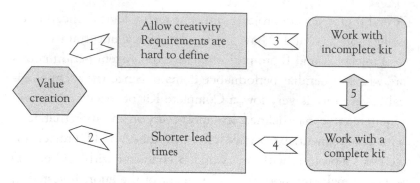

Figure 12.2 The Complete Kit conflict in R&D

implementation of the Complete Kit concept is highly important. Implementation is not difficult and leads to quick results:

- A branch of a local bank decreased the waiting time for a loan by 90 percent using the Complete Kit concept in loan approval processes.

- A branch of a mortgage bank decreased the process of approval of loaning against the mortgage by 60 percent using the Complete Kit concept.

- At a large life insurance company, implementation of the Complete Kit concept led to savings in resources and a substantial decrease in response times.

- The Complete Kit concept was implemented in the court system where plaintiffs had to present needed documents before the proceedings. In car accident claims, for example, the plaintiff was required to present necessary documents, such as a medical opinion statement. The medical opinion statement written by the plaintiff's doctor tended to be more pessimistic than that written by the defendant's doctor. In most cases, the judge had to assign a court-appointed doctor to get an independent medical opinion. The Complete Kit for the proceeding now includes a court-appointed doctor's medical opinion.

In Sales

Salespeople need Complete Kits for sales appointments. This kit includes customer details, expected throughput from the customer, information regarding the customer's needs, current competition, information regarding the customer company and its decision makers.

In Health Care

The Complete Kit is very useful in health care systems (Leshno and Ronen, 2001). Before undergoing an operation, the Complete Kit for patients could include their medical history and test results, information regarding the planned procedure, and the patient's consent form. In the operating room, the Complete Kit includes all the instruments, devices, materials, the necessary personnel, and so on. The OutKit at the end of the operation includes the medical report, further treatment instructions, prescriptions, and so on.

Working with an incomplete kit can endanger the patient and waste valuable bottleneck resources (such as the surgeon, the anesthetist, or the operating room itself), and puts the medical staff and the hospital at risk of malpractice claims.

In Human Resources

Implementation of the Complete Kit concept in human resources' departments can be very useful:

- A Complete Kit of background information and guidelines can help new employees adjust better to the company and motivate them.

- Defining the Complete Kit for managerial development activities, training and development programs, and recruitment, can make the human resources department more efficient and improve its quality of service.

In Purchasing

Implementation of the Complete Kit concept in purchasing departments can lead to a decrease in response times and an increase in effectiveness. This is achieved by:

- Defining a Complete Kit for purchase requests

- Ordering parts and materials in sets that include Complete Kits for the tasks

In Information Systems

The Complete Kit concept can be implemented in information systems departments by defining the Complete Kit of needs and requirements for developing new information systems and for the maintenance and upgrading of existing systems.

Implementing the Complete Kit Concept

Implementing the Complete Kit concept in an organization should be done according to the following guidelines:

1. The introduction of a Complete Kit concept should be parallel to implementations of other advanced managerial approaches, such as just-in-time, quality management, and so on.
2. Top management must be involved in the process. Without the support of top management there is tremendous pressure from second-line managers to start processing incomplete kits, in the

belief that this speeds up the work. Top management and all managers and employees should be trained in the concept.

3. External customers and main suppliers should be involved in the process.

4. A gater should be appointed in main departments and processes who is responsible for the completeness of the kits.

5. The process must be monitored:

   - Monitor the number of tasks starting with a Complete Kit.

   - Use a Pareto analysis of the tasks starting with incomplete kits and the reasons for the lack of components.

   - Regular follow-ups and problem analyses should also be applied.

6. The Complete Kit content for a task should be reexamined from time to time according to the changing circumstances.

According to the Complete Kit concept, incomplete kits should not be released into the system to be worked, even if local measurements, such as resource utilization and cost per unit are impacted.

Summary

The Complete Kit concept is based on common sense and is applicable in all fields of management in all kinds of organizations. Implementing the Complete Kit concept leads to faster response times, better quality, and higher throughput and productivity.

13

Performance Measures and Managerial Control

Global Performance Measures

As we have seen in previous chapters, local performance measures may distort the decision-making process and lead to suboptimization. A measure such as cost per unit may result in the production of large batches, which leads to excess inventory and due-date delays. A measure such as the number of speeding tickets issued by the police does not reduce the number of traffic accidents or smooth traffic flow. A cellular services provider will not increase its value to its shareholders if the main measure of performance of salespeople is the number of subscribers. We need *global performance measures* that yield the following benefits:

- *Clearly communicated management policy regarding organizational goals.* People behave according to how they are measured (i.e., Tell me how you behave and I'll tell you how you are measured.). Clear and simple measures broadcast management policy in an unambiguous way. Using the right measures should improve the value of the firm in a business environment and advance organizational goals in a not-for-profit environment.

- *Decision-making aids.* It is easier for top management to consider different alternatives versus the organizational goals, so that the chosen alternative enhances the value of the firm for its shareholders. However, middle management may find it difficult to see the link between actions in the field and enhancement of the value of the firm directly. Thus, we need performance measures that translate the organizational goal into operative language.

Therefore, performance measures are an intermediary between the decision makers and organizational goals. For example, in managing a research and development (R&D) project, time to market is an important measure for value enhancement. If the project manager is measured by time to market, then he or she will be motivated to reduce this parameter and thus create value to the organization.

- *Control.* Middle management may use performance measures as tools for routine control. If measurement reveals problems, then managers can look for opportunities to correct those problems. If measurement reveals improved performance, then management can use those instances to learn from that success and to replicate it elsewhere in the organization. Performance measures enable an organization to monitor its progress toward goals in the short and long term, and to plan the types of corrective actions that are needed to improve performance.

- *Reward and evaluation.* Good performance measures can serve as part of a system of evaluation and reward in the organization to improve workers' motivation and advance organizational goals.

- *Ability to decentralize.* Appropriate performance measures, by which the CEO and his or her subordinates are measured, allow for decentralized management and decision-making processes.

Appropriate performance measures should have the following characteristics:

- *Global and effective*. Effective measures should significantly advance the achievement of organizational goals and enhance the firm's value in business organizations, and they should advance organizational goals in not-for-profit organizations as well.

- *Simple and clear*. "What will not be simple—simply will not be." Measures should be clear, simple, and easily measured.

- *Based on the satisficer approach*. Measures should be satisfactory, not necessarily perfect or optimal. Implementing performance measures in an organization is not simple and, therefore, it is advisable to proceed gradually. The desire to implement a set of accurate and perfect measures may prove too difficult and lead managers to abandon the process.

- *Founded on easy and simple data collection*. In the organization, it is desirable to use data from existing databases and to have the users of those measures be the agents of data collection.

- *Customized to the organization*. The attempt to adopt measures that have succeeded elsewhere may end up causing disappointment. The organization must gradually build its own appropriate measures or properly adapt others.

Table 13.1 lists a generic set of six performance measures that can be expanded or reduced according to the needs of every organization. The first three measures were defined by Goldratt (Goldratt and Cox, 2004) and the others were defined by Eden and Ronen (1993). These global performance measures represent output measures, input measures, and process measures.

Table 13.1 Six global performance measures

1	Throughput — T
2	Operating Expenses — OE
3	Inventory — I
4	Lead Time — LT
5	Quality — Q
6	Due Date Performance — DDP

Throughput

Throughput: *The effective output of the organization. In business organizations, the cash flow or actual sales minus the real variable costs of those sales.*

Actual sales: *Completed sales transactions, minus returns and cancelled sales.*

Real variable costs (RVC): *Raw materials, components, subcontractors, commissions, and so on.*

The throughput of traffic police is to reduce the number of accidents and to improve traffic flow. It is not the number of tickets issued.

The most important thing in a hospital operating room should be the number of procedures and surgeries, not the hours of operation. The focus should be on output, not input. Throughput is the contribution volume of the procedures.

An example of the use of the throughput measure in decision making: Every month, a company is committed to deliver 100 units of product A, 100 of product B, and 100 units of product C at the selling price of $10 per unit. The company has no work in process (WIP) inventory, and there is no finished goods inventory at the beginning of the month. The real variable costs for each unit are $4. The company actually produced 200 units of A, 150 units of B, and no units of product C.

This seems like a strange decision. If there are well-defined demands, why not produce accordingly? In reality, firms frequently do not produce according to market demands, and they justify their actions on grounds of economies of scale, reducing per unit cost, savings in additional administrative work, or savings on additional machine setups. Sometimes a measure is the number of units produced with no regard to market demand, which results in inappropriate production decisions. Use the data in Table 13.2 to calculate the throughput in this system:

$$T = 100 \times (10 - 4) + 100 \times (10 - 4) + 0 = \$1,200$$

The calculation of the output of products A and B is based on the 100 units that were actually sold (the surplus units will be counted as inventory). In our example, production is 350 units (compared to a demand of 300), but the throughput is only $1,200,

Table 13.2 Calculation of throughput

	Product A	Product B	Product C
Demand (units)	100	100	100
Selling price (per unit)	$10	$10	$10
Real variable cost (per unit)	$4	$4	$4
Actual production (units)	200	150	—

less than the potential throughput of $1,800 (if the plant had produced and sold what the market demanded).

Occasionally, middle management is measured by misleading measures such as the number of units produced; this is organizational language. Such organizations still talk about units sold, tons, and so on. In the insurance industry, the measure of production (total new premiums sold in a period) is still abundant. The use of these kinds of measurements may lead to erroneous decisions and reduced profit.

Measuring throughput in monetary units (dollars) sends a message throughout the organization that we mean business, and helps meet due date performance versus customers by focusing employees on creating effective output. In one organization, we encountered a department manager who successfully implemented the philosophy and refused to produce surplus saying, "this does not give throughput to the firm." This reflects a successful implementation of measures and indicates that measures become part of the organizational language.

Operating Expenses

Operating expenses: *The sum of all* fixed expenses *of the organization during the measurement period.*

The operating expenses (OE) include:

- Direct labor

- Indirect labor

- Other fixed expenses, such as, rent, and so on

Another definition of operating expenses states that the operational expenses are the fixed costs used for converting inventory into throughput (Goldratt and Cox, 2004).

These expenses are the short- and medium-term fixed expenses of the organization. Fluctuations in demand only marginally affect direct labor costs. By measuring operating expenses, the whole organization is examined to evaluate whether expenses have increased or decreased. Suggestions for change or improvement should be evaluated by the manager to determine if operating expenses will increase or decrease, or if they would impact throughput.

A large enterprise hired the services of a consulting firm. After analyzing some data and comparing the enterprise to similar companies in the market, the consultants advised a cutback of 10 percent in the costs of indirect labor. The CEO summoned the division managers and instructed them to cut 10 percent of indirect labor costs. This was immediately implemented despite the tense labor relations between the workers' union and management. How was this achieved? Very simply—some indirect workers were reclassified as direct labor. It is obvious that operating expenses did not decrease nor were any savings achieved.

Inventory

Inventory (I) is classified into three categories that require different treatment:

1. Raw materials (RM) inventory

2. Work in process (WIP) inventory

3. Finished goods (FG) inventory

The value of these three inventory types should be measured in terms of the cost of *raw materials only*. Hence, the value of WIP inventory should not include any additional components reflecting the work invested, and the same is true for FG inventory. Inventories are measured in terms of raw materials because all conversion costs are considered fixed operating expenses. This type of measurement provides convenience and transparency in calculating and analyzing inventories. For example, an increase in WIP inventory is obviously not a result of a change in the way various costs have been loaded, but rather a result of a real increase in quantities. This type of measurement allows quick corrective actions.

Note: This measurement method is different from the way WIP inventory is measured in financial accounting. Accounting measures gradually increase the value of WIP inventory according to the labor hours invested in it.

Lead Time

Lead time (LT) is a general term used for various time measures including cycle time, time to market, and response time. For more accurate definitions, refer to the *APICS Dictionary* (Cox and Blackstone, 1998) and *The Constraint Management Handbook* by Cox and Spencer (1998). Each organization must identify its main processes and measure its lead times.

Appropriate measures of LT look at the process from the perspective of the *customer*. The measurement should include the actual LT, without special allowances for responsibilities that belong to someone else. For example, a patient's main concern is the total amount of time he spends in the medical system, including various waits. He does not care who is actually responsible for his longer than reasonable wait.

Quality

Measures of quality (Q) contribute to organizational value enhancement. Every organization must define its relevant quality measures. For example:

- Percentage of products or services achieved correctly the first time

- Costs of non-conformance quality (the garbage plant)

- Customer satisfaction

- Value/number of returns

- Number of customer complaints

Due Date Performance

Due date performance (DDP) reflects the organization's reliability in meeting deadlines. Due date performance can be measured in several ways:

- *Percentage of on-time performance.* Measuring the percentage of products, services, or milestones that were completed on time. Even though this is a very simple measure, in situations with a high variability in the value of services or products, this measure can distort reality by encouraging the production of inexpensive and easy products. In such cases, the products should be classified into families of products, and measuring DDP should be done for each family separately.

  Occasionally, organizations set a standard for providing a service or delivery: *Quoted lead time* (QLT) and you should measure adherence to this standard.

- *Delayed revenue collection as a result of not meeting due dates (backing orders).* This measure calculates at the end of every period the amount of money of orders not yet delivered. For example: Order X, valued at $200,000, has not yet been delivered, as well as order Y, valued at $100,000. The total value of nonreceived payments due to backing orders is, therefore, $300,000. This measure is simple, useful, understandable, and easy to monitor. However, it does not take into account the length of the delays.

Table 13.3 Example for DDP using the dollar-days measure

Order No.	Order Value ($)	Delivery Date	Days Late	Dollar-Days for June 1
351	100,000	January 1	150	15,000,000
352	200,000	February 1	120	24,000,000
353	300,000	March 1	90	27,000,000
Total dollar-days for delayed orders				66,000,000

- *Dollar-days.* This method calculates DDP as the sum of products of the cash value of orders multiplied by the number of days delay. Table 13.3 presents an example with three delayed orders.

This measure better reflects the economic value of the delays, but is not intuitively appealing to managers and workers, and is barely used. We recommend that organizations try to first use the backing-orders measure of the previous section, and only then move to the dollar-days measure.

Calculating Profit

We can conceptually define the profit of the firm using the measures just discussed as:

Profit of the firm = Throughput of the firm − Operating expenses
$$P = T - OE$$

The importance of this relation is that it forces decision makers in an organization to think globally. Saving two labor hours in some activity or seven minutes of service time, are not necessarily relevant. The important issues are the impact of decisions on global performance measures—the throughput or operating expenses—and as a result, on profit. Therefore, in organizational decision-making processes, the following questions must be asked:

- Does organizational throughput increase as a result of the decision?

- Does operating expenses decrease as a result of the decision?

- Does the decision increase profits? ($P = T - OE$)

Long-term decision making must also take into account the impact of decisions on investments and tax issues.

Adapting Global Performance Measures to a Supermarket Chain

A system of performance measures must be adapted for every organization. Let us consider the six global measures in the management of a supermarket chain:

Throughput   Actual sales minus the RVCs of these sales.

Note: The wage expenses of the employees in the branches are considered fixed costs and are part of the operating expenses. However, the costs associated with temporary seasonal workers or workers of a subcontractor who do not work on a regular basis (where the number of workers can be changed in response to work load) are considered RVCs.

Operating Expenses   Sales and marketing costs, employees' wages, general and administrative costs, rent costs.

Inventory   There are three important measures:

1. Inventory value in the branches
2. Inventory value in the logistics center
3. Number of inventory turns

Lead Time   Lead time of the logistics department—average time from order placement until actual supply to the branch.

Quality   There are two measures:

1. Customer satisfaction as compared to the competitors' as measured by customer questionnaires
2. Average waiting time at the cashier during peak time as compared to the competitors

Due Date Performance   Percentage of on-time deliveries to customers' homes or offices according to the quoted delivery time.

The six global measures form a good starting point for performance measures. You may delete some of them and/or add others as appropriate.

In a supermarket chain, there are other relevant measures such as monthly lost sales. This important metric is measured for each branch separately and accumulated at company level. Lost sales are the daily average sales times (×) the number of zero inventory days of an item during a month times (×) 50 percent. Multiply by 50 percent assuming that 50 percent of the time, the customer will buy an alternative item or will postpone his or her purchase until the next visit to the supermarket. The other half of the time, the customer will buy the product somewhere else or will not buy it at all.

Average daily sales × Zero inventory days × 50 percent
= Monthly lost sales per item

Note: In not-for-profit organizations, there is a tendency to perform extensive and seemingly endless research to find the appropriate performance measure. Those organizations should adopt a satisficer approach. First, start with two to three acceptable, yet not ideal, measures so that you can start measuring right away. Then, measures can be refined and others added as needed. There is no sense in delaying measurement until the perfect measure is found. We do recommend using the satisficer approach in this issue.

Performance measures for project management and development processes are presented in Chapters 20 and 21.

Measures' Profile in Global Decision Making

The measures' profile is a tool for aiding in global decision making. This tool examines alternative decisions using organizational global performance measures. The use of the measures' profile examines alternatives using the six global measures presented earlier. This is a two-dimensional matrix with columns that present the different alternatives and rows that present the performance of the measures (Table 13.4).

The measures' profile presents a succinct picture for each alternative and enables an easy comparison of the impact of each alternative on the various dimensions of organizational performance. The use of this profile across an organization contributes to the decision-making process by having everyone speak the same common and understandable language.

The six global measures are not the only measures useful for decision making. As seen in the previous examples, some of these measures may be deleted (if not relevant) and/or others added.

Later chapters present some uses of the measures' profile in various decision problems and a detailed example of an actual measures' profile is presented in Chapter 16.

Table 13.4 The measures' profile

Performance Measure	Alternative A	Alternative B
T—Throughput		
OE—Operating expenses		
I—Inventory		
RT—Response time		
Q—Quality		
DDP—Due date performance		

Summary

Performance measures are control tools that assist managers of an organization in guiding and navigating. In many situations, an appropriate implementation or adaptation of performance measures can bring about fast and significant improvement in organizational performance and enhance organizational value.

The global performance measures presented in this chapter help an organization focus on activities that improve performance, and thus better achieve the goals of the organization.

14

The Effects of Fluctuations, Variability, and Uncertainty on the System

Fluctuations

Uncertainty related to faults and disruptions is referred to as *fluctuations*. This word serves as a general term for all of the seemingly unexpected situations—problems, malfunctions, interruptions, and disturbances.

Murphy's Law says that if something can go wrong, it will, and it will cause maximum damage at the most inconvenient time. Occasionally, this law is referred to as the bread and butter law. If a buttered slice of bread can drop to the floor, it will; if it drops, it will fall butter-side down, damaging the new carpet. Some people would add that if the slice fell butter-side up, we had spread the butter on the wrong side. The O'Toole principle adds that "Murphy was an optimist."

Sources of Fluctuations

Fluctuations can be classified by their source:

Demand fluctuations
- Variability in demand

- Seasonality

- Technological changes and changes in preferences

Capacity fluctuations
- Variability of work rate at different stations

- Variability in set-up times, both physical set-ups and mental set-ups

- Malfunctions such as machine failure, computer crashes, and so on

- Employee absenteeism

- Scheduling and timing problems

- Incomplete kits

Quality fluctuations
- Unexpected defects

Availability fluctuations
- Problems with quality of materials and components

- Delays in supply

- Supply problems (less than ordered, different from what was ordered, and so on)

For example, fluctuations in the development department of a high-tech company might involve:

- Technological uncertainty (knowledge gap)

- Changes in customers' requirements

- Unavailability of critical purchased items

- Delays of subcontractors

- Uncertainty of market demand

Evolution of Fluctuations in a Process

Consider the planning of a new line of services, products, or development as depicted in Figure 14.1. Every task that enters the system (a patient receiving treatment, a request to develop a smart piece of software, or assembly in production) must go through departments 1, 2, and 3.

Let us assume that $15M has been targeted to create this process. The developers are faced with three alternatives for buying equipment, each costing $15M. Figures 14.2 to 14.4 present each alternative using a cost-utilization (CUT) diagram. The CUT diagram shows, as we have seen before, the *average* utilization of the resources.

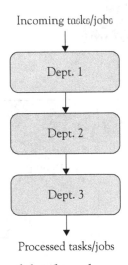

Figure 14.1 Description of the planned process

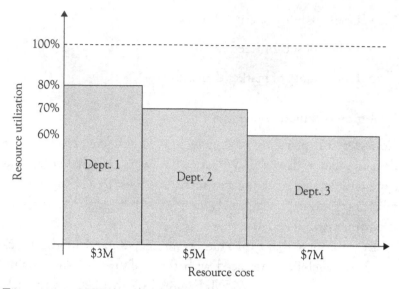

Figure 14.2 CUT diagram for alternative A

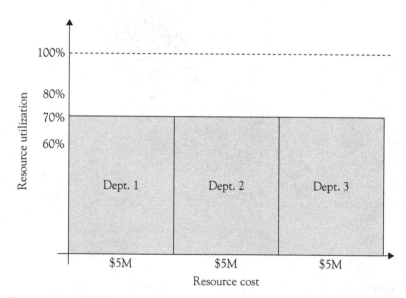

Figure 14.3 CUT diagram for alternative B

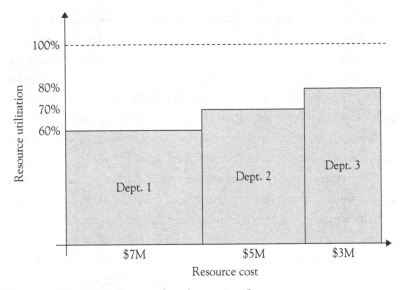

Figure 14.4 CUT diagram for alternative C

Choosing an Alternative

All three alternatives seem to provide a reasonable solution—excess capacity. However, the CUT diagram only presents the average utilization of the resources. In reality, utilization is not constant and varies due to fluctuations. Considering average utilization only, can lead to bad decisions. Types of fluctuations in utilization might include:

- Internal fluctuations

- Cumulative fluctuations

Internal Fluctuations   Internal fluctuations come from the *station itself* and affect its performance. Internal fluctuation can result, for example, from a computer crash at a station, which in turn idles the station and increases the work rate for the rest of the time. Other sources of fluctuations can be worker absenteeism, quality problems, or having a good day with above average achievements.

Cumulative Fluctuations   Cumulative fluctuations result from *performance in preceding stages* of the process. Consider, for example, a group of hikers marching in single file. Where would you rather be: at the head of the line or at the end of the line? The average speed at the head of the line is seemingly the same as that at the end of the line. However, experience has shown that those at the end occasionally have to run to keep up or may have to halt as a result of cumulative fluctuations of all the hikers ahead of them. The standard deviation of a hiker at the end of the line is larger than those at the beginning of the line (Goldratt and Cox, 2004). The behavior of fluctuations in the line is similar: the further a resource is from the beginning of the process, the higher the cumulative fluctuations.

Examine the CUT diagrams of the three alternatives where the diagrams present both the average capacity and the variance of the capacity resulting from internal fluctuations of the stations and the cumulative fluctuations of the preceding stations (Figures 14.5 to 14.7).

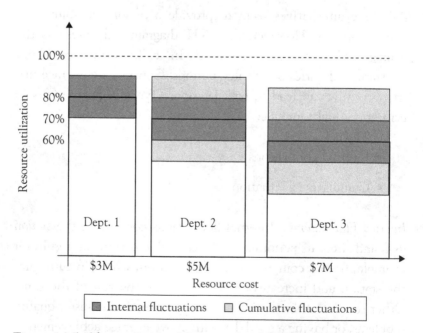

Figure 14.5 Alternative A with internal and cumulative fluctuations

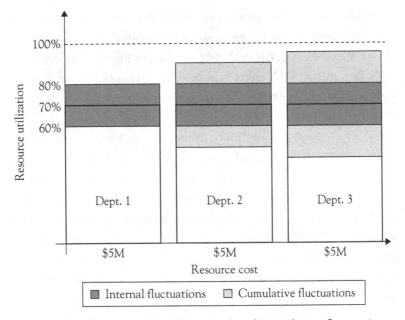

Figure 14.6 Alternative B with internal and cumulative fluctuations

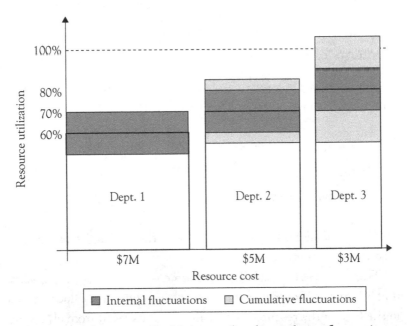

Figure 14.7 Alternative C with internal and cumulative fluctuations

Studying the information presented in these figures, it is clear that alternative A is the preferred choice because even at peak utilization, there is no bottleneck despite the cumulative fluctuations.

With alternative B there is almost a bottleneck part of the time and so it should be treated as if there were an actual bottleneck during those times.

Some of the time, cumulative fluctuations create a bottleneck at department 3 of alternative C. This situation is typical for testing, evaluation, calibration, or other departments located at the end of the process. Such departments are underutilized most of the time because of delays in earlier stations. However, when a wave of work arrives, there is a shortage of resources and the station becomes the process bottleneck. Even though on average such departments have adequate capacity, they become a bottleneck most of the time.

We also present other ways to protect against cumulative fluctuations, such as building a buffer in front of department 3, which is the system bottleneck.

Elements of Capacity

The maximum (theoretical) capacity can be broken down into three parts (see also Cox and Spencer, 1998):

1. Nominal capacity of the resource
2. Protective capacity of the resource
3. Excess capacity of the resource

The *nominal capacity* of a resource is the average capacity utilized for performing its tasks.

The *protective capacity* of the resource is that part of the capacity that is targeted to *overcome* the internal and cumulative fluctuations in the load of the resource. These fluctuations result from changing demand, availability of personnel, availability of raw materials, malfunctions, and so on. This capacity protects the system against routine fluctuations. It is not intended to protect against large and unexpected fluctuations, such as hurricanes, ongoing strikes, and so on, which are rather rare.

System bottlenecks are usually expensive or scarce resources, and the system has difficulty creating a protective capacity for them. However, systems must create *protective capacity* in noncritical resources. This ensures that bottlenecks are not idle because of workflow delays in noncritical resources.

The *excess capacity* of the resource is that part of the maximum capacity of the resource that is not used—not during routine operations and not during increased utilization resulting from fluctuations.

Several conclusions emanate from this analysis:

- During the planning stage for services, products, or development, it is not enough to consider nominal capacity. Planning according to averages can be compared to the situation of the statistics professor who drowned in a lake that had an average depth of 12 inches

  Demand should be sorted by seasonality. For example, in an emergency department there is an obvious difference between pressure during the day and during the night. A system analysis in a hospital should consider two separate emergency departments, a day and a night department.

- In situations of large fluctuations during peak times, system usage must be planned to meet the peaks and to find ways to sell excess capacity during off-peak times. For example, a restaurant with its primary business during evening hours can try to increase sales during lunch by offering business lunch menus.

- A system needs protective capacity. On a local level, this can be viewed as excess and waste. However, from a global perspective, the protective capacity protects the throughput of the bottlenecks and assures that maximum output is achieved for the whole system.

- Resources with a capacity utilization exceeding 85 percent are considered bottlenecks and must be managed accordingly.

- While planning a service or production, we need to arrange sufficient protective capacity. The Japanese tend to build service and production systems with an average utilization of 70 percent.

- The concept of line balancing is not consistent with a reality that has fluctuations in the system. Experience has shown that a service or product line consists of resources with differing costs, some being scarce or expensive. We should maintain adequate protective capacity for the less expensive resources so that they can operate continually and allow us to focus on bottlenecks.

Traditional Approaches to Managing Fluctuations and Uncertainty

Traditional management employs a variety of approaches to different types of fluctuations including:

Managing demand fluctuations
- *Finished goods inventory.* The problems of demand fluctuations may be solved by carrying a large finished goods inventory, along with many warehouses in proximity to customers. This solution is usually expensive.

- *Special sales.* When there is a decline in sales or with the accumulation of a large inventory, special discounts are offered. Sales personnel focus on selling what they have on hand as opposed to selling what is in demand by the market.

Managing capacity fluctuations
- *High levels of WIP inventory.* To overcome capacity fluctuations, and concurrently meet market require-ments for quick response, organizations sometimes build up high levels of WIP inventory. Organizations do this to ensure that bottlenecks do not become idle because of insufficient work flow from preceding stations or due to the lack of available materials or parts. The evils of such inventories are obvious, as discussed in Chapter 10.

- *Buying excess capacity.* It is not uncommon to see organizations create big and expensive excess capacities to meet demand fluctuations.

- *Expediting.* Expediting orders can solve local problems for some customers, but introduces tension into the system and diminishes economic output.

- *Automation and full computerization of the organization.* Automation or complex computerization is sometimes used as a (expensive) solution to overcome market fluctuations. However, without a change in processes or work procedures, the organization may just carry on as before, reaching the same undesirable consequences in a faster and more orderly fashion.

Managing quality fluctuations
- *Overproduction (spares).* Lack of control and an abundance of rejects frequently pushes managers to

overproduction, thus protecting against an unexpected high number of rejects.

- *Repairs.* Creation of repair teams and repair stations is intended to solve problems of failure and rejects.

- *Final inspection and product sorting.* With this approach to quality management (see Chapter 17), at the end of each process, a sorting station is established to sort good quality products from poor quality ones. This is a wasteful approach that does not prevent continued production or development of inferior products. Even so, in many instances, software development companies establish labor-intensive testing departments.

Managing availability fluctuations
- *Raw materials and parts inventory.* Carrying high levels of raw materials and components to overcome situations of delays in supply and delivery. Obviously, such inventories affect the company's cash flow and add carrying and holding costs.

- *Inspection for incoming materials and components.* In situations where a customer cannot depend on the quality of work from his suppliers, there may be a need to establish a testing center for sorting and screening the incoming shipments.

These remedies of traditional management are usually based on fixing the bad outcomes of fluctuations or investment in expensive resources.

Focused Management Approach

Fluctuations must be *managed* (rather than *responded* to) in an effective manner, and with minimal costs. Two possible ways to manage and deal with fluctuations are:

1. Protecting against fluctuations
2. Reducing fluctuations

Protecting against Fluctuations

Creating protective capacity is just one of several methods to protect against fluctuations. The various approaches are:

- *Building a buffer ahead of the bottleneck.* Building a buffer and managing it using the drum-buffer-rope (DBR) approach is a simple and effective way to reduce fluctuations. Building only one buffer does not spread work in process (WIP) across the entire system, and that is what makes this approach unique. This brings about quick results in terms of increasing output and reducing response times.

- *Creating protective capacity or excess capacity.* Creating this protection is immediate. Excess capacity can be achieved through the purchase of resources or through agreements with subcontractors. This is a relatively expensive approach.

- *Building a buffer of finished goods inventory.* In situations of a market constraint when customers request fast response times, you must build a buffer of finished goods to cushion the demand fluctuations.

- *Building an overflow buffer after the bottleneck.* In industrial plants, storage space and storage facilities should be arranged to follow the bottleneck. This keeps the bottleneck working even when there are delays in stations that follow it.

- *Building a buffer of raw materials and parts.* Building a buffer of raw materials and parts protects the system against the expected fluctuations in their supply.

Protection against fluctuations by creating excess capacity, protective capacity, or by creating the right buffers in the right places can be achieved rather quickly. The impact of these protective measures, specifically the right buffers and the DBR mechanism, is immediate and yields short-term results. The problem is that this improvement, as big as it may be, is a one-time achievement. After the initial results, further improvement in protective methods against fluctuations is slow and lengthy and must be accompanied by activities to reduce fluctuations.

Reducing Fluctuations

There are several mechanisms to reduce fluctuations. While the implementation of protection against fluctuations is immediate and brings about quick results, the reduction of fluctuations is usually a slow process whose impact is realized in the medium and long term. For example, the approaches for managing quality and process control according to Deming (1986) are approaches that require a change in the thinking of most people in an organization. Implementing such approaches and observing significant results take considerable time, even years. Let us now examine approaches to reduce fluctuations:

- *Reducing lead time.* Reducing system lead time allows for a better prediction of demand that in turn, allows significant reduction of fluctuations in the system. In addition, the shorter the lead time of the process, the smaller its standard deviation. For example, purchased goods arrive every eight weeks on average, with a standard deviation of plus or minus one week. The firm can protect against a late arrival of materials by creating a week's safety inventory through ordering a week before the original order. If lead time is reduced to eight days, purchases would arrive every eight days on average with a standard deviation of plus or minus one day.

Fluctuations are naturally smaller and so are the required levels of safety stock.

- *Working in small working batches and small working packages.* Small working batches allow for a more continuous process, with less WIP, with a shorter lead time, and as a result, with fewer fluctuations.

- *Sharing information with customers and suppliers.* Sharing information reduces uncertainty. When customers provide suppliers with demand forecasts, the suppliers' uncertainty is reduced and this allows them to obtain raw materials, plan personnel, and so on. Even a forecast that materializes only 70 percent with periodic updates may provide important value to the supplier. Supplier performance improvement contributes to customers by reducing the number of fluctuations that they face.

- *Ability to create a common core for several products or services (the mushroom effect).* Producing or providing service for every product or service separately, as depicted in Figure 14.8, requires separate planning of resources (and raw materials) for every line. Creating a common core for several products (the mushroom effect), as shown in Figure 14.9, allows reduction of the variance in the planning of resources and raw materials. In service organizations, this translates into more flexible and versatile service.

- *Standardization of components and raw materials.* Standardization of raw materials and components used by the firm reduces the variability in work processes and also allows lower levels of inventory to be maintained.

- *Uniting finished goods warehouses.* The variance of overall demand for finished goods stored in one central

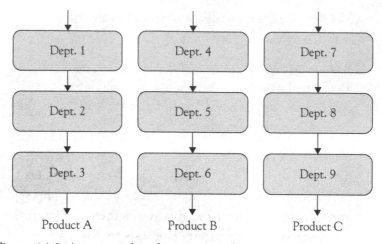

Figure 14.8 A separate line for every product

warehouse is smaller than the sum of demand variances if the finished good are stored in several decentralized warehouses. This results in fewer shortages and less transport among warehouses.

- *Using a single buffer for the entire project using the critical chain approach.* On average, using a common buffer for

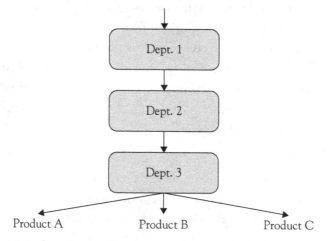

Figure 14.9 Creating a common core for several products—the mushroom effect

all project activities reduces the lead time of the project along with the variance around the finishing date.

- *Reducing overspecification and overdesign.* Overspecification and overdesign reduction reduces project time to completion and time to market. It may also lower the variance in the number of development cycles and decrease fluctuations in the development department.

- *Quality improvement and process control.* Quality improvement and process control contribute significantly to the reduction of fluctuations. These methods are discussed in Chapter 17.

Summary

Managing fluctuations and variability is an important issue that management must consider in planning services or producing products and for routine operation with the organization's resources. Fluctuations that are not properly managed may turn noncritical resources into bottlenecks, thus increasing response time, decreasing throughput, and increasing the amount of WIP. Fluctuations can be managed by a variety of protection and reduction activities.

Reducing fluctuations, especially through the use of quality management and process control, contributes to the output of the organization and enhances its value. However, implementation of measures to reduce fluctuations is more difficult and results are usually only achieved in the medium or long term, while the involvement of most players in the system is usually required.

It is not surprising that many quality improvement programs do not achieve their objectives because of these difficulties. Protecting against fluctuations, especially through approaches of management by constraints, is not sufficient, even though improvements are obtained in the short term.

A combination of both approaches seems to be the right solution—starting the implementation of improvements via management by constraints, and at the same time, starting the implementation of quality management approaches. In the case of implementing steps for improvement, it is safe to say that quality comes second.

15

Evils of Traditional Cost Accounting

Loss of Relevance

The issue of loss of the relevance in traditional cost accounting was raised during the 1980s (Goldratt, 1986, 1990; Johnson and Kaplan, 1987). Traditional cost accounting methods were developed in the 1920s in leading U.S. firms and were suitable for the production environment of those days: mass production of a limited number of products, utilizing economies of scale, and learning curves. Direct labor wages were a major component in costs and were considered true variable costs, taking into consideration the labor relations at that time. The indirect costs were low and assigning them to products based on direct wages (or another volume-based variable like machine hours) was a reasonable approximation for making business decisions, such as continuation or discontinuation of the production of a product, investment decisions, make or buy decisions, and so on.

For example, the cost structure of one unit of product A was:

Materials	$10
Direct labor	4
Overhead allocation	2
Total product cost	$16

In the business environment of the past, traditional cost accounting allowed the breakdown of business outcomes at profit centers by individual product and preparation of a separate balance sheet for each product. Managers could make decisions about *one product* (e.g., increasing/decreasing production, using subcontractors) without *concurrently checking the impact of the decisions on other products.* This is the *separation principle* that created a convenient decision-making tool for management.

Decisions regarding a product, based on the separation principle, required managers to know only the relevant data for a specific product. For example, if the market price for product A was only $13, then a decision about ceasing its production was obvious (compared to the total production cost of $16). If a subcontractor was willing to produce the product for $12, the make or buy decision was easy to make. In another situation, if the market price was $22 per unit, then traditional cost accounting, which is based on the product cost, led decision-makers to provide a positive answer. Several factors are responsible for the loss of relevancy of traditional cost accounting:

- *Changes in the relative weight of indirect costs.* When traditional cost accounting was created in the 1920s, indirect costs were 5 percent to 10 percent of production costs. Today, indirect costs (overheads) constitute 20 percent to 80 percent of the total cost of the product. The bulk of this increase comes from costs related to operations support (i.e., planning, operations control, scheduling, engineering, quality control), information systems, marketing force, and the managers of finance and human resources. The weight of traditional, fixed, indirect costs of production (e.g., depreciation, insurance, property taxes) has remained stable over time.

- *Changes in the character of salary costs.* In the past, direct labor costs were a *variable expense.* Today, direct wages are

mainly a *fixed cost* in the short and medium terms. However, it is still customary for accounting to assign indirect
costs based on direct wages, causing severe distortions.

- *Expanding the variety of services and products.* Today's
  services and products are congruent with customer
  needs and preferences. Technological development,
  along with the desire to adapt services and products to
  customers, brought about a large increase in the variety
  of products, services, and treatments available today.
  The competitive need to expand the variety of services
  and products presents managers with a challenge: How
  do you expand product variety while maintaining the
  advantages of the organization's focused operations?
  The cost accounting system must provide support with
  relevant information. Traditional cost accounting does
  not provide answers to the challenge of production
  complexity, development of prototypes, or providing a
  variety of services.

- *Distinguishing between bottlenecks and noncritical resources.*
  Today, there is a clear distinction between resources
  that are bottlenecks and noncritical resources. The
  noncritical resources have a built-in protective capacity
  that should protect the system against external fluctuations in demand and internal fluctuations resulting
  from malfunctions. Traditional cost accounting does
  not recognize this distinction.

- *The dominance of financial accounting.* In recent decades,
  the sophistication of capital markets and the stricter
  rules for financial reporting have brought about a drive
  for research and regulation in financial accounting,
  with emphasis on financial reporting. However, managerial accounting has remained at a virtual standstill

and is only considered a secondary supportive system. When resources are channeled into managerial improvement, the financial manager (who is frequently also responsible for information systems) usually prefers to invest in financial accounting tools needed for reporting to the stock exchange or the internal revenue service, rather than investing in managerial accounting (e.g., decision support measurement tools).

Undesireable Effects of Traditional Cost Accounting

"It Costs Us More"

A large company purchased a new machine at a cost of $2 million. This machine replaced an old, very labor intensive, line. It produced high quality products with very short response times, in sufficient quantities to meet all local market demand. All of this was accomplished with a capacity utilization that did not exceed 60 percent. The return on investment was less than two years. The cost to produce a unit of the product was calculated by the accountants:

Raw materials	$10
Direct labor	2
Overhead	8
Total cost	$20

A foreign customer wanted to purchase 10 percent of the machine's output for $16 per unit, although the regular selling price was 23$. Even though the customer was from a different geographical region, and even though he would have sold the product under a different name and for a different use, management refused to sell claiming "it costs us more" and "we can't sell a product at a loss." The idea of considering costs that are not relevant for decision making is well known and has been discussed in the literature for decades. However, many managers still use total cost data for decision making.

"Large Batches"

The new CEO immediately pushed to reduce the product cost. The average production batch size (which was congruent with the market) was 10 units. Production resources were at excess capacity. Set-up time was two hours, and the marginal time to produce one unit was one-fourth of an hour. The average time to produce one unit in a batch size of 10 was calculated as:

$$T(10) = (2 + 1/4 \times 10)/10 = (2 + 2.5)/10 = 0.45 \text{ hours/unit}$$

To reduce the cost per unit (a local measure that has no business meaning), management decided to work with batches of 100 units to capitalize on economies of scale:

$$T(100) = (2 + 1/4 \times 100)/100 = (2 + 25)/100 = 0.27 \text{ hours/unit}$$

Phantom savings were achieved and the cost per unit was decreased . . . Note that production costs did not decrease at all. Due to increased work in process (WIP) inventory, the indirect costs increased, along with finished goods inventory and all of their ramifications.

"Efficient Production"

A public company decided to make production more efficient. They realized that the overhead multiplier was 6.2 (for every dollar spent on direct labor in production, there was an overhead of $6.2). The product cost was:

Raw materials	$40
Direct labor	10
Overhead	62
Total product cost	$112

The desire to make production efficient brought about a drastic reduction in direct labor, and interfered with the company's bottleneck. After a 30 percent reduction in direct labor, the cost of the product became:

Raw materials	$40
Direct labor	7
Overhead	43.4
Total product cost	$90.4

The company was thrilled with their savings despite the reduced production throughput. Moreover, they shared the cost reduction with customers by offering them an additional 10 percent discount.

"Savings"

Department A in a company had a temporary manpower shortage. The manager of that department asked his colleague, the manager of department B with excess personnel, for help. The colleague agreed to transfer some staff for the needed time but demanded compensation for the full cost of the staff. The manager of department A, with the manpower shortage, eventually decided to hire outside help at a lower cost. The result—the company increased its expenses while excess workers in B remained idle and received full pay.

Summary

Traditional cost accounting lost its relevance because the underlying assumptions that it is based on are no longer valid, as seen in Table 15.1.

The conclusion from Table 15.1 is that the assumptions of traditional cost accounting, which were relevant at the beginning of the twentieth century, are usually no longer valid; therefore, the use of traditional costing may lead to poor managerial decisions.

Table 15.1 Loss of relevance of the assumptions underlying traditional cost accounting

	Beginning of Twentieth Century	Today
Overhead (indirect expenses)	<5%	20%–80%
Direct labor	Real variable cost	Fixed cost
Resources	Ability to adjust personnel	Coexistence of bottlenecks and noncritical resources (having excess capacity)

More appropriate tools are required for proper decision making. The next chapter presents alternatives to traditional cost accounting that are appropriate for the modern business environment.

16

Marketing, Costing, and Pricing Considerations in Decision-Making Processes

In recent years, two approaches have been developed to handle the irrelevancy of traditional cost accounting and to aid managers in decision making:

1. *Activity-based costing.* This cost accounting method is actually a refinement and improvement of classical cost accounting (absorbing accounting) and was first introduced by Cooper and Kaplan (1988). Activity-based costing (ABC) analyzes indirect costs and assigns them in sophisticated and precise methods across various services or products.

2. *Throughput accounting.* This accounting method was introduced in the 1940s and is an improvement on contribution accounting. Throughput accounting was improved as a managerial decision-making tool by Goldratt (1991). In this chapter, we discuss the basics of throughput accounting and improve on it by adding a structured methodology (global decision making, GDM) and other simple tools that aid managerial decision making.

Activity-based costing only partially aids decision-making processes and is, in fact, using cost allocation that is somewhat arbitrary and not relevant (Eden and Ronen, 2002).

The load of organizational resources is a critical factor in decision-making processes regarding pricing, investment, or make or buy decisions. Two environments that decision makers may encounter include:

1. Decision making in a resource constrained environment
2. Decision making in an excess capacity environment (market constraint)

Decision Making in a Resource-Constrained Environment

Today's competitive business environment is usually an environment with excess capacity in operational resources or services, and the market is a buyers' market. However, there are many situations in which organizations are constrained by bottlenecks. These include departments that are permanent bottlenecks (like development, or marketing and sales) and situations where a bottleneck results from shortages of very expensive resources, shortages of skilled professionals, peak or seasonal periods, or temporary or continual raw materials shortages.

In a resource-constrained environment, managers have to make decisions on the following problems:

- *Problems of product mix.* A resource-constrained environment cannot allow the production of *all* products with market potential or deliver *all* possible services to the customer. System performance is limited by its constraints, and a resource constraint forces managers to decide on a product or service mix: on one hand, managers must decide which products to manufacture and sell (or which services to sell) and, on the other hand, managers must decide which products or services to exclude.

- *Make or buy decisions.* This is a common managerial decision problem. Decisions about using subcontractors require strategic and tactical judgment. The advantage of subcontractors is the elevation of the resource constraint that allows the organization to effectively expand manufacturing or service ability. The decision about which jobs should be performed inhouse (make) and which should be purchased from subcontractors (buy), while considering system resources, is an important one.

- *Pricing decisions.* At what price should a product or service be offered to the market? How should we price products that pass through bottlenecks, and at what price should we sell a product or service that does not pass through one (free goods)?

- *Decisions about stopping production or ceasing service.* This decision must be made while considering the global perspective and system constraints of the whole organization. As we have seen, decisions based on traditional cost accounting can lead to system failure.

- *Decisions about introducing a new product or service line.* These decisions must be taken from a global perspective, making wise use of information regarding system resources and understanding the impact on critical resources.

- *Decisions about investments.* The best investments are those that enhance the value of the firm. Global decision making supports the increase of throughput and the reduction of operating expenses, or the increase in the difference between them. In the case of a system constraint, controlled investments that increase the capacity of the bottleneck are usually the ones that lead to increased profits and value enhancement for the firm.

- *Decisions about acceptance and pricing of projects.* A project environment, which is common to high-tech industries, is usually an environment with constraints on development resources. Managers must determine project priorities and how to price them.

- *Decisions about bidding for contracts.* As we have seen before, managers who use traditional cost accounting cannot distinguish between work hours of excess capacity resources and work hours of constrained resources. The strategic and tactical tools that are presented in this chapter should help managers make decisions about bidding for contracts.

- *Decisions about product differentiation and market segmentation.* Product differentiation and market segmentation are important marketing tools. In many industries (e.g., cosmetics, automotive), segmentation and differentiation have been customary for years. However, many organizations have yet to capitalize on the differentiation and segmentation potential. Smart use of critical resources can lead to better segmentation and differentiation decisions.

Tools

The tools in the following list are suitable and helpful for decision-making processes in both resource-constrained environments and in environments with excess capacity (market constraint):

- Global performance measures, as discussed in Chapter 13

- Global decision-making methodology (see the next section)

- The measurements' profile

- Cost-utilization (CUT) diagram

- Specific contribution (unique to resource-constrained environments)

Global Decision-Making Methodology

The GDM methodology (Geri and Ronen, 2005) is a simple and practical methodology used in global decision making. It helps managers with decisions about pricing, make or buy decisions, decisions about stopping the production of a product or shutting down a line of products or services. The three steps of the methodology are:

1. *Make a global economic decision from the perspective of the* CEO. The decision should be such that it would achieve the maximal contribution to the organization's objective function and should reflect the CEO's perspective. The decision uses two tools we have introduced:

   a. Measurements' profile

   b. CUT diagram

2. *Take strategic considerations into account.* Strategic considerations relate to the long run, and to considerations that involve intangible benefits. Step 1 generates an economic decision. Now, managers can add strategic considerations that may change the global economic decision and they can calculate the cost of those strategic considerations for the organization. Decisions are frequently made without in-depth analysis, with claims that it was a strategic decision. The strategic considerations of management are important, but they are more appropriate if they carry a price tag.

3. *Change local performance measures, if needed.* Local performance measures frequently distort the decision-making process. A manager may occasionally prefer to make a bad decision,

rather than a decision that would better serve the organization, if it would maximize local or personal performance measures. Managers should examine and adapt local performance measures to maximize organizational objective functions. The use of local measures such as profit per product or service, cost per service or product, or number of units produced or served, may distort decisions, and should, therefore, be changed.

Decision Making in an Excess Capacity Environment

The GDM methodology is valid both in a resource-constrained environment and in an excess capacity environment (market constraint). The following example highlights the use of the GDM methodology in make or buy decisions in situations of excess capacity.

In a large company, the project manager considers whether electronic cards should be made by the company's production department (inhouse) or through a subcontractor. The company estimated the work package at 1,000 direct labor hours. The hourly rate (operating expenses divided by direct labor hours) of the department is $35 per hour. For the next two quarters, it is forecasted that the load of the production department will be about 50 percent. Thousands of labor hours in this department are still available. The production department estimates that the work can be done within one quarter. The purchasing manager of the project is also considering outsourcing the work for $25,000. Which decision should the project manager make? Please note that the project manager is evaluated quarterly according to the project's profit and loss (P&L).

> *The analysis:* In a world of local performance measures, it seems reasonable for the project manager to turn the work over to the external subcontractor (buy) rather than perform the task inhouse (make) because this would be $10,000 better for P&L. *Seemingly,* the project manager saves $10,000 by making this decision. Actually, the project manager spent $25,000 out of pocket, and the fixed costs of the company were not changed. (Variable costs would have been incurred in both cases.)

In the next section, we examine this decision using the GDM methodology.

Global Economic Decisions from the CEO's Perspective

A CUT diagram for the production department is presented in Figure 16.1. This is a situation with excess capacity, and even if production is completed inhouse, the situation remains the same and there is still no bottleneck. Table 16.1 presents the measurements' profile for this decision.

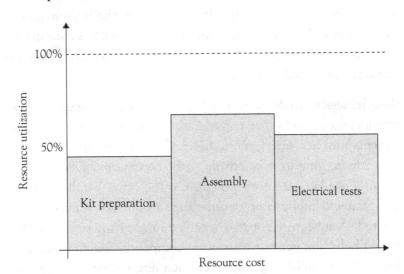

Figure 16.1 CUT diagram for the production department

Table 16.1 Measurements' profile for the make or buy decision

Measurement	Make	Buy
T—Throughput	X	X-$25,000
OE—Operating Expenses	Y	Y
I—Inventory	?	?
LT—Lead Time	?	?
Q—Quality	?	?
DDP—Due Date Performance	?	?

The throughput of an organization is defined as actual sales minus real variable costs of these sales. Thus, the costs paid to the subcontractor in a *buy* decision reduce the firm's throughput by $25,000.

Operational expenses (in conditions of excess capacity in the company) do not change. The total cost for salaries, rent, and machine maintenance remains constant, whether the work is done inhouse or outside of company. The *bottom line* is that giving the work to the subcontractor reduces profits.

Every measure must be dealt with separately, considering pros and cons for each alternative. It is clear from the measurements' profile that if the last four measures (I, LT, Q, DDP) are similar for the two alternatives, then the *make* (inhouse production) decision should be preferred to the buy (subcontractor) one.

Take Strategic Considerations into Account We must take long-term considerations and other considerations that relate to intangible benefits into account. On one hand, the firm may have an interest in preserving its relationship with the external subcontractor because of planned future growth. On the other hand, the negative strategic implications of using the subcontractor must be considered. A subcontractor may receive important information that would help him become a strategic competitor. At this stage, we know the financial implication of each alternative and may thus make the decision on economic grounds.

In many situations, strategic considerations may include the following question: Is the relevant technology a *core competency* of the organization?

Figure 16.2 presents the core competence matrix, which assists managers in making or buy decisions. The matrix combines the strategic technology and efficiency dimensions of the relevant department.

A department situated in quadrants 1 or 2 in the core competence matrix is of strategic importance to the organization—this is the core competence of the organization. The tasks of these departments should be performed inhouse (e.g., a development department in a high-tech firm, or project management department in a company that oversees construction).

The tasks of departments in quadrant 1 should be performed inhouse. Departments in quadrant 2 have core competence that should be kept within the organization, but they should not operate at low efficiency. We must find ways to improve the performance of such departments, make them more efficient, and shift them to quadrant 1.

Tasks of quadrant-3 departments should be taken outside to subcontractors or outsourcing services—these tasks do not have

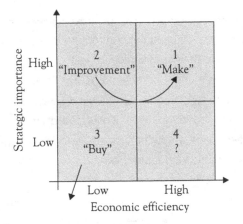

Figure 16.2 The core competence matrix

core competence and are not efficient (e.g., dining or cleaning services in a high-tech company).

Decisions regarding departments in quadrant 4 should be evaluated individually according to the current strategy of the organization.

The decision to assign tasks to subcontractors is management's strategic decision. An attempt to resolve the make or buy decision on local economic grounds may be detrimental to the organization. A decision based on the economic wisdom of allowing *market forces* to dictate actions, empowers internal customers within the organization to form make or buy decisions. This approach allows management to disengage itself from the problem, perhaps leading to the *drying out* of strategic technological departments. Such an approach also prevents future investments in cutting edge technology and information that may be needed to preserve the technological ability of strategically important departments.

A policy of performing jobs outside the organization only because of local economic considerations may bring about the loss of core competence and the loss of clear strategic advantages.

A high-tech company used subcontractors for all its system engineering needs in data communication, although that was defined as the company's core competence. Over time, the entire body of knowledge relating to data communication system engineering moved outside the company. This created a strategic and economic dependence on subcontractors and limited the influence the company had on the future development of data communication products and technologies.

A public company specializing in the production of testing equipment realized that the production of its products had become rather
standard. They outsourced production to a multinational firm in
Asia, which allowed considerable savings in production costs. The
realized savings encouraged management to outsource sales and
marketing as well. Putting strategic marketing abilities in foreign
hands resulted in a steep drop in sales and finally the company
filed for bankruptcy.

Management and control are strategic capabilities in many
organizations. Giving those abilities away makes the organization
vulnerable to a loss of control of its operations.

Change or Refine Local Performance Measures   Reaching the right
decision, situations like this may be delayed by some factors,
such as local performance measures (hourly rate) or project profits.
We must aspire to address these factors and change them if necessary. Measurement of project profit can be refined by using an
external, alternative transfer price. Another possibility is to
make the production unit into a *cost center* (instead of a *profit
center*), which management wants to keep inhouse for strategic
reasons (Horngren, Foster, and Datar, 2000).

Decisions about Stopping Production or Ceasing Service

The GDM methodology can be used in decision problems about
whether to stop production of a product. We can use the same
techniques to analyze the cessation of some service.

Suppose management is wondering whether to stop production
of a certain product. The production line used for this product is at
excess capacity and in the coming year there is no planned effective

use of this capacity. The market price of the product is $4.00 and the production costs (using *traditional cost accounting*) are:

Raw materials	$2.00
Packaging	0.50
Direct labor	0.75
Processing	0.31
Depreciation	0.20
Indirect costs	1.10
Total product cost	$4.86

Projected sales of the product are 10,000 units per month. According to traditional cost accounting, the company is losing $0.86 for every unit sold. As a result, management is considering stopping production of this product. It should be noted that the company will not lay off workers if they close the line because they are needed for other tasks.

Make a Global Economic Decision from the CEO's Perspective

Let us examine the situation using the GDM methodology. The CEO should draw the CUT diagram for the production line and consider the various alternatives. The CUT diagram reveals excess capacity. Table 16.2 shows the measurements' profile of the two alternatives.

Table 16.2 Measurements' profile for production example

Measurement	Continue Production	Stop Production
T—Throughput	X	X-$15,000
OE—Operating Expenses	Y	Y
I—Inventory	=	=
LT—Lead Time	=	=
Q—Quality	=	=
DDP—Due Date Performance	=	=

In this example, throughput will be reduced by $15,000 because the selling price is $4.00 per unit and the variable costs are $2.50 [10,000 × ($4.00 − $2.50) = $15,000].

The real variable costs for production are raw materials and packaging. Some of the processing costs can also be considered variable (energy and parts). The manager should consider other variables as needed.

Fixed costs are not changing. Therefore, the economic decision should be to continue manufacturing. The contribution of sales in this case helps cover the fixed costs and should not be given up.

Make Strategic Considerations

In stopping production of the product, the important strategic considerations are: Does the stoppage of sales negatively impact the firm's reputation? Will competitors capture the market share given up by the firm? In any case, step 1 of the methodology presents the cost of each strategic decision to management.

Change Local Performance Measures if Needed

If a department manager is measured by a local balance sheet of a product line, this measure must be changed. Performance measures that take throughput into account could be appropriate substitutes.

Product Mix Decisions

In the modern service and production environment, there is an abundance of operational excess capacity. The question about what should be done with this excess is an important one.

Let us consider the following product mix example: A company is considering what price to charge for a new product. The variable costs (mainly raw materials and components) are $55 per unit. The other costs are fixed and the company has an excess capacity that allows it to produce up to 1,000,000 units monthly.

Table 16.3 Demand as a function of price

Scenario	Price per Unit ($)	Demand (Units per Month)
A	100	100,000
B	80	200,000
C	60	500,000

The marketing consultants envision three scenarios for market demand as presented in Table 16.3. The demand curve is represented graphically in Figure 16.3.

The natural solution is to choose the price that maximizes profit. However, the maximum profit would be realized if the product was offered *at all three prices*: segment the market to those who will pay $100, those who will pay $80, and those who will pay $60.

Global Economic Decisions from the CEO's Perspective

Examine this example using the GDM methodology. We first examine the problem using the measurements' profile as shown in Table 16.4. The global economic decision is to sell the product at three different prices. This yields the highest contribution to the company, hence the highest profit.

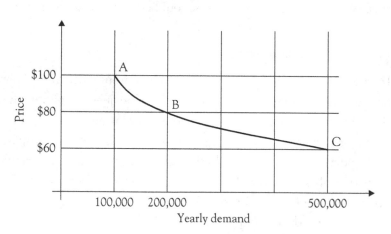

Figure 16.3 Demand curve for product mix example

Table 16.4 Measurements' profile for product mix example

Measurement	Not to Sell	Sell A	Sell B	Sell C	Sell at All Prices
T—Throughput	X	X + $4.5M	X + $5M	X + 2.5M	X + $8.5M
OE—Operating Expenses	Y	Y	Y	Y	Y
I—Inventory	=	=	=	=	=
LT—Lead Time					
Q—Quality	=	=	=	=	=
DDP—Due Date Performance	=	=	=	=	=

Take Strategic Considerations into Account

Long-term strategic considerations place several *threats on the organization* when selling products at three different prices:

- *Falling prices in the market.* Selling the product to type C customers can lead to a *price drop* for A and B customers:

  —The salespeople, who feel that the only sales margin is variable costs, will sell the product to all customers at lower prices (close to $55) in the future. Salespeople always want to sell (occasionally at any price) and they will justify this by the marginal positive benefit to the company.

  —A type A customer, who finds out that the product is sold to market segment C at a lower price, will demand the lower price as well. In addition, the customer will feel cheated.

  —Type A and B customers may demand the lower rates, even for past purchases. They may now demand lower prices for other products as well.

There is the danger that the excess capacity will quickly be filled up with product sold at lower prices. These dangers can be overcome by:

- *Product differentiation and market segmentation:* The product may be sold in different forms to different market segments and priced at the perceived value of these segments. There are many industries that have specialized in market segmentation and product differentiation (e.g., the cosmetics industry, airlines), and there are other industries that have not done so. A first-class passenger on a flight may pay up to five times more than a passenger in economy class, but neither passenger feels he is not getting his money's worth. Moreover, two passengers sitting next to each other in economy class may have paid different prices for the same flight because their tickets may be different kinds—reflecting restrictions or other differences. The electronics industry differentiates products by performance or by brand names that reflect the perceived value of the products to their customers.

The high-tech industry differentiates products by performance, mainly by downgrading performance. The automotive industry differentiates by model type (e.g., two door, four door, coupe, sedan, or station wagon), by the number of features, type of transmission, or brand (e.g., GM has several brands such as Chevrolet, Buick, Pontiac and Oldsmobile).

In most cases, the costs in providing differential services or producing differential products is relatively small in relation to the price differences customers are willing to pay. Therefore, the dimension of differentiation includes:

- Performance

- Brand name

- Size

- Quality

- Reliability

- Quantity

- Repetitiveness of purchases (e.g., one time or frequent flyer)

- In season or out of season

- Packaging

- Warranty

- Service level

- Geographic differentiation

- Response times

Correct product or service differentiation and market segmentation can provide answers to the potential dangers of upper-market segments pushing prices down.

Change Local Performance Measures if Needed

Local performance measures such as price per unit may lead to failure that will prevent correct product differentiation and market segmentation.

Summary

The GDM methodology presented in this chapter is a simple and efficient tool for decision making. It bypasses the need to determine product cost or product profit and their inherent problematic natures. This methodology is useful in pricing decisions, make or buy decisions, pricing new products or services, stopping production or services, determining transfer prices, determining bid prices, determining product mix, and evaluating investments.

With all the benefits provided by this methodology, we must not ignore its largest danger, which is lack of threshold. Traditional cost accounting, with all that it lacks in common sense, determines a cost threshold. The disadvantages of a threshold are known: It is arbitrary and leads to loss of business opportunities. However, it provides a barrier to the pressure from salespeople to sell more at any cost, while causing price attrition.

The user of this methodology must maintain a constant mechanism for management to determine performance thresholds for every product or family of products or services. This threshold is determined by market prices, availability of resources, and strategic considerations. Such a mechanism requires a high level of management that enables differential treatment of products or services.

An organization that uses this methodology must have a common language among staff in finance, marketing, development, and operations. Understanding the managerial approaches behind this methodology will bring about better decisions, both at strategic and tactical levels.

17

Quality Management and
Process Control

One of the major breakthroughs in management over the past decades is in the area of quality management and process control. Today, quality is one of the most important factors in the competitive environment of any organization.

Poor quality does have a very negative effect on the value of an organization, both by contributing to a decrease in income and an increase in expenses. The opposite is also true—good quality has positive effects on income and expenses.

Quality should be viewed as an important value enhancer and as a tool for improving processes, products, and services. This chapter presents a goal-oriented business approach to quality and process control. We show that good quality and a reduction of expenses can be achieved simultaneously by utilizing a number of different approaches:

- Operational approach

- Economic approach

- Customer approach

- Uniformity (consistency) approach

Operational Approach

This approach, characterized by Crosby (1979), states that quality means *conformance to requirements*. A product, service, or proto-type has quality only if it conforms to the requirements dictated by the customer. According to this definition, there is no difference in the quality of a brand new Rolls Royce that meets customer requirements or a VW beetle (an older model) that was manufac-tured to meet all of its required specifications. Service provided at a fast-food chain like McDonald's can be considered high quality if it meets standards of waiting times, service rules, and food prepara-tion procedures as specified by the company. The first step in creat-ing quality according to Crosby is to *define requirements*. We often realize that services or products do not have well-defined require-ments. Development of new products is frequently completed with incomplete specifications, resulting in many development cycles and delays in project completion.

Economic Approach

In the economic approach, quality is defined by Schonberger (1986) as two dimensions that reflect the process quality of an organization and are closely related:

1. Achieving a minimal garbage plant
2. Doing it right the first time

Garbage plant: *Activities that do not add value to the cus-tomer, the product, the service, the prototype, or the process.*

Some examples of garbage plant activities are labor hours, money and materials wasted on repairs, rework, errors, or customer compensation for defective services or products, and time devoted to solving these problems. This is also considered the noneffective time of specialists and marketing and sales personnel. Garbage plants have *nonconformance quality costs* that occupy large percentages of employees' or managers' time. Some examples of garbage plants include:

- In a billing department, a large quantity of staff members spend time correcting billing errors.

- In a high-tech organization, the systems integration stage is about 8 to 15 weeks. Most of this time results from out-of-date specifications, unreported changes, and unreliable test procedures.

- In a department that manufactures components, several technicians spend most of their time analyzing and correcting problems.

- Many salespeople report that 40 percent to 60 percent of their time is ineffective because of repeat or cancelled meetings and incomplete kits.

- The customer service department of a large financial services company reports that dozens of employees spend hours on the phone trying to resolve problems that arise from mistakes or ambiguities in customers' bills.

- In the development department of a high-tech organization, relatively simple cards required six development cycles. Most of the unnecessary cycles stemmed from faulty requirements (incomplete kit), although the missing information actually existed in the organization.

- In a certain restaurant, about 10 percent of the customers received the wrong dish because waiters tried to memorize orders and did not write them down. This resulted in delays in food delivery, food that had to be discarded, waiters and cooks wasting time, and unhappy customers, some of whom will not return to the restaurant.

Garbage plants can be avoided. It is clear that we cannot always provide a service or produce a product with zero defects. However, by reducing the garbage plant from 50 percent to 30 percent, we can achieve economic advantages and value enhancement for the organization.

When a task is done right the first time there is no need to redo any of the steps or to correct problems that may have occurred.

Right the first time: *Every step in the process of performing a task is completed successfully the first time around without failures or quality problems.*

Customer Approach

This approach is derived from Juran's definition of quality (1989). Juran, one of the founding fathers of quality theory, claims that one of the most important dimensions of quality for the customer is *fitness to use*. This fitness emphasizes the centrality of the customer. The customer sets the standards, and the whole organization, including all products, services, prototypes, and employees, should be subordinated to the customer's requirements. The product or service must be fit to the customer's use. Juran views the work processes as a chain of *internal suppliers* who work to fulfill the needs and requirements of *internal customers*. At the same time, every element in the value chain of the organization should serve the *external customer*.

Uniformity (Consistency) Approach

Taguchi, a Japanese engineer and one of the founders of the modern quality theory, emphasized *uniformity*, *consistency*, and *minimal variance* as critical components of quality (Taguchi, 1986). According to this approach, a service or product that is offered with minimum variation and consistent performance is a testimony for a *controlled process*.

In *service organizations*, uniformity or consistency means a *process* that repeats itself again and again with minimal variation over time.

In the health care system, waiting times in a clinic are one measure of service quality. If patients wait once for 10 minutes and other times for two hours, the resulting variation is problematic. If they have alternatives, such inconsistency in the level of service may drive patients to the competition.

In the McDonald's fast-food chain, consistency is one of the key parameters of quality. A consistently high level of service that conforms to requirements of time standards, performance, and service must be maintained. In every McDonald's restaurant, a customer expects to receive the same quality burgers and fries produced using the *same* methods. This consistency is a value enhancer for the chain, and it produces a reputation that brings customers back again and again.

The Howard Johnson's restaurant chain is an example where the lack of consistency had severely negative effects. For years, customers knew what to expect at any restaurant in the chain. At some point, variability between restaurants increased, and the lack of uniformity (consistency) in what customers were receiving, eventually led to the disappearance of this restaurant chain.

In *production*, uniformity and consistency mean having good control over a process. This means that companies should have the capability to produce the same product again and again, even thousands of times, regardless of other factors that may introduce *variability* into the system. Such factors may include:

- Suppliers of raw materials
- Raw materials and components

- Employees

- Production specifications

- Equipment and computerization

The fact that an organization is able to maintain uniformity and minimal variability despite the "noise" by these factors, demonstrates that it is possible to achieve near complete process control. This control assures the continual production of the same product at the same quality across time.

In research and development (R&D) departments, uniformity and minimum variability mean the design process needs to be structured and uniform. Such a process encourages thorough design and cooperation among all the partners in the R&D process. Usually, the main problems in R&D are not lack of creativity or an inability to overcome technical gaps. Many problems in development are due to ambiguous and incomplete requirements kits, lack of communication between marketing and development, overspecification, overdesign, an unstructured design process, poor duration estimation, and low levels of control and follow-up. These problems can be solved using structured processes with minimum variability. This does not mean that *all* processes will have the same format or will be managed the same way. Usually, we classify processes into various groups, where each group may have a different process to fit its special requirements and needs.

We have presented four of the more popular approaches to quality. There are other definitions of quality, which describe quality as *meeting* or even *exceeding* customer expectations. Other definitions break quality down into several dimensions like reliability, performance, perceived quality, response time, and life cycle.

Eventually, improving processes of service, production, and development, yield improvement no matter what definition of quality is used. An organization using a particular approach to quality can enhance its value by taking quality improvement actions to implement this specific approach.

Stages in Managing Quality and Process Control

There are three main stages in quality management and process control:

Stage A: No quality management or feedback exists.
Stage B: Inspection—Quality control at the end of the process.
Stage C: Process control.

Stage A: No Quality Management or Feedback Exists

Organizations in this stage are usually monopolistic organizations, and they lack customer awareness or feedback systems for process control and improvement. At this stage, the organization is doing its best and solves problems in an ad hoc manner. Customer complaints are usually answered with "we worked by the guidelines," or "the customer doesn't understand, is not right, or is responsible." More serious complaints are solved by apologies or gifts.

Stage B: Inspection—Quality Control at the End of the Process

At this stage, the organization adds quality control at the end of the process through the use of *inspection*, which is usually performed by an independent body. Inspectors examine the final products and screen out defective ones, as depicted in Figure 17.1.

Because there is some control over the quality of the final product or service, stage B (with inspection performed at the end of the line) is preferable to stage A. However, experience shows that inspection, as good as it may be, neither prevents nor screens defects. Moreover, the mere existence of a quality control department relieves responsibility from the operations staff, who believe

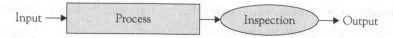

Figure 17.1 Adding inspection at the end of the process

that quality control staff members are responsible for quality. There is also undesirable tension between personnel in the two areas. Because there are no preventive measures introduced, the garbage plant continues to produce defective services and products. This approach is *open circle control* that identifies current problems, but usually does not prevent future ones.

Stage C: Process Control

Every organization that wishes to survive in today's competitive environment must reach stage C the sooner the better. This stage is also referred to as *Deming's theory* (Deming, 1986). At this stage, we have *closed circle control,* which is control with feedback at constant and short intervals (Figure 17.2).

The principles of process control include:

- *Continuous improvement of organizational performance.* This improvement usually focuses on increasing the throughput of the organization.

- *Continuous improvement of processes.* Many managerial cultures focus on the short term and on achieving immediate and one-time results. The improvements and advantages achieved by one organization, may also be

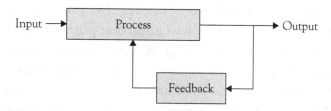

Figure 17.2 A closed circle control system

achieved by competitors, after a while. To establish a continuous competitive edge, there must be a continuous improvement of processes in marketing and sales, production processes, and engineering processes.

- *Emphasis on process improvement.* Quality is achieved through correct processes.

85/15 rule: *85 percent of failures are caused by inappropriate processes and are the responsibility of management. Only 15 percent of failures are the responsibility of employees.*

Processes under the responsibility of management include employee selection, recruitment and training, setting and measuring work processes, measuring and rewarding employees, working with complete kits, sales processes, marketing, pricing and costing, and so on.

When a problem occurs in an organization, everybody is mobilized to solve it. However, organizations that do not embrace the conceptual change in spirit of Deming's theory begin the unavoidable hunt for those responsible for a problem, right after the problem has been solved.

The process control approach suggests that after solving a problem, the following question must be addressed: What was wrong in the *process* that caused the failure, and what can be changed in the process so this failure does not reoccur in the future?

In a certain regional airline, one major cause of plane crashes was planes flying into birds. When the process was investigated, it was discovered that bird migration repeats itself with high precision every year. As a result, corrective measures were taken to significantly reduce the number of bird-related crashes.

- *Prevention rather than fixing.* The major focus should be
  on appropriate process design and on measures that
  avoid failures.

In one high-tech company, the authors observed a manager of
a large project who decided to withhold the start of the project
until all the necessary specifications were complete. About 30
development people were not allowed to begin work (not even
one line of code), until the completion of the specifications, which
took about six weeks. The organization was able to gain from the
project manager's reluctance; the project was delivered on time
to satisfied customers and made a profit for the company. Pay-
ing attention to the problems before they occur made the project
successful.

- *Use of data.* Process control is possible only if the organization routinely collects data about what is happening
  with the process and analyzes them. ("In God we trust.
  All others should bring data.")

- *Use of graphical tools.* The recommended control
  tools are process control charts, Pareto diagrams, and
  additional graphical tools (Deming, 1986). These tools
  enable focused and effective analysis of the data, and
  identification of negative phenomena that require
  intervention and corrective measures. The continuous
  improvement in work processes achieved in this way
  brings about value enhancement.

- *Quality management and process control by the employees
  themselves.* The modern approach to quality management and process control states that a person doing a
  job is also *responsible for* its quality. This requires setting

initial conditions in appropriate work environments:

—Managers must clearly define what they consider a good product or service.

—Employees and managers must be given the tools they need to evaluate the quality of a service or product.

—Managers must specify rules and procedures that define clearly what has to be done when a failure occurs or a defective product or service is detected.

- *The 10 times rule.* The later the stage a problem is detected, the more expensive it is to fix (i.e., 10 times more expensive). This rule is presented graphically in Figure 17.3.

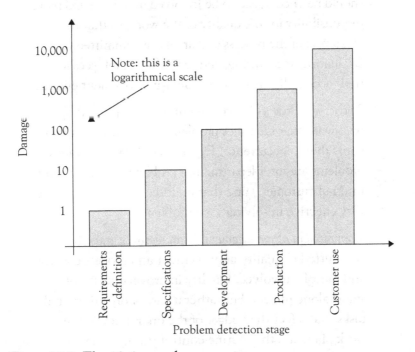

Figure 17.3 The 10 times rule

If a defective component in an electronic device could have been detected while inspecting the incoming shipment, then fixing it would be 1/10 the cost of fixing the problem if it had been detected during production and 1/100 of the cost of fixing the problem if it had been detected during the final quality control inspection.

The conclusion is that most of the emphasis of control and inspection must be shifted to the *beginning* of the process, rather than to the end (as is customary in stage B of quality control).

- *Participation of managers and employees.* A quality product, service, or development can be achieved through a quality process where employees and managers feel ownership over the process and are actively involved in process design and control. Employees should be encouraged to be involved and delegated more responsibility for the quality of the work, so that they feel a part of the process and are more committed to it. Evaluating, recognizing, and rewarding employees for their accomplishments is a quality-improvement engine.

- *Teamwork.* Process improvement is accomplished by teamwork that identifies problems, solves them, and prevents their reoccurrence. Experience shows that many problems are interdepartmental problems (suppliers and internal customers) and that multidisciplinary teams are very effective in solving such problems.

- *Commitment of management.* Management must be committed to quality improvement and process control and must be involved. Quality improvement is not a stand-alone project, but rather a part of organizational tasks that affect the budget of the organization, the work plan, and the routine control through the use of the regular tools of the organization.

- *Centrality of the customer.* The customer must be the focus of attention of all levels of the organization. In an era of excess capacity in services and production and an era of fierce competition, there should be subordination to the market in all decision making.

- *Working with a small number of quality suppliers.* By studying the global, long-term life cycle cost of products and services, we realize that quality processes save money. Managers must work in cooperation with suppliers by using problem identification and the goodwill of both sides to solve them. This kind of cooperation can only be achieved by working closely with a small number of quality suppliers.

    The approach of developing mutual long-term relations with a small number of suppliers is contrary to the approach and the statutory responsibility of most public organizations to publish offerings for bids before any substantial agreement is signed. The bidding approach can reduce costs in the short term, but it makes it difficult for the organization to maintain and assure a quality service or production process. The savings in costs are frequently offset by losses resulting from poor quality. We do not recommend going to the other extreme of "putting all your eggs in one basket" by working with a single contactor. This exposes the organization to commercial and economic risks.

Implementing Quality Improvement Processes

The implementation of quality improvement processes in organizations should be done using a business approach in combination with additional managerial approaches. The purpose of quality improvement in not-for-profit organizations is to improve organizational performance, and in business organizations, it is to enhance the value of the firm.

Implementing only partial or limited quality improvement, confined to areas of operations (service and production), yields limited improvement in performance. Customers want a high quality product or service, but they also want fast response, reliable supply times, good performance, and services and products that are congruent with their needs, and they want all of this with competitive prices. In other words, management must evaluate the organization in a global manner as a complex entity whose individual components must function better. In most organizations, profit increases achieved by improving marketing, development, and engineering are more significant than profit increases achieved by improving production processes. Unfortunately, many managers equate quality improvement to improvements in production processes or improvements in service.

Management must focus on the important issues of the organization. Identifying critical issues must be done by adopting a global perspective. Managing critical issues should utilize effective and efficient management tools. In other words, a successful implementation of quality improvement implies combining quality improvement using Deming's theory with approaches such as management by constraints, just-in-time (JIT), managerial measurement and control, the Complete Kit concept, and advanced strategic approaches. Experience shows us that applying just one managerial approach yields only partial success.

Quality improvement should be implemented *gradually*:

- Improve operational systems by implementing JIT approaches, management by constraints, measurement and control, and the Complete Kit concept. This step provides fast results of increased throughput, reduced response times, and quality enhancement, mainly through the reduction of work in process (WIP).

- Use quality improvement and process control methods, work with departmental and interdepartmental teams, and implement process control charts.

- Leverage strategic advantages of quality improvement, such as the ability to turn to markets that pay more for better quality, the ability to increase prices in certain markets, and the ability to compete with lower prices in other markets. This is possible through implementation of quality work processes, reduction of variable costs (especially raw materials), and increased throughput.

Throughput World versus Cost World

The objective of quality improvement is to increase organizational profits, mainly through increased throughput. This can be done by increasing throughput from increased sales and better uses of raw materials. Deming believes that the organizational objective is to increase profits and create more jobs by increasing market share, reducing response times, adapting the product or service to the customer at a higher quality (Deming, 1986). This philosophy that focuses on increasing the throughputs of the organization is referred to as *throughput world* (Goldratt, 1990a).

In contrast to throughput world, there is a philosophy that focuses on cost reduction in the organization, which quickly translates into management's desire to reduce the size of the workforce. This is known as *cost world*, and it occasionally conflicts with quality objectives. In organizations that do not have job security for workers, it is difficult for management to involve the workforce in making changes. In many cases, big money is not made by reducing costs, but rather by increasing throughput or improving quality.

Quality Improvement Myths

According to Deming's theory (Stage C), quality management and process control break several myths that relate to quality management:

> *Myth*: Quality work takes more time.
>> *Reality*: Quality work requires a good and structured process, and it takes less time. For example, working with a Complete Kit in a development, sales, or production process requires fewer cycles in the process and naturally a smaller time investment and shorter cycle time.

> *Myth*: Quality costs more money.
>> *Reality*: High quality work and a quality process cost less money because they cause less rework and fewer cycles, and reduce the garbage plant. Thus, quality costs less and generates higher contributions to profit. Many customers are willing to pay a premium for quality services and products.

> *Myth*: It is not possible to provide a quality service or quality product in large quantities.
>> *Reality*: It is possible to provide customers with a quality service and to produce a quality product even in large quantities, if the process is good, consistent, and reliable. For example, customers of a cell phone company may receive quality service if the company develops a quality process—a good software system to support its call center and to provide answers to most queries, and a quality process of selecting, training, and managing employees.

Summary

Quality improvement and process control are means that an organization must employ to survive and exist in a competitive environment. Organizations that do not meet the required quality standard that increases year after year, will not survive. Organizations that use quality improvement as a competitive tool can enhance their value. Quality improvement, in combination with the approaches detailed in Part Two of this book (i.e., management by constraints, JIT, the Complete Kit, Pareto rule), may all enhance organizational value without substantial (if any) financial investment, which enables the organization to do more with existing resources.

Part III

Strategy and Value Creation

18

Strategy, Positioning, and Focusing

Strategy

Strategy is the route chosen by management to reach its goal. The strategy of an organization should address the following questions:

- Which market is the organization competing in?

- What are the core competencies of the organization, and how can they be conserved?

- What are the weaknesses and the threats of the organization, and how can the organization defend itself against them?

- What is the strike plan for the company?

- What products and services are sold by the organization and where should they be positioned in the market?

- What are the pricing, quality, and focusing policies of the organization?

- What is the proper growth rate for the company?

- What are the required investments?

- What capabilities does the company have that form sustainable competitive advantages?

- What are the dimensions of differentiation for the company's products and services against the competition?

- Where should the constraint of the company be located?

- What should be the capital structure of the company?

- What should be the business and the organization structures of the company?

The answers to these questions actually shape the functional strategies of the organization in marketing, sales, finance, technology, information systems, operations, logistics, quality, human resources, and risk management.

This chapter presents several angles of strategy that can significantly increase value for shareholders. We focus on certain value drivers that may change or improve company strategy using the Focused Management philosophy:

- Assess strategic moves.

- Improve the good old SWOT analysis.

- Watch your assets:

  —Implement a conservation strategy.

  —Implement a defense strategy.

  —Implement a strike strategy.

- Determine where the constraint should be located.

- Define a *mafia offer* or a *viable vision*.

- Translate strategic decisions into action items.

- Utilize the focused arena strategy (FAST).

At the end of this chapter, we demonstrate the use of these concepts through a case study analysis of an international high-tech organization competing in a global market.

Assess Strategic Moves

Sometimes there is a feeling that decisions and moves with strategic tags attached to them do not require scrutiny. In many cases, strategic considerations are not quantified and decisions are made without justification.

Any strategic move has its own price tag. The cost associated with such moves should be justified by future cash flow and added value. A structured business plan should be used as a justification tool. If benefits are difficult to assess, or intangible benefits are involved, a scenario explaining the value derived, followed by a rough estimate of any kind of cash flow, may be sufficient.

A leading company in the communications industry was developing, producing, marketing, and selling sophisticated components and subsystems for large-scale communication systems. The company faced continuous price erosion in the communication component and subsystems market. Management was about to make a drastic move and they had created a strategic plan to become a system integration house.

An attempt to assess cash flow led management to develop a full business plan for the move in which they analyzed, among other things, the gross margin of existing and future systems, subsystems, and components.

The analysis revealed that there was no economic justification for neglecting the development, production, and sales of components and subsystems. A three-tier strategy was developed: the company decided to continue manufacturing components, to

(continued)

---

sustain its leading position in the subsystems market, and also to become a large systems integrator. A decentralized business and organizational structure that supported this strategy was implemented.

A large distributor of pharmaceuticals and medical supplies faced a declining demand in the market. Many large hospitals were starting to buy pharmaceuticals and supplies either directly from the producers or from other agents.

To compensate for the loss of business, management decided to make a strategic move by becoming a player in the international market. Initial studies resulted in a list of potential countries, and the company started negotiating with potential local partners in each country. There was a feeling that the company was securing its future by making this move.

A full strategic process, including an economic analysis, was completed. The analysis revealed that the move was too risky and would not increase the company's value.

As a result, management decided to terminate the plan to go international. Instead, management formulated a strategy to regain most of the lost business by adjusting customer service strategies to bring more value to the customer.

Improve the Good Old SWOT Analysis

The strengths, weaknesses, opportunities, and threats (SWOT) analysis is one of the main tools in the strategy formation process. Unfortunately in many cases, SWOT analysis is completed without focus. Namely, all strengths, weakness, opportunities, and threats are considered in the analysis.

A more effective focused SWOT analysis would:

- List all company strengths in a short, concentrated list of two to three *core competencies* by using a core competencies tree (CCT) diagram.

- List all company weaknesses in a short list of two to three *core problems* by using a focused current reality tree (fCRT) diagram. The use of the fCRT was previously discussed in Chapter 7.

- Limit the list of opportunities to three.

- Limit the list of threats to three.

Watch Your Assets

In the formulation of a company strategy, emphasis is usually given to the strike side of the strategy (or the strike strategy). In a strike strategy, a company may plan new capabilities to exploit certain opportunities that exist in its business environment (e.g., new products, new markets, repositioning). The strike strategy may be appealing, but you should remember to act against threats and keep competencies of the company current.

Current competencies should be secured by a *conservation strategy*. Core competencies of the company may have brought value to the company in the past. These competencies should be conserved by a conservation strategy to ensure that the company continues to receive the value created by them.

Threats should be counterbalanced by a *defense strategy*. A defense strategy is created by assessing the main threats against relevant threats through the use of a focused SWOT analysis and an analysis of the core problems revealed by the CRT. A strike strategy is created by assessing the main opportunities against the relevant core competencies and the opportunities identified by the focused SWOT analysis.

The formation of conservation, defense, and strike strategies is discussed in the FAST methodology section and the case study later in the chapter.

Determine Where the Constraint Should Be Located

An important strategic task is to determine where the system constraint should be located. Until now, we have considered tactical issues within a given system where the goal was improvement. To strategically plan the constraint, we must consider three strategic questions about the resources of the organization (Goldratt, 1990a):

1. Where should the constraint be located?

   Should the constraint be *internal* (resource constraint) or *external* (market constraint)?

   If the constraint should be a resource constraint, which resource should be constrained?

2. Where is the constraint located now?

3. How do we transfer the constraint to its proper location?

These issues were discussed in Chapter 6.

Define a Mafia Offer and a Viable Vision

In parallel with the orderly formation of conservation, defense, and strike strategies, the company has to strive to define a *mafia offer* for its customers. A mafia offer is an offer the customer cannot refuse. Mafia offers use the core competencies of a company to address certain customer needs, which adds substantial value to these customers. A good mafia offer results in a real competitive edge for the company. For example, in a market where the quoted lead time was three months, one company offered their customers a two-week lead time in a make-to-order policy. They were using the methods described in previous chapters and were also confident enough to assure the deliveries by including contract penalties. The company doubled sales and tripled its value in less than 18 months.

Finding ways to exploit mafia offers and/or some other value drivers of the company may lead to a *viable vision* for the company (Kendall, 2004). A viable vision as defined by Goldratt is a road map for achieving a multifold increase in the value of a company by taking strategic advantages out of operational and logistics excellence. Other ways may lead to a Blue Ocean for a company (Kim and Mouborgne, 2005), where in certain cases you make the competition irrelevant.

Translate Strategic Decisions into Action Items

Even the most brilliantly formulated strategy in an organization is not worth much if it is not a part of a strategic implementation process. Strategic decisions should be translated into a set of action items. These action items are then fed into a focusing table and a focusing matrix. Finally, the preferred action items are chosen. The organization strategy and the resulting action items should be presented to all the relevant employees and managers in the organization. As part of an ongoing strategic process, the strategy should be reexamined and updated at least annually.

Utilize the Focused Arena Strategy

The focused arena strategy (FAST) methodology is an integration of traditional strategy-planning methodologies with state-of-the-art managerial philosophies from the focused management approach. This model, developed by Coman, was broadened for strategy formation and implementation in conjunction with the focused management approach (Coman and Ronen, 2002).

The steps of the FAST methodology include:

1. Identify the organizational goal, vision, and mission.
2. Define performance measurements.

3. Analyze internal and external environments with a focused SWOT analysis.

4. Identify core competencies using the core competencies tree.

5. Identify core problems using the focused current reality tree.

6. Focus on the main opportunities and threats.

7. Perform a gap analysis.

8. Decide where the constraint should be located.

9. Determine what actions to take, then execute and control those actions.

Step 1: Identify the Organizational Goal, Vision, and Mission

The *goal* of an organization reflects the reason for its creation. The goal of a business firm is to increase its value for shareholders. In nonprofit organizations, the goal can be defined by answering the following question: "What is the purpose of the organization?" A broader discussion on the goal of an organization is presented in Chapter 4.

The *vision* of an organization is what the organization strives to get. For instance, a certain global information technology security company states that its goal is "to be the global leader in information security."

The *mission* of the organization addresses the questions: What kind of an organization are we? What kind of environment do we work in? An example of a corporate mission statement for the technology company mentioned previously might be "We supply information security solutions, products, and services for large corporations and institutions."

In the initial step, it is important to get a *consensus* among top management and board members on the goal, vision, and mission of the organization. The definition of the goal, vision, and mission of an organization should genuinely reflect the intention of management and the owners. Each sentence in this declarative document should be backed by well-planned action items.

Step 2: Define Performance Measurements

The set of performance measures defined in this stage as control tools for the board of directors and management should reflect the goal, vision, and mission of the organization. In a business, the relevant measurements are profit, cash flow, company's value, and the economic value added (EVA). The EVA measure is discussed further in Chapter 19. You must add nonfinancial measures to the financial measures mentioned previously because they are strategically important for the company (e.g., customer satisfaction, time to market (TTM), and innovation).

Step 3: Analyze Internal and External Environments with a Focused SWOT Analysis

The analysis of SWOT is one of most basic and important tools in the strategy development process. The analysis of strengths and weaknesses reveals information about the internal environment of the organization, while the identification of opportunities and threats refers to the external environment. Any SWOT analysis should be focused and value oriented.

An analysis of strengths usually includes about 8 to 12 very desirable effects (VDEs). These are the core competencies of an organization and the main assets that helped the organization reach its present value and position in the market.

The analysis of weaknesses usually includes about 8 to 12 undesirable effects (UDEs). Among the UDEs, we find those problems that inhibit further enhancement in the value of the organization.

A SWOT analysis also identifies up to three business opportunities and three business threats that an organization faces, which could considerably improve or deteriorate the value of the organization.

Step 4: Identify Core Competencies Using the Core Competencies Tree

The core competencies tree (CCT) is a logical tree that shows the interrelationships among the various competencies of an organization and is aimed at identifying the *core* competencies. The process of building a CCT as demonstrated in this chapter's case study is similar to the process of building an fCRT (as described in Chapter 7):

Take 8 to 12 very desirable effects (VDE) from the SWOT analysis, which are the competencies that enhance the value of the organization. Links among the VDEs reflect managerial insights and logic. The leading VDE of the organization is "shareholders' value increased."

At the bottom of the CCT, identify one to three core competencies that are the strategic competencies of the organization. These core competencies are considered strategic because they represent those strengths that should be continuously augmented and supported by the whole organization.

Following the CCT analysis, define the *conservation strategy* for the core competencies of the organization. The most effective action items should be selected with the aid of the focusing table and the focusing matrix.

Step 5: Identify Core Problems Using the Focused Current Reality Tree

The creation of the focused current reality tree (fCRT; see Chapter 7) enables managers to identify the core problems of their organization. The leading UDE is always "the value of the organization is insufficient." Current core problems are the main reasons that the value of the organization is inadequate.

Step 6: Focus on the Main Opportunities and Threats

From the list of opportunities and threats originating from the SWOT analysis, choose three main opportunities and three main threats on which to focus. The two criteria for choosing these opportunities and threats are:

1. The added value of the organization if the opportunity materializes, or the decreased value if the threat materializes, and

2. The probability that these events will take place.

The focusing matrix can be an invaluable aid for sifting through the various opportunities and threats.

Step 7: Perform a Gap Analysis

At this step, a gap analysis should be performed separately for each of the main opportunities and threats. The ultimate objective is to formulate the *defense strategy* against weaknesses and threats and to shape the *strike strategy* for opportunities realization.

Gap Analysis for the Main Opportunities   Define the critical success factors (CSFs) that are required for each opportunity to realize full exploitation of the opportunity and to enhance the value of the organization. CSFs could be: low price, advanced system engineering capabilities, fast response time to the market, technological innovation, financial stability, contacts and respect among the leading customers of the industry, contacts and understanding among the regulating bodies of the industry, influence in international standards committees, or effective marketing channels.

The CSFs have to, on the one hand, be supported by the core competencies of the organization. On the other hand, realization CFSs should not be affected by the core problems and weaknesses of the organization. Therefore, you should contrast the core competencies and core problems and threats against the critical success factors for each opportunity. Figure 18.1 shows a gap analysis diagram for the realization of an opportunity.

The interrelations between the CFSs, the core competencies, and the core problems that emerge from the gap analysis diagram fall into four categories. The four categories as illustrated by Table 18.1 are:

Quarter 1 opportunities: Core competencies support the CSFs and the weaknesses (the core problems) do not

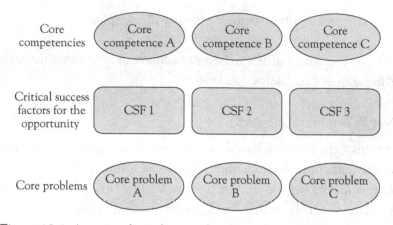

Figure 18.1 A gap analysis diagram for the realization of an opportunity

Table 18.1 Opportunities mapping matrix

Core competencies support the realization of the opportunity

	No	Yes
Yes	#1 Go for it	#2 Rectify core problems
No	#4 Consider adding new competencies	#3 Opportunity can not be realized

Core problems prevent opportunity realization

interfere. Those are opportunities that can be realized quite easily.

Quarter 2 opportunities: Core competencies support the CSFs, but the weaknesses *do* interfere. In this case, the core problems should be corrected to allow the realization of these opportunities.

Quarter 3 opportunities: The organization has no core competencies that are relevant to the CFSs (namely, no strategic edge), but weaknesses inhibit the realization of the opportunity. The organization will not be able to realize such opportunities.

Quarter 4 opportunities: The organization does not currently have core competencies to support the CFSs and there are no hindering weaknesses. In such cases, management has to build new capabilities to realize these opportunities. Building core competencies is a lengthy and complex process.

When all opportunities in the matrix are analyzed, the *strike strategy* for opportunities exploitation can be formulated.

Gap Analysis for the Main Threats   Each of the threats should be scrutinized. For each threat, define a list of the critical defense factors (CDFs) that are crucial to cope with the threat. Potential CDFs are similar to the potential CSFs: low price, advanced system engineering capabilities, fast response time to the market, technological innovation, financial stability, contacts and respect among the leading customers of the industry, contacts and understanding among the regulating bodies of the industry, influence in international standards committees, and so on.

An organization's ability to cope with a threat should be analyzed taking into account the strengths (core competencies), the weaknesses (core problems), and the CDFs that are relevant to this threat.

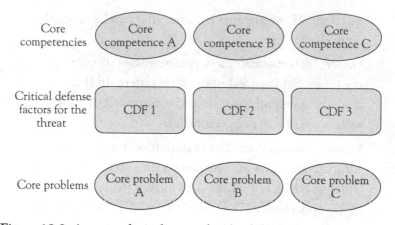

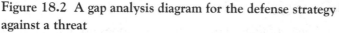

Figure 18.2 A gap analysis diagram for the defense strategy against a threat

Figure 18.2 demonstrates a gap analysis diagram for defense against a threat.

The interrelations between the CDFs, the core competencies, and the core problems that emerge from the gap analysis diagram fall into four categories as illustrated by Table 18.2:

> *Quarter 1 threats:* Core competencies support the critical defense factors, and the weaknesses (the core problems) do not interfere. These are threats that can be blocked quite easily.

> *Quarter 2 threats:* Core competencies support the critical defense factors, but the weaknesses do interfere. In this case, the core problems should be corrected to allow those threats to be defeated.

> *Quarter 3 threats:* The organization does not have core competencies that are relevant to the CDFs, and the weaknesses inhibit the ability to defend against the threat. Such threats are insurmountable and constitute a real risk to the organization. The organization can deal

Table 18.2 Threats mapping matrix

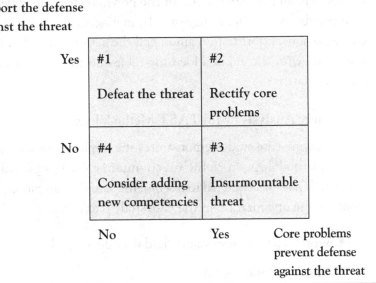

Core competencies
support the defense
against the threat

	No	Yes
Yes	#1 Defeat the threat	#2 Rectify core problems
No	#4 Consider adding new competencies	#3 Insurmountable threat

Core problems prevent defense against the threat

with the risk by insuring itself (if possible) or finding ways to divert the risk to others.

Quarter 4 threats: The organization does not currently have core competencies to support the CDFs, and there are no hindering weaknesses. In such cases, management has to build new capabilities to fight the threat. However, building core competencies is a lengthy process.

When all the threats in the matrix are analyzed, the *defense strategy* for the organization can be formulated.

Step 8: Decide Where the Constraint Should Be Located

This issue, which was discussed in Chapter 6, is an important one, and connects the organization's strategy to its resources.

Step 9: Determine What Actions to Take, Then Execute and Control those Actions

In this step, all the action items of the previous steps are collected with possible action items suggested by management during strategic discussions. Prioritization among all the action items should be completed with the aid of a focusing table and the corresponding focusing matrix.

Case Study Analysis by the FAST Methodology

The following case study demonstrates the implementation of the FAST methodology in a high-tech international organization. The details have been altered to disguise the actual organization. The profile of the organization in the case study is as follows:

- World leader in a specialty field they developed

- Annual sales of $40M

- 200 employees

- High-tech

- Two product lines:

    —Components (modules) for the electronic communication industry

    —Subsystems for leading customers in the electronic communication industry

- Sales to original equipment manufacturers (OEMs).

- Strong marketing and sales departments active mainly in the United States

- Fast development capability

- Strong position in important standard committees

- Excellent human resources, as well as good management and positive working atmosphere

- Subcontracted production activities

The company faces a drastic slowdown in demand. The slowdown is part of a trend in the whole market and is considered a threat to the company's cash flow. Let us implement the nine steps of the FAST methodology for this firm.

FAST Step 1: Identify the Organizational Goal, Vision, and Mission

- *Goal.* To increase shareholders' value with an improvement in the employees' welfare and the contribution to the community.

- *Vision.* To stay the world leader in its specialty field in technological innovation and the ability to customize solutions to the customer.

- *Mission.* To be the main supplier for the leading international customers in components and subsystems that offer the functionality invented by the company.
  To sell OEM products in the electronic defense market. To supply tailor-made solutions that address specific customers' needs through fast and effective development.

FAST Step 2: Define Performance Measurements

The strategic performance measures for the company are:

- The investors require a return of 10 percent on the capital, and they expect an annual EVA of $5M.

- Technological innovation measures are defined by management.

FAST Step 3: Analyze Internal and External Environments with a Focused SWOT Analysis

Interviews with top management, examination of the financials, examination of marketing and operations reports, and field surveys led to the following SWOT analysis:

Strengths
- Sales to leading customers in the market
- Fast development of products integrating diverse technologies
- Influence in standards committees
- Strong sales division
- Technological innovation and professionalism
- R&D and production divisions
- Interdivisional communication
- High motivation of employees
- Business relations with leading companies
- Excellent and devoted employees
- Technological leadership

Weaknesses
- Inadequate strategic gating in the assignment of development tasks
- Insufficient differentiation of products
- Company is loosing money
- Lost sales
- Insufficient awareness of mergers and acquisitions
- Excessive focus on technology

- Not enough contact with the final customers

- A small player in a giants' market

- Product specifications infected with overspecification and overdesign

- High cash burn rate

- Focus on a single technology

Opportunities
- Development of an innovative product for a specific market segment

- Acquisition of the company by one of the giants

Threats
- Declining component market

- Delayed growth in the subsystems market

- Unfavorable company standards

- Undesirable partnerships between customers and the company's competitors.

FAST Step 4: Identify Core Competencies Using the Core Competencies Tree

The strengths that were identified in the previous step are fed into the core competencies tree (CCT). To validate the CCT, we start with the accomplishments of the organization, which are attributed to its capabilities and later translated into a short list of core competencies as illustrated by Figure 18.3.

The core competencies of the company are:

- Technological leadership

- Excellent and devoted employees—team spirit

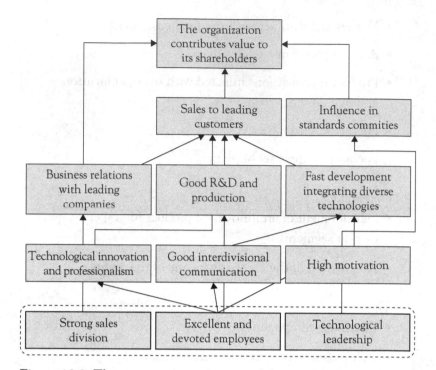

Figure 18.3 The core competencies tree of the company in the case study

- Strong sales division—sales and business relations with the leading companies

Management has decided to use the following conservation strategy for the core competencies of the company:

- Conservation of the technological leadership:

  —Continue to recruit only excellent employees, even if that lengthens the recruitment processes and short-ages of resources will delay milestones and deliveries.

  —Encourage technological upgrades and updates for the development team members.

- Conservation of excellent and devoted workers:

  —Keep divisional independence.

  —Keep the good working atmosphere in the company.

  —In cases where manpower downsizing is required, do it with full empathy, concern, and commitment for new jobs for those people (even if it involves higher costs for the company).

- Strong sales division:

  —Create a most valuable customers (MVCs) program to help focus the salesforce on the most important customers.

  —Continue to recruit stars for sales.

FAST Step 5: Identify Core Problems Using the Focused Current Reality Tree

The core problems that emerged from the focused current reality tree (fCRT) analysis, as illustrated by Figure 18.4, were:

- Focus on a single technology

- Excessive focus on technology

- Small player in a giants' market

Management formulated a defense strategy against these weaknesses, which includes enhancing business thinking of the development staff by offering specific training and facilitation, and by giving preference in the recruitment for candidates with experience and business training. The weakness of being a small player in a giants' market will be addressed by strategic partnerships with one of the giants or by being acquired by one of them or by a large competitor.

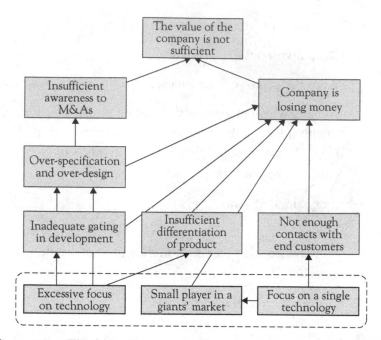

Figure 18.4 The focused current reality tree of the company

FAST Step 6: Focus of on the Main Opportunities and Threats

The main opportunities:

- Development of an innovative product for a specific market segment

- Acquisition of the company by one of the giants

Examine opportunity number one as an example of the treatment of an opportunity. The first opportunity is the development of an innovative product for a specific market segment. The critical success factors for such a development are:

- A well-known brand

- Fast development

- Partnership with a leader in the market

- Size

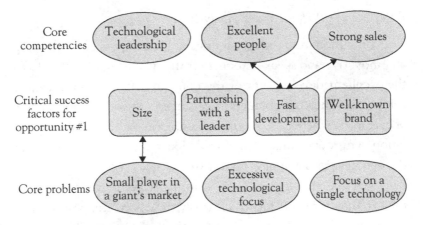

Figure 18.5 Gap analysis diagram for the realization of opportunity number 1 in the case

The Gap analysis for opportunity number 1 is depicted in Figure 18.5.

The main threats identified in the SWOT analysis are:

- Declining component market

- Delayed growth in the subsystems market

- Unfavorable standards for the company

- Undesirable partnerships between customers and the company's competitors

In examining the declining components market, we can identify the following opportunities:

- Partnerships with customers

- Focus on the subsystems market

- Low price

- Customization to customer's needs

FAST Step 7: Perform a Gap Analysis

The conclusion from the gap analysis is that it is possible to develop an innovative and special product for the specific market thanks to the excellent development of the company and its technological leadership. The core competencies support the realization of this opportunity, whereas the core problems don't hinder such a realization. This opportunity is obviously located in the first quarter of the opportunities mapping matrix (go for it).

The strike strategy for this opportunity is to find partners among the leading customers for which (or with which) the product will be developed.

Let us analyze now one threat as an example. The gap analysis for threat number 1 is depicted in Figure 18.6.

The conclusion from the gap analysis regarding this threat is that core competencies support the defense against this threat, whereas the core problems have no influence. This threat is in the first quarter (defeat the threat).

The defense strategy against this threat is the improvement of capabilities for merger and acquisition in the company and the formation of partnerships with other players in the market.

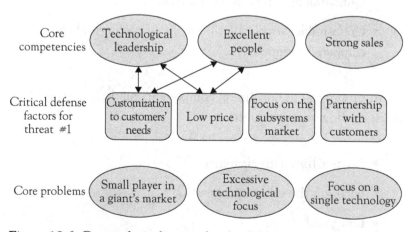

Figure 18.6 Gap analysis diagram for the defense against threat number 1 in the case

FAST Step 8: Decide Where the Constraint Should Be Located

The constraint of the company should be its management capabilities, flexibility, and prowess. All decisions in the company should be subordinated to this constraint. The operations division is not currently a constraint and it should not become the constraint in the future. As you might expect, marketing and sales and the development staff are permanent bottlenecks in the company.

FAST Step 9: Determine What Actions to Take, Then Execute and Control those Actions

This step is the summary step performed with the aid of the focusing matrix (Figure 18.7). The various action items that constitute the conservation, defense, and the strike strategies are examined.

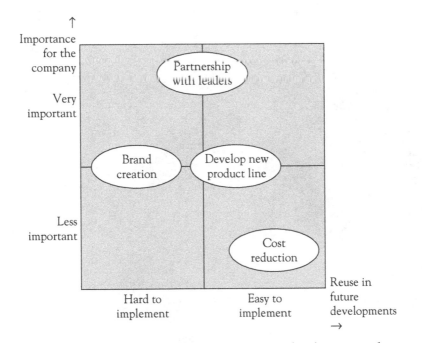

Figure 18.7 The focusing matrix of action items for the case study

Summary

The formation of an organization's strategy is actually the formulation of the actions required to realize the aspirations of the organization for the medium and long term. In this chapter, we introduced conservation, defense and strike strategies, the mafia offer and viable vision, and the FAST methodology. The FAST methodology serves as a platform for strategic discussions. The strategic process must finally form a list of action items. It is the responsibility of management to incorporate these action items into the work plan of the organization.

19

Value Creation

One of the major problems managers face is how to initiate the process of enhancing value or improving performance, and what priorities to set on the various possible improvements. For example, should they first perform improvements in marketing and sales, production, or perhaps change the organizational structure? Should management focus on improvements in research and development or should they focus on logistics and purchasing?

A manager cannot afford to spend more than 10 percent of his time on pursuing improvements because most of his time is spent managing current and emergency situations. There is no doubt that managers of every department in every organization can and should perform significant improvements in their specialty. However, the major problems of the organization are interdepartmental. Thus, only joint proactive efforts by management can lead to improvements. For example, improvements in marketing and sales cannot be made by the vice president of that department acting alone because the work process also involves finance, research and development, production, customer service and other departments.

Value Creation from Managerial Activities

This chapter presents a holistic and global approach to management's focus based on the importance of the improvement and the ease of implementing it.

The goal of the organization is to increase shareholders' value. The goal of management, therefore, is to bring about a constant creation of value for the shareholders, and it is incumbent on management to constantly strive to achieve this goal. Increasing shareholders' value usually brings with it better job security, financial benefits, and self-fulfillment for the employees, as well as value to the well-being of the community. Value creation can arise from activities in two areas:

1. Finance activities.
2. Other managerial activities.

Creating value from financial activities focuses mainly on changing the capital structure, mergers and acquisitions, and distributing dividends. This activity is carried out at the level of the firm's management and board of directors. We will not cover these activities.

In this chapter, we focus on the creation of value using management activities because they have a significant potential to increase firm value, and because this subject has been addressed to a lesser extent in practice and in academic research. Such value creation is caused by strategic changes, changes in business or organizational structure, increasing throughput in operations and logistics, improvement in inventory levels, improvement in the information systems, and shortening of development times.

Changes in cost accounting and performance measures, or improvements in decision-making processes, can contribute substantially to improving firm value. Moreover, as we have seen in previous chapters, the "blind" use of traditional cost accounting and the use of local performance measures can lead to a decrease in the value of firms and organizations.

Sometimes, business decisions concerning investments, or organizational changes do not necessarily contribute to improving the value of the firm. In many cases, this is caused by the absence of a global perspective and lack of knowledge and a structured methodology for improving the firm's value. Management's time is wasted, and its attention diverted from matters that are important to the firm and which, if properly addressed, could increase its value. In Chapter 20, we discuss the topic of firm value and the various methods of assessing it, and present a model for value-focused management (VFM) that links changes in the various areas of the organization to the increase in its value.

Assessing the Value of the Firm

Firm value is a concept commonly used by investors, managers, owners, and boards of directors. Its use is particularly prevalent when the firm is being bought A or sold, during mergers, and in negotiating with interested parties. There are several approaches to assessing firm value, including:

- *Market value.* The firm's value as assessed by the stock market. This immediate assessment is relevant to traded public firms. However, experience shows that when the level of trade is low, a substantial gap may be created between the "true" value of the firm, as reflected in purchasing transactions, and its value according to the latest stock market prices resulting from a low and insignificant trading.

- *Actual transactions.* The value can be determined by actual transactions, events of raising capital, exchanging shares, and/or mergers and acquisitions.

- *Asset value.* The asset value or worth of the firm's equity is the worth of the assets minus the worth of the liabilities.

- *Discounted cash flow.* The basic assumption of discounted cash flow (DCF) is that the value of the business is the present value of the cash flow over time. The firm's operational assets and the components of the working capital are needed to attain the cash flow, and their worth to the business is expressed by the DCF. In analyzing value, the present value of the unleveraged free cash flow is assessed. This amount represents the value of the activities. We must add the value of the *available* assets, which are not required to create cash (e.g., investments in real estate that are not for purposes of the firm's operations, cash surpluses). From this result, we subtract the worth of the net financial liabilities on the day of the valuation to obtain shareholders' value. Academically, this method is considered more acceptable and correct. It is suitable for measuring the contribution of management to improving firm value, enabling the measurement of cash flow arising from the activities of the different sectors of the firm and their sources of finance. For more details the reader may refer to Copeland et al., 2005.

The approach of this book in general, and of this chapter in particular, is to enhance the economic value of the firm as it is reflected in the cash flow over time. We believe that in the long run the economic value of the firm will level out at its market value.

Economic Value Added (EVA) Metric

The economic value added (EVA) metric measures the periodic (e.g., annual) increase in shareholders' value. We can demonstrate this metric with a simple numerical example:

Suppose there are two firms in the market. Firm A has equity of $600,000 and achieved an end-of-year net

operating profit after tax (NOPAT) of $100,000. In
parallel, Firm B has equity of $1,000,000 and achieved
a NOPAT of $150,000.

In this example, which of the two firms achieved the better result? The answer is not simple. True, the manager of Firm
B achieved a higher profit, but he also used a larger amount
of capital. We assume, for simplicity, that all investments were
made using the equity of the firms and that they did not have
any debt.

The EVA measure will give us a satisfactory answer. First presented by Stewart (1994), it measures the periodic value creation
of the firm.

Measuring the EVA presents a systematic way that takes into
consideration the requested rate of return on the firm's capital. The
EVA is expressed in tax-free terms.

EVA is defined as the difference between the net operating
profit after tax (before finance costs) and the annual cost of the
firm's capital (the equity and the debt used to generate this operating profit):

$$\text{EVA} = \text{NOPAT (Net operating profit after tax)} - \text{WACC}$$
$$\text{(Weighted average cost of capital)} \times \text{(Invested capital)}$$

The meaning of the EVA measure is that an economic value
added is created for the shareholders only when the operating
profit after tax and before financing costs (NOPAT) is higher than
the annual cost of the capital taken for financing the firm's investments (and all in tax-deducted terms, which take into account the
tax shelter for the firm's interest expenses). When the NOPAT is
smaller than the annual cost of the capital invested in the firm,
there is a reduction in the shareholders' value. It should be noted
that firms with negative EVA are not necessarily losing firms. They
are rather firms that do not compensate the investors for their

Table 19.1 Return on Assets and EVA

	Firm A	Firm B
Assets	$600,000	$1,000,000
NOPAT (Net operating profit after taxes)	$100,000	$150,000
ROA (Return on assets) NOPAT/Assets	16.67%	15.00%
Required profit according to a rate of return of 10% net	$60,000	$100,000
EVA (Economic value added) Profit after deducting required profit on capital	$40,000	$50,000

inherent risk and sometimes even represent a rate of return that is lower than the rate of return on risk-free assets.

Table 19.1 shows that the ranking of firms by the EVA measure is different from their ranking by other common measures (such as return on assets—ROA). Profit alone does not take into account the capital invested in the firm.

Table 19.1 shows that even though Firm A has a higher ROA, its EVA is lower. A possible situation is a firm that has a positive NOPAT and a positive net profit but a negative EVA, that is, it diminishes its shareholders' value.

The EVA measure has attracted much managerial attention and today many firms commonly use it. It can be seen as a measuring tool that determines if the business is earning more than the real cost of the capital invested in it. In other words, EVA is a measuring tool that enables managers, shareholders, and potential investors to examine whether the business created value during the last period (e.g., year) or diminished the value for the shareholders (Stern and Shiely, 2001).

It should be noted that criticism has been leveled at the use of EVA as the main measure for evaluating the level of performance. For instance, AT&T, which was one of the first to adopt the EVA measure at the beginning of the 1990s, reported after several years of implementing it that it had been forced to add two additional nonfinancial measures to it: customers' value added and employees' value added. Following the appointment of a new president in 1997, the firm decided to stop using the EVA measure (Horngren et al., 2000).

Nevertheless, we are convinced that despite this criticism, the use of EVA is far preferable to the use of any other financial accounting measure proposed to date. Moreover, it should be remembered that a measure is not a substitute for effective management, and managers have to identify loopholes that exist in any performance measurement system and close them.

Value Focused Management Model

The value focused management (VFM) model is an effective tool for increasing the firm's value. The VFM model helps managers focus on those areas in which the potential for increasing the firm's value is greatest, bearing in mind the limited management resources. The model is based on the principles of value-based management (VBM), as presented by Copeland, Koller, and Murrin (2005), together with additional elements.

The VFM model incorporates the following two dimensions:

1. It details the action plan required in the field for creating value.
2. It focuses managerial attention on the important activities that give the highest value, taking into account the organization's limited resources, particularly the managerial resources that are in short supply.

The stages of implementing the VFM model that we discuss next are:

1. Determine the goal.
2. Determine the performance measures.
3. Identify the value drivers.
4. Decide how to improve the value drivers.
5. Implement and control.

Determine the Goal

The goal of the firm is to increase shareholders' value. This should be clear to all the managers and employees. The goal can be sustained over time if at the same time the interests of the employees, the suppliers, the customers, and the community are borne in mind.

Determine the Performance Measures

The performance measures include the financial statements and the global performance measures of the system (see the six global measures in Chapter 4). The EVA metric examines the increase in the firm's value periodically.

Identify the Value Drivers

A value driver is defined as an important factor that can significantly affect the value of the firm (such as increasing sales, shortening response time, reducing inventories).

Four approaches are used to identify the *relevant* value drivers:

1. *Balance sheet and profit and loss statements approach.* All sections of the balance sheet and the profit and loss statement are reviewed to identify potential areas for improvement against the ease of carrying out the improvement, using the focusing matrix (as described in Chapter 7).

2. *Functional review approach.* Bottom-up: The major functions in the organization are reviewed systematically and examined for the existence of relevant value drivers. Such functional areas may include:

The organization's strategy

Marketing and sales

Human resources

Information systems and information technology

Finance

Technological innovation

Product and service quality

Logistics and purchasing

Operations

Cost accounting and performance measurement

Organizational structure

Risk management

Customer service

Project management

The function review is carried out by interviewing management and the organization's key personnel, touring the premises, perusing the financial and management statements, interviewing customers and suppliers, and benchmarking against similar organizations. With the aid of the focusing matrix, attention is then directed to the most important value drivers among those selected. The importance of each value driver is measured according to the incremental value it affords the firm.

3. *Global performance measures approach.* The global performance measures (see Chapter 4) are reviewed, and the potential increment to the firm's value from improving them is examined.

4. *Core problems approach.* Top-down: After collecting the data in stages 1, 2, and 3, the undesirable effects are mapped by the focused current reality tree (fCRT) and the core problems are identified (see Chapter 7).

The relevant value drivers (up to 10) are collected using these four methods. Using the focusing table and the focusing matrix, an assessment is made regarding the potential of each value driver to add to the firm's value and the ease of implementation. This process ends with the selection of the value drivers to be used for increasing the firm's value.

Decide How to Improve the Value Drivers

A detailed implementation plan for improving each value driver is prepared, using the novel managerial techniques described in Parts Two and Three of this book.

Implement and Control

The realization of the plan and its control are the responsibility of management.

Value Creation: The Supermarket Chain

The following example describes the implementation of the value focused management (VFM) model in a supermarket chain. The balance sheet and profit and loss statement for the last year, which is considered representative of the activities of the firm in the past and the future, appear in Appendix A to this chapter.

We implement the VFM approach to examine the potential increase of the value of the chain as follows:

Stage 1: Determine the Goal

The goal of the company is to increase shareholders' value.

Stage 2: Determine the Performance Measures

The performance measures are:

- Financial statements performance measures

- The six global performance measures

- EVA

- Company's value

Stage 3: Identify the Value Drivers

We now apply the four methods to identify the firm's value drivers:

1. *Financial statements approach.* The relevant sections of the financial statements are:

   Relatively short suppliers' credit terms compared to the competition

   High inventory level

2. *Functional review approach.* Bottom-up: We now review the potential for increasing value by identifying value drivers scanning the firm's functional areas:

   Organization's strategy: The chain's strategy is outdated and not well defined. The chain is located in a suburban area and caters to the lower middle class residents. It does not sell private labels and has no logistics center to control supplies.

   Marketing, sales, and business development: There are sales efforts, but no clear marketing plan. There is no structured format for sales promotions. There is no precise definition of the relevant market segments. No new branches have been opened in recent years. A pilot study showed that the average customer basket is 7.8 percent lower in value than that of the competitors'.

Human resources: There is a high turnover among the marketing, sales, business development, and other main office staff members. However, there is a strong sense of loyalty among the branch staff members who have been with the chain for many years. The workers are organized by three unions in the various sectors. Labor relations are good.

Information systems: The information systems do not provide an up-to-date picture of the various inventories, or distribution of customer purchases. The managers complain that the systems lack managerial information. "Profit per branch" is calculated once a quarter, 20 days after the quarter's end. The inventory system has been upgraded in recent years, but it is not yet connected to the control system. Branch managers do not have current access to the inventory system, so sometimes they find out about shortages by going out and physically checking the shelves.

Finance: The finance people are well versed in their work. The capital structure does not need to be changed. The number of suppliers' credit days can be increased to bring it into line with that of the leading chains. The firm has valuable real estate assets (particularly the main office) that can be sold. In addition, the firm can rent areas of real estate for some of the branches instead of ownership of real estate assets.

Engineering development and innovation: There is no technological innovation, though there is an interest in "smart trolleys" designed to serve the customers in the branches.

Quality: The quality of the goods sold is guaranteed by the suppliers. The firm has been certified to meet the ISO 9002 standard. A customer service department, a part of the human resources division, is occupied mostly with customer complaints and conducting "hidden customer" surveys. A comparative survey among the chains found that the customers' satisfaction from the chain was lower than that of the competing chains and that customers spent more time waiting in line at the checkout counters.

Operations, logistics, and purchasing. The purchasing people are well qualified, and the chief buyer does his job well and succeeds in obtaining good prices in comparison to the other chains. There is no logistics center. On a typical day, more than 30 different suppliers come to each branch, which interferes with operations. The chain has a central fruit and vegetables storeroom and a central imported goods storeroom.

Cost accounting and performance measures: Profit and loss measures are carried out quarterly for each branch. The branches are not measured by any operating performance measures. Service quality is measured by headquarters and the branch managers are informed of the results.

Organizational structure: The organizational structure is centralized and the branch managers are given little freedom of action. All financial expenditures for branch maintenance, for sales promotion, or hiring temporary or permanent personnel have to be authorized by the main office.

Risk management: There is no risk management function or activity. The insurance portfolio is managed by the finance people.

Customer service and support: The customer service department is part of the human resources division. This department takes care of customer complaints, but there is no structured feedback process for corrective action.

Project management: No project management expertise and tools are used in the company.

3. *Global performance measures approach.* When reviewing the performance measures, the following potential value drivers are relevant to the organization:

Lost sales

Lead time for items supplied to the branches—from demand to their supply to the branch

Inventory levels

4. *Core problems approach.* Top-down: In order to identify the company's core problems, a focused current reality tree was constructed using the relevant undesirable effects (UDEs).

UnDesirable Effects

The UDEs were elicited from the interviews with managers and other employees, the functional areas' survey, the financial statements, and the performance measures, all in comparison with the two leading competitors. The following UDEs represent undesirable effects that prevent the firm from increasing its value:

- Main UDE: Firm's value is not sufficient.

- Profit after tax is too low.

- Lost sales are high.

- The average purchase is too small.

- The branch managers have too little autonomy.

- There is no private label.

- Strategy is not updated.

- There are no branches in prime locations.

- The information system is inadequate.

- There is no logistics center.

- Inventories are too high.

- There is no structured shelf management.

- Real estate assets are not bettered.

Figure 19.1 presents the focused current reality tree for the supermarket chain.

Potential Value Drivers

The following potential value drivers were selected following the identification process:

1. Increase the average customer purchase.
2. Establish a logistics center.

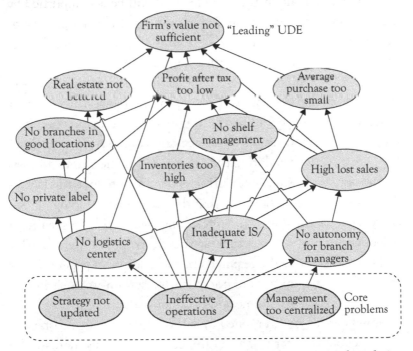

Figure 19.1 A focused current reality tree for the supermarket chain

3. Introduce a private label.

4. Enhance shelf space management.

5. Increase the managerial and professional quality of the administrative and operations personnel.

6. Increase the shelf space area at the expense of storerooms in the branches.

7. Increase the number of suppliers' credit days.

8. Open new branches in prime locations.

9. Sell the main office real estate.

10. Make the transition to long-term rental of premises for the firm's branches.

Increase the Average Customer Purchase   Increasing the average purchase of the customer by 5 percent will lead to an increase in income of 5 percent in the first year, after that, It is assumed that the sales will remain at the same level. It will be accomplished by means of periodic sales promotions, training of check out personnel, stationing sales promotion personnel in the branches, tasting promotions, advertising, lotteries, and so on. Service improvement, too, is an important part of increasing customer wallet share. Attention should also be paid to improve/enhance the customer shopping experience and to try to give the customers more than they expected with regard to service and courtesy. The checkout lines are a bottleneck during peak hours. Using the Pareto analysis of the cashier's wasted time during peak hours, reduce the factors that cause this waste. Ensuring that the cashier has a Complete Kit at the start of the day or at shift changeover can help greatly in reducing the noneffective time at the checkout counter. The kit includes cash to give the required change, additional paper rolls for the cash register, up-to-date price lists for certain items, information on special offers, promotions, coupons, and so on.

Lines can also be shortened by stationing a packing assistant at the checkout counter to offload the cashier and thus increase the throughput at the counter (faster passage at the checkout counter will also lessen the heavy pressure on the parking lot at some of the branches, which will no doubt increase the number of customers).

The assumption is that the cost of all these actions will not exceed 0.5 percent of sales turnover. The difficulty of implementation is 4 on a scale of 1 (difficult) to 5 (very easy). That is, the implementation is relatively easy.

Establish a Logistics Center   Establishing a logistics center is compatible with the just-in-time (JIT) and theory of constraint (TOC) management philosophies. These philosophies support the creation of a single logistics center to which the suppliers send their goods and which will dispatch them to the branches. This centralized delivery system has the following advantages:

- *Reduction of the number of deliveries arriving at the branch daily*. Centralized delivery relieves the branch managers of the job of supervising unloading of deliveries, leaving them more time for improving service and promoting sales.

- *Reducing unloading time*. Arranging the goods for speedier unloading reduces the waiting time of the delivery vehicle.

- *Optimizing deliveries*. A single aggregate delivery is cheaper and more efficient than 10 or 20 deliveries of different suppliers. Since both the suppliers and the chain benefit from the change, the suppliers may be charged for the additional service given by the logistics center.

- *Reducing shortages and more efficient management of inventories*. Supervision and control enable savings and increased returns. It will result in reducing lost sales and managing inventories from a global perspective.

It is estimated that the lost sales will fall by 50 percent
and the extra time made free for the branch manager
will lead to a 1 percent increase in sales, which will
give a total increase in sales of 3.3 percent, starting
from the second year. The estimated cost of constructing a logistics center is $10 million, with another
$4 million per year for maintenance and operations.
Aggregated delivery to the branches will allow an
annual saving of $500,000, starting from the second
year. That is, the net costs will increase by $3.5 million.
Moreover, it will be possible to charge the suppliers
1 percent of the sales, starting from the second year, for
transportation and handling. At the same time, total
inventories will decrease by 10 percent, starting from
the second year. Managers estimate that the implementation will be difficult—2 on the 1–5 scale, since
it requires establishing new procedures and substantial
changes in working with many of the suppliers.

Introduce a Private Label   The chain is considering launching its
own private label. According to the plan, in the first year, private
label (coffee, soft drinks, and washing detergents) sales will reach
5 percent of the turnover. This percentage will increase in the second year to 7 percent, in the third year to 10 percent, and in the
fourth and fifth years to 15 percent.

The new private label will be introduced by placing the products on the shelves in areas with good access, granting discounts,
advertising, and sales promotions. The chain will also hire sales promotion personnel to arrange the shelves and assist in the sales
promotion activities (as do the suppliers of the leading brands).

The chain's economists calculated that it is possible to buy private label goods at 80 percent of the brand price. This will also
enhance the chain's bargaining power over the leading brand suppliers, though due to conservative practices we will not include

this benefit in the calculation. The cost of introducing a private label is estimated as follows:

In the first year	$2 million
In the second year	$1.5 million
In the third, fourth, and fifth years	$1 million

Difficulty of implementation is 3 (moderate).

Enhance Shelf Space Management   Shelf space management is a relatively easy task that has a high potential to increase shareholders' value.

- Not enough attention is paid to shelf space management and product display. It is estimated that effective shelf space management, supported by a software package, can increase the average consumer purchase by 3 percent, which will increase revenues by 3 percent each year. Furthermore, sales can be increased by 1 percent by thinking in terms of specific throughput (see Chapter 5), and removing items with poor specific throughput from the shelves. Altogether, sales will increase by 4 percent.

- In a large branch some 10,000 different items are displayed on the shelves. The number of stock keeping units (SKUs) that the suppliers would like to offer is more than 100,000. Thus, there must be a system of strategic gating of products (see Chapter 5). Though the choice is limited (you should always sell milk and bread in a supermarket), management still has substantial degrees of freedom over 20 percent of the shelf space. Since the system constraint is the shelf space, one of the considerations in displaying goods on the shelves or removing them is the throughput per unit of shelf space (or the throughput per unit of shelf length)—the specific throughput.

- The costs of purchasing shelf-space management software, applying the specific throughput of products concept, and sales promotion expenses are estimated as follows: A one-time expenditure of $500,000 will be required in the first year. In this year the increase in sales will not be felt, due to the need to introduce the system into the branches. Starting the second year, there will be a variable cost increase of about 0.2 percent of the annual sales turnover, in each of the subsequent years. It is estimated that sales will grow by 4 percent compared to the base line, and will remain at this level in the subsequent years.

The implementation difficulty is 5 (relatively easy).

Increase the Managerial and Professional Quality of the Administrative and Operations Personnel   One of the main challenges of the chain is the need to replace some of its mid-level managers. At the same time, the turnover of those managers the chain wishes to retain, has to be reduced. Management recruiting, training and development programs, and plans to retain competent employees are likely to induce the following results:

- In the first year, there will be no change in revenues.

- From the second to the fifth year, sales will be 3 percent higher than the base year due to better management causing a further increase in the average customer purchase. These improvements are in addition to the activities described in the previous paragraphs. A 10 percent decrease in lost sales is expected. Due to increased efficiency, the inventories will remain at the base year levels, despite the increase in sales.

The estimate for the expenses in the first year is $1,000,000. These expenses include recruiting and training managers, and a program to retain competent employees. From the second to the fifth year, the expenses will amount to $700,000 per year. The implementation difficulty is 3 (moderate).

Increase the Shelf Space Area at the Expense of Storerooms in the Branches   Apparently, deliveries to the branches are mostly made once a week (except for fresh products, which arrives daily). Currently, about 25 percent of the branch area serves as an internal storage space. The proposal is that the delivery rate be doubled, in order to halve the storage space and add to the shelf space. Clearly, the transportation costs will increase. However, there will be no need for "monster" trucks that are difficult to maneuver and cost a lot to maintain. It will be sufficient to maintain a fleet of small and faster delivery vehicles

- Pilot studies carried out by the chain on increasing the existing shelf space and displaying new categories of goods in the newly created space showed that the throughput increased almost in proportion to the increase in the shelf space.

- We assume that the shelf space will increase by 8 percent after one year, and that it will remain at this level for the next five years. Thus, the increase in throughput will be as follows:

  —In the first year—no increase

  —In the second year—8 percent

  —In the third, fourth, and fifth years—8 percent compared to the base year.

- Making the transition to increased supply frequency involves negotiating with the suppliers and constructing a logistics center, reorganizing the branch premises and increased transportation costs. The additional expenses (beyond the cost of building the logistics center) will amount to $2 million per year, apart from the first year when they will be $1 million.

The implementation difficulty is 4 (relatively easy).

Increase the Number of Suppliers' Credit Days   The suppliers enjoy a lower number of credit days than demanded by the competing chains. The intention is to increase the number of credit days by 10 percent. Even then, it will still be lower than the credit days demanded by the competing chains. The process of increasing the suppliers' credit days will be carried out by negotiating with the suppliers, and it does not therefore involve any expenses.

It is estimated that the matter will be difficult to implement, mainly because of opposition from the leading suppliers. Thus, the difficulty of implementation will be 1 (very difficult).

Calculate the Potential Value Creation

In calculating the effect of the changes on the value of the firm, we make the following assumptions:

- Any change in the volume of sales is expressed in proportional change to the cost of sales, to the accounts receivable and the accounts payable, and to the inventories.

- The operating expenses are fixed.

- The accounts payable are sufficient to finance the maintaining of inventories and the accounts receivable.

- At the end of each year, all available cash flows are distributed to the shareholders as dividends.

Selecting the Value Drivers

At a meeting of the board of directors, it was decided that as a first stage no investment would be made in opening new branches, and the main effort would be concentrated on realizing the existing potential. In view of the complex tax problems involved, the board decided not to address the issue of selling the main office real estate assets or making the transition to renting premises for the branches.

The first seven potential value drivers were examined using the focusing matrix. The importance of each value driver is the added value that it will bring to the firm. The results of the potential value creation are presented in Table 19.2.

Appendix B depicts an example of a calculation of one of the value drivers. The focusing matrix in Figure 19.2 gives a graphic representation of the candidates for the value driver portfolio.

Out of the potential value drivers, the first six were chosen for implementation. The seventh—increasing suppliers' credit days—is problematic and its throughput is not high. As a first stage, the board of directors decided to accept management's recommendation to start implementing value drivers 1, 2, 4, 5, 6. Value driver 3—introducing a private label—will be implemented in the second stage due to the large amount of management time it requires and out of a desire to avoid dispute with leading suppliers.

Stage 4: Decide How to Improve the Value Drivers

For each value driver, a detailed work plan will be drawn up, including a full description of the activities, a schedule for their implementation, and the name of the person responsible for each activity.

Stage 5: Implement and Control

It is important to note that the implementation and control need to be an integral part of the firm's management tasks. Increasing

Table 19.2 Focusing table for the potential value drivers

	Value Driver	Importance – Additional Value ($M)	Ease of Implementation (5 – Relatively Easy, 1 – Very Difficult)
1	Increase the average customer purchase	44	4
2	Establish a logistics center	66	2
3	Introduce a private label	97	3
4	Enhance shelf space management	43	5
5	Increase the managerial and professional quality of the administrative and operations personnel	35	3
6	Increase the shelf space area	93	4 (Dependent on the establishment of a logistics center)
7	Increase the number of suppliers' credit days	4	1
	Total potential increase in value	**382**	

the value of the firm is the main management role, and all the organization's procedures, measuring and reward system, and information and control systems should be used to this end. The process of value creation should not be viewed as parallel or external to the organization's ongoing management. The firm's management has to serve as a steering committee to each of the value driver

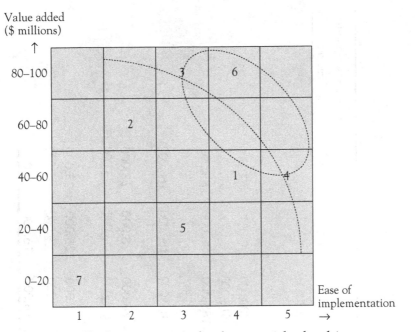

Figure 19.2 The focusing matrix for the potential value drivers

improvement projects. The process of implementation will be reported to the board of directors at their meetings and the various problems encountered presented.

Summary

Enhancing an organization's value is the goal of its managers. In this chapter, we presented a practical approach to increase the value of the firm, especially through managerial (nonfinancial) value drivers and measuring their contribution to the firm value.

The VFM methodology enables managers to decide correctly where they should devote their time and energy, and in which areas the contribution will be marginally small.

Appendix A

Table 19.3 Base Evaluation—Business as Usual

	Base Year	Year 1	Year 2	Year 3	Year 4	Year 5	Notes, Assumptions and Factors
				Thousands $			
Income Statement Summary							
Sales	700,000	700,000	700,000	700,000	700,000	700,000	1
Cost of goods sold	512,000	512,000	512,000	512,000	512,000	512,000	0.73
Gross profit	188,000	188,000	188,000	188,000	188,000	188,000	
Selling, General and Administrative expenses	160,000	160,000	160,000	160,000	160,000	160,000	1
Earnings before interest and taxes	28,000	28,000	28,000	28,000	28,000	28,000	
Interest expense	3,000	3,000	3,000	3,000	3,000	3,000	5%
Earnings before income taxes	25,000	25,000	25,000	25,000	25,000	25,000	
Income taxes	9,000	9,000	9,000	9,000	9,000	9,000	36%
Net income	16,000	16,000	16,000	16,000	16,000	16,000	

Balance Sheet Summary

Current assets

Accounts receivable	65,000	65,000	65,000	65,000	65,000	65,000	Changes in proportion to sales
Inventories	43,000	43,000	43,000	43,000	43,000	43,000	Changes in proportion to sales
	108,000	108,000	108,000	108,000	108,000	108,000	

Short-term non-interest liabilities

Accounts payable	105,000	105,000	105,000	105,000	105,000	105,000	Changes in proportion to sales
Other current payables	32,000	32,000	32,000	32,000	32,000	32,000	
	137,000	137,000	137,000	137,000	137,000	137,000	
Net working capital	−29,000	−29,000	−29,000	−29,000	−29,000	−29,000	
Net property plant and equipment	274,000	274,000	274,000	274,000	274,000	274,000	
Total capital required	**245,000**	**245,000**	**245,000**	**245,000**	**245,000**	**245,000**	Total capital demand
Short-term bank credit	11,000	11,000	11,000	11,000	11,000	11,000	
Long-term debt	52,000	52,000	52,000	52,000	52,000	52,000	
Shareholders' equity	182,000	182,000	182,000	182,000	182,000	182,000	
Total capital resources	**245,000**	**245,000**	**245,000**	**245,000**	**245,000**	**245,000**	

(Continued)

Table 19.3 *(Continued)*

	Base Year	Year 1	Year 2	Year 3	Year 4	Year 5	Notes, Assumptions and Factors
			Thousands $				
Cash Flow Available to Investors							
EBIT (Earnings before interest and taxes)	28,000	28,000	28,000	28,000	28,000	28,000	
Taxes on EBIT	10,080	10,080	10,080	10,080	10,080	10,080	36%
NOPAT (Net operating profit after tax)	17,920	17,920	17,920	17,920	17,920	17,920	
Depreciation expense	18,000	18,000	18,000	18,000	18,000	18,000	6.6%
Gross cash flow	35,920	35,920	35,920	35,920	35,920	35,920	
Increase (decrease) in Working capital	0	0	0	0	0	0	
Capital expenditures	18,000	18,000	18,000	18,000	18,000	18,000	
Total gross investment	18,000	18,000	18,000	18,000	18,000	18,000	
Cash flow available to investors	17,920	17,920	17,920	17,920	17,920	17,920	

Economic Value-Added Calculation

NOPAT (Net operating profit after tax)	17,920	17,920	17,920	17,920	17,920	17,920	
WACC (Weighted average cost of capital)	8.3%	8.3%	8.3%	8.3%	8.3%	8.3%	10% Cost of equity
Debt/equity ratio	0.35	0.35	0.35	0.35	0.35	0.35	3.2% Debt price 5%, tax advantage 36%
Invested equity (beginning of year)	182,000	182,000	182,000	182,000	182,000	182,000	
Financial liabilities (beginning of year)	63,000	63,000	63,000	63,000	63,000	63,000	
Total invested capital	245,000	245,000	245,000	245,000	245,000	245,000	
Capital charge	20,216	20,216	20,216	20,216	20,216	20,216	
EVA (Economic value added)	−2,296	−2,296	−2,296	−2,296	−2,296	−2,296	

(Continued)

Table 19.3 (Continued)

	Base Year	Year 1	Year 2	Year 3	Year 4	Year 5	Notes, Assumptions and Factors
				Thousands $			
Valuation at the Base Year							
Discounted cash flow							
First five years	71,078						8.3% discounted by WACC at the third year
Residual value	146,097						1.487
Total valuation of invested capital	217,175						
Net financial liabilities	63,000						
Excess assets	0						
Value of the company to its shareholders	154,175						

Appendix B

Table 19.4 Value Driver No. 4—Shelf Space Management

A one-time increase of sales in year 2. Later, sales remain the same level.

	Base Year	Year 1	Year 2	Year 3	Year 4	Year 5	Notes, Assumptions and Factors
			Thousands $				
Income Statement Summary							
Sales	700,000	700,000	728,000	728,000	728,000	728,000	1.04
Cost of goods sold	512,000	512,000	532,480	532,480	532,480	532,480	0.73
Gross Profit	188,000	188,000	195,520	195,520	195,520	195,520	
Increase in costs		500	1,456	1,456	1,456	1,456	0.2%
Selling, General and Administrative expenses	160,000	160,000	160,000	160,000	160,000	160,000	1
Earnings before interest and taxes	28,000	27,500	34,064	34,064	34,064	34,064	
Interest expense	3,000	3,150	3,156	3,156	3,156	3,156	5%
Earnings before income taxes	25,000	24,350	30,908	30,908	30,908	30,908	
Income taxes	9,000	8,766	11,127	11,127	11,127	11,127	36%
Net income	16,000	15,584	19,781	19,781	19,781	19,781	

(Continued)

Table 19.4 (*Continued*)

A one-time increase of sales in year 2. Later, sales remain the same level.

	Base Year	Year 1	Year 2	Year 3	Year 4	Year 5	Notes, Assumptions and Factors
			Thousands $				
Balance Sheet Summary							
Current assets							
Accounts receivable	65,000	65,000	67,600	67,600	67,600	67,600	Changes in proportion to sales
Inventories	43,000	43,000	44,720	44,720	44,720	44,720	Changes in proportion to sales
	108,000	108,000	112,320	112,320	112,320	112,320	
Short-term non-interest liabilities							
Accounts payable	105,000	105,000	109,200	109,200	109,200	109,200	Changes in proportion to sales
Other current payables	32,000	32,000	32,000	32,000	32,000	32,000	
	137,000	137,000	141,200	141,200	141,200	141,200	
Net working capital	−29,000	−29,000	−28,880	−28,880	−28,880	−28,880	
Net property plant and equipment	274,000	274,000	274,000	274,000	274,000	274,000	
Total capital required	245,000	245,000	245,120	245,120	245,120	245,120	

Short-term bank credit	11,000	1,000	11,120	11,120	11,120	11,120	
Long-term debt	52,000	52,000	52,000	52,000	52,000	52,000	
Shareholders' equity	182,000	182,000	182,000	182,000	182,000	182,000	
Total capital resources	**245,000**	**245,000**	**245,120**	**245,120**	**245,120**	**245,120**	

Cash Flow Available to Investors

EBIT (Earnings before interest and taxes)	28,000	27,500	34,064	34,064	34,064	34,064	EBIT
Taxes on EBIT	10,080	9,900	12,263	12,263	12,263	12,263	36%
NOPAT (Net operating profit after tax)	17,920	17,600	21,801	21,801	21,801	21,801	NOPAT
Depreciation expense	18,000	18,000	18,000	18,000	18,000	18,000	6.6%
Gross cash flow	**35,920**	**35,600**	**39,801**	**39,801**	**39,801**	**39,801**	
Increase (decrease) in Working capital	0	0	120	0	0	0	
Capital expenditures	18,000	18,020	18,000	18,000	18,000	18,000	
Total gross investment	**18,000**	**18,000**	**18,120**	**18,000**	**18,000**	**18,000**	
Cash flow available to investors	**17,920**	**17,600**	**21,681**	**21,801**	**21,801**	**21,801**	

(Continued)

Table 19.4 (Continued)

A one-time increase of sales in year 2. Later, sales remain the same level.

Thousands $

Economic Value Added Calculation

	Base Year	Year 1	Year 2	Year 3	Year 4	Year 5	Notes, Assumptions and Factors
NOPAT (Net operating profit after tax)	17,920	17,600	21,801	21,801	21,801	21,801	NOPAT
WACC (Weighted average cost of capital)	8.3%	8.3%	8.3%	8.2%	8.2%	8.2%	10% Cost of equity
Debt/equity ratio	0.35	0.35	0.35	0.35	0.35	0.35	3.2% Debt price 5%, tax advantage 36%
Invested equity (beginning of year)	182,000	182,000	182,000	182,000	182,000	182,000	Balance at the begining of the year
Financial liabilities (beginning of year)	63,000	63,000	63,000	63,120	63,120	63,120	Balance at the begining of the year
Total invested capital	245,000	245,000	245,000	245,120	245,120	245,120	
Capital charge	20,216	20,216	20,216	20,220	20,220	20,220	
EVA (Economic value added)	−2,296	−2,616	1,585	1,581	1,581	1,581	

Valuation at the Base Year

Discounted cash flow		
First five years	82,494	8.2% discounted by WACC at the third year
		1.486
Residual value	177,811	
Total valuation of invested capital	260,304	
Net financial liabilities	63,000	
Excess assets	0	Increase relative to the base year
Value of the company to its shareholders	197,304	45,130 30%

Part IV

Applying the Focused
Management Approach

20

Value-Focused Project Management

Projects are a vital part of the activity of many organizations. In research and development (R&D), high-tech, construction, consulting, and defense companies, the business is based on project execution.

This chapter introduces a value-focused approach to project management. The well-established theory and techniques of project management will not be deliberated. We assume that you have some fundamental knowledge of project management. Our purpose in this chapter is to show how the value of the organization can be increased by focused and professional project management, using modern management concepts.

Project Management Environment

Project: A one-time task aimed at producing a product or a service.

A project has a set of predefined outcomes that are achieved using numerous resources within the constraints of a timetable, content, budget, and performance. Projects are usually planned and performed with uncertainty. This uncertainty stems from the inability to foresee the exact environment in which the project is occurring, and the performance of the organization while it executes the project plan. Projects usually require teamwork. The teams are usually interdisciplinary; hence, the resources come from several organizational units.

Because of the uncertainties surrounding projects, there are risks that may harm the value of the organization. However, once properly managed, uncertainties may become opportunities to increase the value of the organization.

Projects have to be executed within the framework of a given timetable, budget, content, and performance. Many projects overrun their predefined costs and budgets. Delays, budget overruns and partial realization of the goals and incomplete performance are common. These problems are not caused by lack of professional or technical know-how, but mostly by insufficient managerial skills and methods. Thus, significant improvement in project outcome can be gained by improving project management.

An organization that excels and delivers projects in a short lead time, on time, on budget, and on scope has a significant competitive edge over its competitors. Namely, excellence in project management is a significant value for the organization.

Project Management

Project management increases the value of the organization by improving its ability to deliver projects in a short lead time, and within its due date, budget, and content, taking the project life cycle cost and the global cash flow of the organization into consideration.

Project management: *The use of knowledge, skills, tools, and methodology along the project life cycle in order to achieve its goals.*

Value Drivers in Project Management

Proper project management leads to increased throughput and hence to increased organization value. The increase in throughput is achieved by:

- Direct increase of the throughput:

  —Improving the capacity of the permanent bottlenecks in R&D (as is discussed earlier and in Chapter 21)

  —Improving the throughput by the strategic gating

  —Reducing usage of materials and subcontractors costs

- Indirect increase of the throughput can be materialized by:

  —Quality improvement (using the methods discussed earlier).

  —Global view of the life cycle of the project and its costs

- Shortening lead times allows increased throughput adding strategic benefits as well as tactical benefits to the organization. This can be done in various ways as discussed in the previous chapters and in Chapter 21. On top of it, these are three topics related to lead time reduction:

  —Uncertainties and risk management

  —Implementation of the critical chain concept

  —Methodological planning

Each of these value drivers may contribute to value enhancement to different extents. In this chapter, we focus on the following value drivers that have the highest value enhancement potential in most organizations:

- Strategic gating and project initiation

- Project planning

- The project manager as a business manager

- Forward-oriented execution and forward-looking control:

  —Drum-buffer-rope (DBR)

  —Forward-looking measurements

- Implementation of the critical chain approach

Strategic Gating and Project Initiation as a Value Driver

To increase the organization's value through project management, you should focus on the initiation and the first steps of the project. This is where the "big money" lies.

Most projects have a similar life cycle:

1. Strategic gating
2. Initiation and specification
3. Project planning
4. Execution, monitoring and control
5. Completion and debriefing
6. Use of the project products and/or customer support

We focus on the first two stages as an important source for value creation.

Strategic Gating

The permanent bottlenecks of marketing and R&D are heavily involved both in the preparation of proposals and the execution of the projects. Consequently, organizations are not able to reply to all the requests for proposals (RFPs), nor to execute all the potential projects. To select which proposal to respond to and which projects to perform, you must prioritize. Prioritization is done according to an initial strategic gating process (see Chapter 5) that is sometimes known as a bid/no-bid or a go/no-go process.

Several questions should be considered when deciding whether to continue with the project initiative:

- What is the total throughput of the project throughout its life cycle (development, production, integrated logistic support (ILS), and so on)?

- Is the specific contribution of the project (or the proposal) higher than the specific contribution of the other alternatives?

- Is there enough bottleneck capacity within the required time frame to execute the project (or the proposal), considering all the existing projects (or proposals)?

  Note: The effort invested by the permanent bottlenecks is both for the preparation of the proposal and the execution of the proposed project, since the same bottleneck resources are usually involved in both tasks.

Experience shows that there is a tendency in organizations to bid for every job and to answer every RFP. Usually, this stems from the fear of missing opportunities (see Chapter 5).

The switch to a focused policy toward a bid/no-bid (go/no-go) process will direct the organization toward those proposals and projects that will lead to an effective increase in the organization's value. In our experience, about 25 percent of the projects and the incoming proposals should be screened out in the strategic gating process.

Initiation and Specification

A project can be initiated from within the organization or by an external customer. In the global and business-oriented view of the project, the goal of the project is always to increase the value of the organization. From this standpoint, the project manager's responsibility is not simply to conform to cost, time, and content. The project manager manages a business that has to contribute to the value of the organization. To avoid overspecification that is common among customers and marketing people alike and overdesign that is common among developers, the project team should focus on satisficing goals to increase the organization's value.

The initiation and specification stage is critical to the success of the project because at this stage the most critical decisions and commitments are made. Figure 20.1 depicts the reality of most projects: in the very short initiation stage, 70 percent of the commitments are taken, whereas the effort put in the project in this stage is only about 1 percent of the total effort.

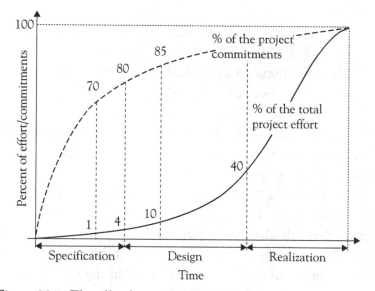

Figure 20.1 The effort/commitments profile of projects

This phenomenon fits with the concept of the 10 times rule (see Chapter 17) that states that late detection and correction of a problem will result in great damage to the project and the organization. In the initiation and specification stage, the project is not yet organized: the project manager has probably not been nominated or the person responsible for the proposal is very busy with many issues. However, at this stage, the crucial decisions are made and most of the budget is committed.

Hence, focus has to be put on this stage, even at the cost of prolonging this stage. All the specifications and decisions have to be made with a Complete Kit or at least with a mandatory kit. The time invested in assuring the existence of these kits will pay for itself at the later stages of the project.

Project Planning as a Value Driver

A structured and methodological project planning process results in the following benefits:

- The process forces the project team to examine and analyze the project in a systematic way.

- The process facilitates the early identification of problems.

- The process diminishes the risks of the project.

- The process creates good communication, synchronization of expectations, and shared commitment of the parties involved in the project.

- The process encourages interdisciplinary thinking.

Methodological planning: A *key success factor for the project. Poor planning will lead the project to time and budget overruns, damages, and bad reputation.*

It is important for the project team to use a structured and methodological planning process for the project. Experience shows that the use of a clear methodology and the orderly, step-by-step planning process are keys to the success of the project. Trying to dump a good methodology for an excellent one will not dramatically change the performance of the project. If the project team is competent and is fully committed to the project, then what actually matters is the adherence to a methodology and the persistent of the project leaders. Teamwork based on the planning process leads to emergence of problems at an early stage. Planning according to a defined methodology is only the platform for an effective process. Hence, a project manager that has a satisficer mindset would look for a satisficing methodology and adhere to it.

As pointed out previously, a structured and methodological planning process has many advantages including:

- Forcing the project team to analyze the project in a systematic way

- Enabling early identification of the problems

- Reducing the uncertainty of the project

- Enabling effective communication and commitment among the participants of the project

- Enhancing interdisciplinary thinking

At the first stage of the planning process, the project team should scrutinize the project specifications and requirements. They should perform a contract review—a review by representatives of all the relevant units in the organization that examines the requirement specification document, the proposed solution outline, and the reuse of existing assets of the organization (experts, knowledge, resources, proven hardware/software solutions, and so on).

Most important, do not accept customer requirement documents (external or internal) as is, but try to see whether they really match the *real* need.

When analysis reveals major problems during the planning stage, these problems can be solved by one or more of the following actions:

- *Improved conformance to due dates.* The duration of the project is governed by the duration of the critical path. To shorten the duration of the project, you have to focus on the activities on the critical path and find ways to shorten them. A Pareto analysis of the duration of the activities on the critical path identifies the longest activities that are, naturally, the best candidates for duration reduction. Though the Pareto analysis is suitable for independent entities, these activities are not necessarily independent. However, as a first-order approximation, we can treat them as if they were independent. Thus, shortening the longest activities of the critical path first is a reasonable route to reduce project lead time.

  Reduction of project duration not only improves competitiveness and reduces costs but also reduces project risks and the tendency to introduce changes in the project content.

- Review for overspecification and overdesign and removing the nonrequired content.

- Addition of resources for critical path activities.

- Management of bottleneck resources.

The Project Manager as a Business Manager as a Value Driver

The prevalent belief is that the goal of the project manager is to conform to the time, content, and budget. That is, if the project manager achieves this goal then the project will bring the maximum contribution to the value of the organization.

This belief is a reflection of the local optimum way of thinking. As seen in previous chapters, the sum of local optima will not lead the organization to the global optimum and sometimes not even to a satisfactory solution.

The following examples clarify this point:

- A project manager considers buying services from another department in the organization. This department has excess capacity (while the organization is not willing to or not able to lay off workers). The project manager's other alternative is to purchase these services from an external subcontractor that offers a lower price than the transfer price required by the inhouse department. This is a classical make/buy dilemma. Most project managers will prefer using the subcontractor as it affects better their measure of performance—it brings more "profit to the project," although it leads to a clear loss for the organization (see the example in Chapter 16).

  A global view that reflects the understanding that the goal of a project manager is to increase the value of the organization by improving the cash flow of the project throughout its life cycle will guide the project manager in finding a satisfactory solution that will also prevent the type of loss described above. Making the buy decision when there is excess capacity in the organization often leads to extensive losses.

- An R&D organization developed a complex system that had an innovative sensor as a component. The sensor prototype conformed to all the required performance and was delivered on time and on budget.

However, it turned out that the sensor could not be integrated into the system and the requirement specification had to be altered. This change dictated an additional cycle of development of the sensor, which in turn led to delays in system delivery.

You could argue that the sensor development project manager did his job flawlessly: the project conformed to every requirement and performance measure and coped nicely with the requested change in the requirement specifications. In other words, from a local standpoint the sensor development project was a success. However, from a global standpoint, the sensor development project led to the failure of the system development project.

From a global view, the project manager has a clear goal—to increase the value of the organization by improving the cash flow of the project along its life cycle. The global view dictates that the project managers have constant communication, frequent meetings, and close collaboration with customers and subcontractors alike.

- Specifications will never be complete and accurate, especially in high-risk projects. Hence, it is impossible to dissect the system into a set of independent subprojects.

- Budgets and resources will never be divided among several units in a fair and just manner.

- The due dates defined for some projects are just a guess and achieving them will not necessarily lead to maximizing the value of the organization.

The belief that conformance to the triangle of commitment (due date, budget, and content) is the project manager's goal may lead to suboptimization of projects.

The global view considers the goal of the project as increasing the value of the organization by improving the project cash flow along the life cycle. It should bring some changes in the organization:

- The project manager should be considered a business manager—a mini-CEO who contributes, together with others, to the increase in the value of the organization.

- The acceptance of the notion that the project manager should make the decisions from the viewpoint of the CEO.

- The drive to find better performance measures for the project, which will motivate the project toward a larger contribution to the value of the organization.

- Improvement of the communication and cooperation between the units involved in the project as well as with customers and subcontractors.

Performance Measurement Gap Tragedy

Every system is a subsystem of a larger parent system, and the optimization of each system leads to suboptimization of the larger parent system. This perspective is well known in systems theory and operations research. It is difficult to derive optimal performance measures for a large system, and there will always be a gap between the goal of the system and its performance measures that aim to lead the organization toward its goal. Also, there will always be a gap between the performance measures of a system and those of its subsystems. This gap is called the performance measurement gap (see Figure 20.2).

Because of this gap, we are not able to define project performance measures that are 100 percent compatible with the performance measures of the organization as a whole. Even if there exist project

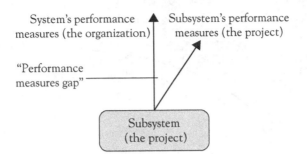

Figure 20.2 The performance measurement gap

performance measures having only a small gap, there may be project managers who will be tempted to abuse the system and improve their project's performance measures on the account of the performance measures of the total organization. By doing so, they might, knowingly or unknowingly, cause harm to the organization. The performance gap will always exist. The best that management can do is try to limit this gap. Mature managers understand that this phenomenon cannot be eradicated, but its effects can be reduced.

Whenever project performance measures are applied, there is some degree of suboptimization and a performance measures gap that has to be reduced. Sometimes managers tend to believe that this suboptimization can be cured by one central decision maker who oversees all projects. This solution is not practical because no single central decision maker (competent as he or she might be) is ever able to tackle all problems of all the concurrent projects in the organization. The performance measurement gap can be reduced substantially by focusing on the main contributors to this gap. The practical tool for this application is the Pareto analysis of the causes of the performance measures gap (Figure 20.3).

The main causes for the gap are the A items that are the "vital few." Such important causes for the gap could be, for instance, measuring the project only according to its profit/loss that will encourage the project manager to an extensive use of subcontractors while

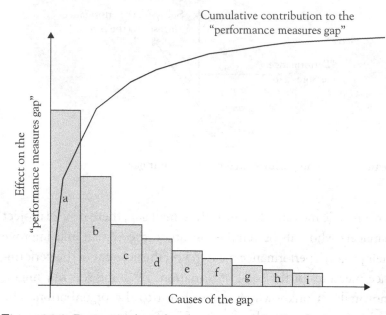

Figure 20.3 Pareto analysis for the causes of the "performance measures gap"

there are idle workers within the company, or the use of inappropriate transfer prices that might lead to missed business opportunities (see Chapters 15 and 16).

Forward-Oriented Execution and Forward-Looking Control as a Value Driver

One of the most effective mechanisms for effective and efficient use of the project scarce resources and to achieve the project goals is the use of tactical gating (see Chapter 5). Thus, all activities and work packages should be released to work only by the gater assigned; all activities and work packages should be smaller than 200 working hours; the amount of activities waiting in front of each employee should not exceed 600 working hours; all activities and work packages should be released having a Complete Kit or a mandatory kit.

In many cases, projects are still monitored by backward-looking parameters such as earned value, and the emphasis of input resource control rather than throughput and a results-oriented one. Projects should be monitored using forward-looking parameters such as time to complete and progress along the critical path.

In status meetings, the project team should focus on future risks and problems and ways to solve them.

Implementation of the Critical Chain Approach as a Value Driver

As seen, projects are prone to delays, budgetary over-runs, and partial achievement of the scope. Goldratt (1997) suggests the critical chain approach as a remedy to the inherent problems of project management.

The critical chain approach is based on the following principles:

- An alternative mechanism for the estimation of activities' durations, which takes into account the existence of the Parkinson's law and the student's syndrome (see discussion that follows)

- A new policy to manage uncertainties

- Focus on the bottleneck resource of the project

Alternative Mechanism for the Estimation of Activities' Durations and Uncertainty Management

A key to the critical chain approach is the understanding of the statistical distribution of the activities' durations. As seen in Figure 20.4, the distribution of the duration of a typical activity is bell shaped but it has a long tail toward longer duration. The duration that has 50 percent probability to end the activity in a shorter time

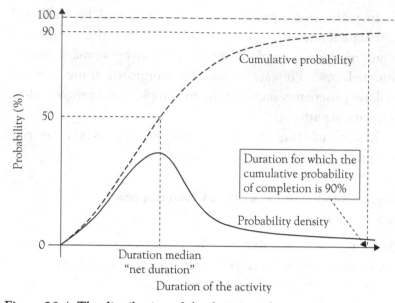

Figure 20.4 The distribution of the duration of a typical activity in a project

is referred as the *duration median* or the *net duration*. Namely, if this activity will be performed in many repetitions, then in 50 percent of the cases the activity will be completed in durations that are shorter than the net duration, and in 50 percent of the cases it will be completed in longer durations than the net duration.

Because of the tailing toward the longer durations, the duration for which the cumulative probability of completion is 90 percent is almost twice as long as the net duration.

When the participants of the project are requested to estimate the duration of an activity (or a work package) that they have to perform, they usually quote the 90 percent duration rather than the duration median. Thus, the 90 percent duration is perceived as the realistic duration estimate: a duration estimate that has a 90 percent certainty that the activity (or work package) will be completed in this duration or sooner. The participants would not like to be committed to duration estimates that will not be met in 50 percent of the cases. Hence, they give overestimates which they feel can be met in 90 percent of the cases (the realistic duration estimates).

As a result, the resources group managers save large buffers for potential problems.

Unfortunately, although local buffers for each activity are introduced, reality shows that a significant percentage of projects is overdue. Goldratt (1997) suggests several reasons for this discrepancy:

- *Parkinson's law.* A task is performed according to the duration that is allocated for it. Hence, given the overestimation, a task will not be completed in a shorter duration than the duration estimate given for it. Also, since people stand behind their estimates and they are expected to be committed to them, the estimate turns into a self-fulfilling prophesy.

  Even in cases where the employee feels that he is able to complete the task before the estimated completion time, this does not happen because of the following reasons:

  - He doesn't want to have his future duration estimates cut by his managers.

  - In the available time, the employee continues to try to improve his work. This tendency to improve the performance of the deliverables is very prominent in R&D projects.

  To sum up, early completion of an activity rarely results in an early start of the next activity, while delayed completion of the activity always brings delays in the start of the subsequent activity.

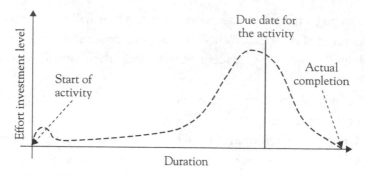

Figure 20.5 The student's syndrome

- *The student's syndrome*. The psychological tendency of people to postpone work until the end of the time allocated for it (Figure 20.5). The employee actually has enough time to finish the job on time, but the late start results in a delayed completion time.

- Because the activity has numerous predecessor activities, the activity can start only when the most delayed predecessor activity has finished. This pattern is very prominent in integration activities during large systems' development.

- When there is a common resource for several activities or several projects, if this resource is delayed in one of these activities or projects, it delays all other activities that are scheduled later on.

- In the bad multitasking (BMT) situation, employees are moving among a large number of open activities thus causing delays in all of them.

An attempt by the managers to arbitrarily trim down all of the duration estimates is not very effective because the next time employees are asked to give their duration estimates for activities and work packages, they will increase their estimates so that after the "trimming down" by management, the durations actually planned for the activities and work packages will be the original realistic duration estimates.

The conflict described is very familiar (Figure 20.6). On the one hand, managers wish to trim all activities down to the net durations in order to reduce the lead time of the entire project and hence to improve the competitive position of the organization; on the other hand, employees feel committed to their duration estimates and therefore they give realistic duration estimates.

This conflict can be solved in two ways:

1. *The differentiation approach.* Ask for net duration estimates only for the activities along the critical path of the project and leave the realistic duration estimates for the activities that are not part of the critical path. This is a partial solution for the situation.

2. *The globalization approach.* Safety margins are not required for all activities. What actually matters is not the fact that each of the activities is on time, but rather that the project as a

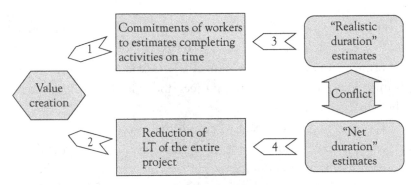

Figure 20.6 The duration estimates conflict

whole is completed on time. In order to protect the due date of the project, you have to introduce a time-buffer at the end of the project that will protect the whole project against possible delays in some activities (Goldratt, 1997).

Statistical analysis shows that the size of a single buffer set to protect the whole project against its uncertainty is smaller than the sum of the safety margins introduced by the realistic duration estimates of all the activities along the critical path.

Goldratt's solution is to ask the employees to give net duration estimates for all the activities and at the same time to set a joint time-buffer for the entire project.

Critical Chain Approach to Project Planning

Critical chain: *The longest set of interrelated activities, leading from start to end, that are related by precedence or by being performed by the bottleneck resources of the organization. The durations of the activities of the critical chain are estimated as net durations and a time-buffer is placed in front of the end node.*

To better exploit the constraint—the critical chain—the ineffective security margins of each activity (hidden in the realistic duration estimates) should be cancelled. Instead, a joint time-buffer is introduced at the end of the project and it is planned to protect the due date of the project.

Goldratt suggests (1997) to cut all realistic duration estimates given by workers and resource group managers by 50 percent and convert them into net durations. Half of the saved time will be put as the time-buffer for the project. This project buffer is placed in front of the end node (Figure 20.7).

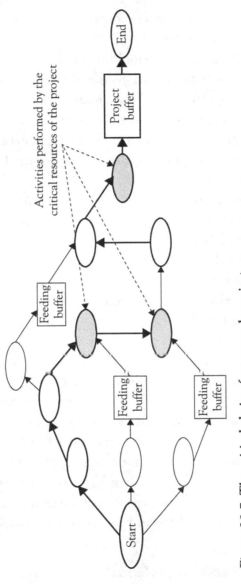

Activities performed by the
critical resources of the project

Figure 20.7 The critical chain of an example project

Planning according to net duration estimates causes time over-runs in 50 percent of all the activities. Therefore, the project buffer is placed at the end of the project in order to buffer these over-runs. This buffering action reduces significantly the probability of a delay for the project as a whole.

Reaching the consent of the employees to the 50 percent trim-ming down of the activities durations is not an easy task because employees fear being blamed for delays. Management should stress the fact that when the work plan is based of net durations there is a probability of 50 percent for delays in the completion of an activ-ity. Also, the role of the project buffer in preventing the project delay should be explained.

The ambitious rule thumb of 50 percent trimming of the realistic duration estimates is not sacred nor is it based on scien-tific analysis. Even a reduction of 10 percent in the lead times of projects can double the value of a projects-based organization rely-ing on permanent bottlenecks. Hence, by proper interaction with the project team, management can achieve consent of a 10 percent to 30 percent reduction of the realistic duration estimates with the obvious value enhancement.

In addition to these actions, all activities, resources, and deci-sions should be subordinated to the constraint of the project—to the critical chain. If we don't want the activities of the critical chain to be delayed by delays in noncritical activities outside the critical chain, we should introduce a feeding buffer (whenever a noncritical path feeds a critical chain activity (Goldratt, 1997). The recommended size for the feeding buffer is 50 percent of the duration of the path leading from the start of the project to the con-nection point. Feeding buffers can be seen in the example shown in Figure 20.7.

Critical Chain Approach to Project Execution and Control   We intro-duced a set of guidelines for project execution and control. These guidelines hold also for a project managed according to the con-cept of the critical chain, including the tactical gating mechanism.

However, the implementation of critical chain concepts brings additional benefits for project control processes:

- Control over the project status can be achieved by analysis of the situation of the project buffer. By monitoring and analyzing the rate at which the buffer is being consumed, you can identify at an early stage the problems in the project. The project buffer is not only a protection mechanism; it is also a command and control system for the project manager. Also, the monitoring and analysis of the feeding buffers provide some control over the noncritical activities.

- The discussion in the project team meetings should analyze the status of the project buffer.

- Analysis of the causes of depletion of the project buffer protection leads the project team to deal with the emerging problems and hints at the priorities of these problem rectification tasks.

- Whenever an activity is completed, especially if this is ahead of time, the person in charge of this activity should report that the activity has been completed. This is important because there is the possibility that the successor activities can be started immediately, leading to a possible reduction in the duration of the whole project.

- When making decisions regarding the allocation of a scarce resource to several competing activities, the criteria for the allocation should be the following:

  —Highest priority to activities of the critical chain.

  —If all the competing activities are noncritical, priority is given to activities that have consumed the entire relevant feeding buffer.

Effects of the Implementation of the Critical Chain Approach The implementation of the critical chain approach brings about a reduction in the lead times of projects and improves the efficiency of usage of bottleneck resources. This enables the completion of more projects in a given time frame, brings higher throughput, and improves the attractiveness of the organization to its customers.

The implementation of the critical chain approach is not trivial, and faces many obstacles and failures (Lecher, Ronen, and Stohr, 2005). This approach has a potential to improve the performance of the organization.

Summary

Project management is a complex issue that has significant potential for improvement of the performance of the organization. Success in the implementation depends on the focus of the people involved in the project: focus on the critical chain or the critical path, focus on bottleneck resources, focus on the initiation and the launch of the project, focus on high risks, and focus on the project buffer.

The global view of the project goals, considering the entire life cycle of the project and collaboration among the parties involved in the project, can turn a complex endeavor into a successful project.

21

Managing Research and Development

Research and development (R&D), a topic of utmost importance because of its complexity, encompasses three interrelated elements:

1. Project management
2. Resource management
3. Technology management (identifying opportunities, marketing the product, managing technological innovation, and more)

This chapter focuses mainly on managing the R&D department that has components of these three elements.

Complexity of R&D Management

Research and development management is characterized by:

- A multiplicity of projects competing for the same resources

- High levels of marketing and technological uncertainty

- Complexity in managing employees with a high level of specific expertise

- A multiplicity of specializations in various technological areas

- Inherent conflicts between the two permanent bottlenecks:

  —Marketing and sales personnel

  —R&D personnel

- Pressure from customers and management to reduce response times and costs

- Continual reduction of the product or technological service life cycle

Improving R&D enhances the firm's value. To achieve this enhancement, there is a need to deal with the main problems faced by R&D management.

Experience with R&D departments demonstrates several typical important problems:

- Business thinking and subordination to the market and its needs

- Effect of project type on management requirements

- Conflict between generic development and specific development

- Overspecification and overdesign

- Viewing development as a process

- Working without a Complete Kit or mandatory kit

- Lack of strategic gating processes

- Lack of tactical gating processes

- Inappropriate measurement

- Business structure

- Substantial garbage plant

- Make/buy decisions

Business Thinking and Subordination to the Market and Its Needs

Two problems that emerge from managing R&D departments are technological thinking that lacks business thinking and insufficient subordination to the market and its needs.

This phenomenon characterizes veteran organizations that operated for years in a sellers' market. It usually arises because of the dominance of technology people over those in marketing and sales. This dominance was accentuated during the high-tech start-up boom of the 1990s where investors were willing to pay a premium for technological vision.

Technological thinking usually results in subordination to technological topics rather than to the market and its needs.

Dealing with this problem is not immediate and it is incorporated in exposing many levels in the organization to business thinking and acquisition of knowledge and techniques. In some cases, the treatment requires enriching the management team by adding managers with a business orientation.

Effect of Project Type on Management Requirements

Many R&D organizations do not have sufficient differentiation among the various R&D projects. The A, B, C, D classification of projects can be helpful, with projects classified by the level of their technological uncertainty (Shenhar, 1998).

Type A Projects

A projects have relatively low levels of uncertainty, that is, the product performances are within a known and accepted "performance envelope." These are projects whose performance requirements are a partial set of performances of products already developed by the organization, or are simply more of the same. Such projects have very little technological uncertainty. All decisions in this type of project will be subordinated to time and cost considerations.

Type B Projects

B projects are those whose majority of performances have been achieved by similar projects developed in the organization in the past. Such projects also have low technological uncertainty.

Type C Projects

C projects involve at least one technology that is new to the organization. They have a high level of technological uncertainty.

Type D Projects

D projects involve breakthroughs, or projects involving several technologies that were previously unknown to the organization. They have a very high level of technological uncertainty. In these projects, it is not clear whether a solution exists for the requirements, and it is unclear if the organization can bridge the technological gaps with its resources and capabilities. In other words, it is unclear whether the technological requirements can be met.

Project Classification Table

Project classification and the possible implications are described in Table 21.1.

Type A projects have a very low level of uncertainty. All decisions in this project will be subordinated to time and cost considerations.

When considering whether to subordinate decisions to time or cost considerations, the answer is usually clear: subordination should be to time considerations. In development projects, most

Table 21.1 Classifying development projects

Project Type	A	B	C	D
Performance requirements	Achieved in the organization in the past	Most were achieved in the past	Integration of new technology in the organization	Integration of several new technologies; solution existence doubtful
Project nature	More of the same	Specific knowledge gap that can be bridged	Technological innovation	Breakthrough
Level of uncertainty	Very low	Low	High	Very high
Constraint	Time and cost	The specific knowledge gap	Setting up an operational prototype	Proving existence/nonexistence of a solution
Subordination to constraint	Subordination to duration of development	Subordination to specific knowledge gap	Subordination to gap in technological know-how	Subordination to existence of solution

(*Continued*)

Table 21.1 (*Continued*)

Project Type	A	B	C	D
Monitoring and control	Linear focus on time	Focus on specific knowledge gap	Focus on gap in technological know-how	Focus on existence of solution
With progress, change project type to:		Project A after overcoming specific gap	Project B after integrating the new technology	Manage as project D throughout development
Manager personality	Planning and organizing	Planning and organizing	Technological knowledge, planning and organizing, and managerial know-how	Technological knowledge, courage, and vision, managerial and technological experience

resources are human resources (usually 85 percent). These resources constitute fixed costs. A typical profit structure of a firm is:

Sales	$100
Real variable costs	15
Fixed costs	80
Profit	$5

Reducing response times by 10 percent with the same resources enables the firm to develop an additional 10 percent sales. Under the assumption that the development personnel are "permanent bottlenecks," the profit structure will be:

Sales	$110
Real variable costs	16.5
Fixed costs	80
Profit	$13.5

The enhancement potential is 170 percent.

As we have seen, it is not certain that such an enhancement is feasible. Because of market competition and declining prices, the declining base line phenomenon results in a lesser, yet significant, enhancement.

Matching Manager Personality with Project Type

There are two types of project managers: a *cost* project manager and a *time* project manager. A cost project manager makes a majority of decisions primarily by cost considerations, where time is only a secondary factor. He calculates how many labor hours were invested, how much a certain system feature will cost, and so on. When the time project manager must decide among alternatives, he puts time to market as his top priority. Experience shows that a time project manager will reach the market faster and with lesser project costs. His project will eventually result in a higher value for the firm.

In type A projects, response time will be the major constraint to which planning, design, and other decision-making considerations will be subordinated. Control of such projects will be based on the time parameter and due date performance, and will be performed linearly (that is, the control points will be spread out uniformly throughout the project life time, where the actual performance will be proportional to time).

A type project managers should have planning, administrative, and organizational skills. His technological knowledge is not critical for managing an A project. Experience shows that if a project manager excels in vision and ingenuity, or is a pure technology person, then the project will suffer from overspecification and overdesign, and will quickly become a C project.

The technological uncertainty of B projects is not inherently different from that of A projects. Focusing on the specific knowledge gap, where the majority of uncertainty is concentrated, will reduce this uncertainty. The work plan for B projects should initially focus on the specific knowledge gap. If necessary, other planning and design considerations should be subordinated to this constraint, leading to a reduction in the uncertainty. The control for B projects should not be linear (as is the case with A projects) because this might encourage the B project managers to achieve higher success rates in early stages, leaving closure of the specific knowledge gap to the end. This is typical for projects where 95 percent of the tasks have been completed, and the last 5 percent take 95 percent of the total time. . . .

B project managers should have similar personalities to A project managers—planning, administrative, and organization, but they should be more experienced and familiar with the technological concepts.

C projects require managers with good technological knowledge. Subordination in such projects is to the specific technological gap, and this gap should be dealt with as early as possible. The project's other components and decisions should be subordinated to this knowledge gap. Establishing an operational prototype that will work and will meet most specifications should be the first assignment of the project.

The C project manager should have a technological orientation, planning and organizing abilities, and managerial knowledge and experience.

The D project managers should have vision and courage. Many D projects don't have "proof of existence" at their starting point. Hence, there are no assurances that the project requirements can be met and it is unclear whether there exists a solution to the problem. The central question at the beginning of the project, to which all planning and design considerations will be subordinated, is: Does a solution to the problem exist?

Evaluating the Project Portfolio

Classifying projects into different types (A, B, C, D) enables an educated evaluation of the firm's project portfolio. First and foremost, it is possible to examine if the project distribution is congruent with the firm's strategy. A firm whose strategic goal stresses innovation and leadership will have to invest much effort in type C and D projects. A firm defining itself as a follower ("me too") will focus on type A and B projects, and occasionally on type C. The existence of a significant gap between the strategic declaration and the development strategy (as is manifested in the distribution of projects) should bring about a series of corrective measures to close the gap. The firm's strategy with respect to the project portfolio will also determine the type of personnel it will recruit.

Project Classification and the Complete Kit Concept

In earlier chapters, we discussed various issues that relate to the Complete Kit and the mandatory kit in development processes. Implementing a Complete Kit/mandatory kit will occasionally not be done in development organizations because the developers claim it is difficult to implement because of the high uncertainty in the environment. The mere differentiation between two project groups with differing levels of uncertainty—the A, B group and the C, D group—allow a differential treatment in implementation. A very high percentage of the development time effort of R&D organizations is invested in A and B projects, both in projects that are initially classified as such, and in A and B components of C and D projects. There is no argument about the low level of technological uncertainty in A and B projects, so there is no reason that the characterization and specifications should not be defined with a Complete Kit.

Implementing a mandatory kit provides an important contribution to R&D organizations. The mandatory kit defines the minimal necessary requirements and specifications needed to begin the task. The classification of projects as A, B, C, or D improves defining the contents of Complete Kits, leading to reduced response times and increased development throughput—all leading to enhancing the value of the organization.

Conflict between Generic Development and Specific Development

One of the dilemmas faced by many development departments is whether to generate a generic solution or a specific/designated one (Figure 21.1). A generic solution is a general solution that is appropriate for a wide array of products/systems, and for a larger number

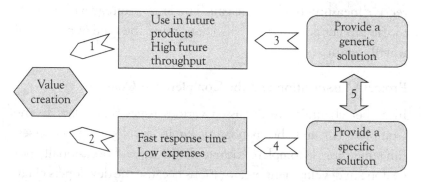

Figure 21.1 Conflict—a generic solution versus a specific solution

of customers. In many instances, it is a modular solution, that can be used to differentiate the product for market segmentation and for future potential growth. A specific solution is an ad hoc solution to the customer's request or for a specific problem.

This conflict must be resolved at the management level. The mechanism for dealing with such issues is through differentiation: Management must decide when a solution should be specific, and when it should be generic. Using a global view of the portfolio of all the projects and resources at the disposal of the organization, there is no doubt that some of the solutions will be generic. Trying to resolve the conflict using a local view of a single project will eventually lead to suboptimization.

Overspecification and Overdesign

To properly deal with the problems of overspecification and overdesign, let us first relate to Rule I of just in time (JIT) in development processes.

Rule I of JIT states: "Work only on what is necessary in quantity, time, and requirements." This rule has a double meaning in R&D organizations:

1. *Working on tasks according to the planned schedule.* Developers should work on activities and tasks at the right time—not after the time but also not ahead of time. This means that performing tasks ahead of time will increase the work in progress, and usually comes at the expense of tasks that should have been performed earlier. Hence, violating Rule I of JIT implies the 40–20–40 phenomenon.
2. *Avoiding overspecification and overdesign.* Work only on "just-in-spec." The overspecification and overdesign phenomena express themselves in:
   - Desire to achieve performances that are better than required (occasionally viewed as safety margins)

- Desire to add unneeded features

- Desire to achieve tighter than needed tolerances

Features that are better than required or unneeded imply that overspecification and overdesign do not contribute to the business and marketing perspective, not from the customer's needs, not from the perceived value by the customer, and not from the actual requirements.

Overspecification and overdesign burden the development process because they are usually very challenging requirements and design that are on the boundary of the technological scope. Complications in the development process are often the result of overspecification or overdesign. Such unsuccessful attempts to achieve the overspecification or overdesign results in time pressure that forces the development team to forgo implementing some requirements that are needed by the customer and that the firm is obligated to. From the perspective of the project life cycle cost, overspecification and overdesign create difficulties in the production processes, the integration, the implementation, and the use of the supplied products and systems.

Sources of Overspecification

In many cases, overspecification is a results of lack of knowledge about the customer's needs during the early stages of the project. The tendency is to define a broad and inclusive specification that includes a wide scope for the customer's needs. This tendency falls on the fertile ground of the development people who are technology-biased, who try to develop "the best" systems and products, or systems and products that are multipurpose (a generic platform for future growth). When the customer has a strong technological orientation, there may develop a "conspiracy" between the customer and the developers that results in overspecification and overdesign.

In an environment with technological uncertainty, there is a tendency to overspecify or overdesign some of the subsystems in order to reduce risks during integration with the overall system. This causes delays in the development process and hinders the production process and the use of technological devices by the customer.

Sources of Overdesign

Overdesign usually results from the developers' desire to create a product that is:

- Better than required due to the challenge of implementing a leading edge technology

- More generic than required so it will be applicable to other products, without coordinating this decision with the appropriate decision makers.

This desire of the developers often results from the personal conflict of the development person, as depicted in Figure 21.2.

As we saw, there are sometimes good business reasons to expand customer's requirements and add features and performances to the project. However, such a decision should be made by management

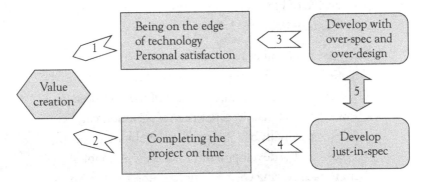

Figure 21.2 The personal conflict of the development person

with a global view of all projects and products, both in the short and long term.

Solutions to Overspecification and Overdesign

The following solutions help to overcome the problem of over-specification and overdesign:

- Existence of a periodic process of evaluation, and relaxation of the specifications by the marketing and development personnel as well as authorized representatives of the external customers (in case of an ordered development). The requirements are evaluated and updated according to the most recent information. The proposed changes go through a strategic gating process of the features and performances, using a focusing matrix that weighs the features' or performance's contribution to the value of the organization versus the bottleneck resources that are required for their implementation.

    It is also recommended to have a detailed discussion with the customer (or with the marketing personnel) about the requirements.

- Implementing business thinking and expanding the perspective of life cycle cost to contribute to understanding the problem.

- The personal conflict of the development person (Figure 21.2) can be relaxed through differentiation. The desire to be at the cutting edge of the technological knowledge and to achieve personal satisfaction can be met by occasionally assigning these development people to type C and D development projects. This enables them to face cutting edge technology and fulfill their technological interest. However, in type A and B projects and type A and B components of C and D projects, development should follow just-in-spec plans.

The conflict may occasionally be resolved by challenging the developers with the economic need of design to cost.

Viewing Development as a Process

There are situations where the development people do not view the development of products and services as a process. They do not consider themselves as part of a process that has to be completed within a specified time but rather relate their work to "art." Indeed, some of the development process is creative and thus resembles art. However, most of the development follows a process: identifying the customer's or market's needs, preparing the work plan and specifications, planning the life cycle, defining Complete Kits in various places, feasibility studies, and staff meetings. Experience shows that most development problems result from inappropriate processes and methods, and only a fraction from insufficient technological knowledge or creativity.

Research also involves a research process, but it is much less structured and requires separate consideration.

Working without a Complete Kit or a Mandatory Kit

As we have seen before, it is of utmost importance to work with a Complete Kit or with a mandatory kit. This is one of the easier tools to implement, and it carries with it significant contribution to the organization. Implementing the Complete Kit and the mandatory kit in development uses the satisficer approach: a firm that estimates that only 50 percent of the time the development people work with Complete Kits will aspire to improve the percentage of tasks using Complete Kits and mandatory kits to, say, 80 percent in the next quarter, and will then try to continue improvement gradually.

Lack of Strategic Gating Processes

The lack of strategic gating processes is a substantial problem in some R&D organizations. The R&D department is a permanent bottleneck in the organization. This is a situation where the number of projects and tasks exceeds the development capacity. As a result, the organization must perform strategic gating.

The strategic gating process selects the projects that will be worked on from among all other potential projects. This process considers the importance of the project, product, or service vis-à-vis the difficulty in implementing it. Importance is evaluated in terms of the monetary contribution to the value of the firm, and the implementation difficulty is determined in one of two ways:

1. Subjective assessment of the task by development management on a scale of 1 to 5 (where 5 is relatively easy and 1—very difficult)

2. Assessing the effort of the permanent bottlenecks (e.g., in person-months) in the development project

Many firms perform a screening process for projects and assess their economic worthiness. In most cases, this screening process can be complemented by three additional components:

1. *A one-shot global view of all projects.* There could be situations where all projects carry a positive net present value, but there are insufficient permanent bottleneck resources in development to be able to accomplish all of them.

2. *Periodic updating of the projects' portfolio using a strategic gating process.* Projects should be periodically screened using a global view. In R&D processes, the external business environment is constantly and dynamically changing—new opportunities arise and earlier forecasts are proven wrong. Periodic strategic gating can improve the important process of screening

projects, especially with respect to ceasing development of some of the existing projects.

3. *Terminating projects versus lowering their priority.* Firms do engage in a prioritization process, but the bottom line is a priority ranking of projects: projects for immediate work, projects for stage 2, projects to be carried out if some capacity opens in development (filler projects), and so on. Such a priority ranking seems good, satisfies all parties in the process, and does not lead to confrontations. However, once a project has been authorized to be worked on (even if it was planned for a later date), management lost much of the control over the project's priority and its start time. In many situations, the field people are the ones who actually set priorities. Development department managers occasionally want to introduce additional projects into the work routine in order to provide work for underutilized people. The desired solution is to *totally stop* work on projects that are no longer in priority.

Lack of Tactical Gating Processes

The lack of tactical gating processes is an important factor in prolonging response times in development processes. In development departments, the roles of the tactical gating process are:

- *Controlled release of tasks using the drum-buffer-rope (DBR) approach.* A controlled release of tasks ensures that the levels of work in process in the development department will not be high, thus avoiding the problem of long lead time and also reducing bad multitasking (BMT). Tactical gating enables the developers to view the project from a global perspective but allows them to work only on tasks that have been released for work. Management determines the size of the buffer. In some development departments, work in process is planned for a level of four to six weeks for each development person. Control of the buffer size is achieved through a controlled release of tasks to the developers.

- *Working with appropriate size activities and work packages.* In the tactical gating mechanism, development tasks are released in activities and work packages of appropriate size. Activity size usually varies between 50 hours and 200 hours. The activity size obviously depends on its functionality.

- *Timing the release of tasks for work.* The tactical gating process enables the release of just those tasks that are needed according to plan.

- *Release of tasks in Complete Kits or mandatory kits.* A task with an incomplete kit will not be released, even at the expense of development people having some idle time.

Inappropriate Measurement

The six global performance measures presented in earlier chapters can form the basis for measuring R&D departments. In R&D organizations that are mainly dealing with projects, performance measures may be introduced as follows:

- Throughput is measured according to the standard definition. The measure looks at revenues and real variable costs.

- Operating expenses are measured as in any other organization.

- Inventory (raw materials and finished goods) are measured as usual, namely only the costs of the raw materials.

- Work-in-process (WIP) inventory relates to the amount of yet uncompleted development tasks. The core activity of an R&D organization is the development process. The most relevant inventory in a development process—the work-in-process—can be measured in several ways:

  —Measuring the labor hours that have been invested in the uncompleted tasks.

  —The number of tasks (work packages) waiting for each development person. This measurement is based on the assumption that the size of the work package is rather uniform (50–200 work hours per package). Controlling this parameter reduces, among others, the BMT phenomenon, that is, frequent and uncontrollable switches among tasks.

- Response time (lead time) can be measured in places where development is homogeneous and repetitive (e.g., engineering departments). In some cases, we can aggregate projects into homogeneous families and measure the response time of each family. In most cases, however, the heterogeneity in response times of development processes is large, and it is preferable not to use this as a measure.

- Quality of development is usually measured by the number of development cycles and the amount of changes in the development process. Another possible measurable quality parameter is the percentage of tasks that went into work as a Complete Kit.

- Due-date performance is the key to reducing development times and avoiding overruns. This is the most important measure. Every project must have a work plan that divides the project into appropriate work packages.

Measure the due-date performance of the projects or various project milestones.

- Percent progress along the critical path or critical chain. This is a very important measure because it provides important information on the effective progress of the project.

Business Structure

Most knowledge-intensive firms and R&D organizations ponder about the appropriate business structure to use for project management. Two alternatives usually show up:

1. *Project structure.* Most of the project's development resources such as system engineers, software people, testing people, and so on, are subordinated to the project manager. The advantages of this structure are the control the project manager has over his resources, the ensuing flexibility, and the identification and loyalty of the project personnel with the project and its goals.

2. *Matrix structure.* The development people are subordinated to the resource managers; they are assigned to the various projects to perform specific tasks and follow orders and priorities from the project managers. The advantage of the matrix structure is in the uniformity of methods and exploitation of resources. Figure 21.3 presents a typical matrix structure.

The conflict of the organizational structure of an R&D organization is presented in Figure 21.4. Before analyzing the conflict, let us clarify some points: The project structure should be the default structure. In development projects, loyalty and accountability of the project personnel are an important component of

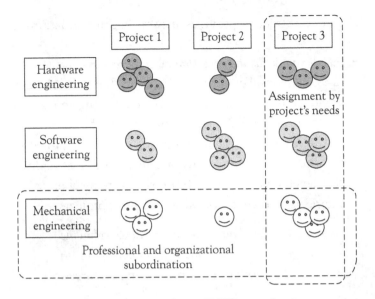

Figure 21.3 **A matrix structure in an R&D organization**

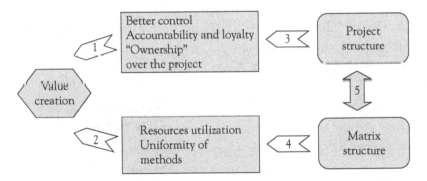

Figure 21.4 **The organizational structure conflict of an R&D organization**

the project success. The project manager's control over his or her people allows flexibility and access to each individual, thus resulting in the ability to shorten response times. Being the direct supervisor of the developers makes the project manager's authority rather large.

The matrix structure provides answers in some situations:

- *Inability to divide the development resources among the various projects.* For example, in a firm that develops and produces high-precision sophisticated testing components, there are 150 ongoing projects and 50 software people whose involvement is needed in all the projects. Another example: A knowledge-intensive firm employs 800 development people, 10 of whom are mechanical engineers who are involved in dozens of projects.

- *Lack of professional and experienced labor within the resource group that is a permanent bottleneck.* This requires an optimal exploitation of the existing resources.

- *Existing problem with product quality as a result of varying standards and lack of uniformity in the development methods among the various projects.*

The conflict can be resolved, in most cases, by appropriate differentiation, thus achieving fast lead time and worker commitment, as well as good use of the scarce resources:

- *Differentiation by resource types.* The project's critical resources should remain under the control of the project manager. The other resources will be assigned to the resource groups' managers. For example, marketing and system engineering will be under the project manager, and the remaining resources will maintain a matrix structure. This enables the project manager to control the important decisions, and the entire firm will benefit from uniform methods and appropriate resource utilization.

- *Differentiation by project size.* A small number of large and long-term projects will be managed according to a project structure. The medium and small projects—in a matrix structure.

- *Differentiation between the organizational affiliation and the physical location of the project personnel.* One way to establish loyalty and commitment to the project in the matrix structure is physically locating the project team in one place. This enables proximity, effective communication, identification, and commitment to the project.

- *Ascription of people to the project.* In long-term projects, it is common to ascribe people to a specific project, thus creating identification, commitment, and accountability to the project.

Many of the problems of the matrix structure can be solved by a strong and professional management that can assign clear priorities to the resource managers.

Substantial Garbage Plant

As we have seen, we must exploit and extract the permanent bottlenecks in the development process.

Garbage plant: *In development, all the labor hours that do not add value to the firm, the customer, the project, the process, the product, or the service.*

The garbage plant in a development environment is estimated at about 50 percent. Namely, about half the development resources are not effectively utilized. This garbage time includes:

- Unnecessary or irrelevant experiments

- Unnecessary development cycles

- Participation of unneeded people in discussions

- Development that ended late

- Working with an incomplete kit or without an appropriate mandatory kit

- Repeated deliberations resulting from unclear definitions

- Bad multitasking—skipping from topic to topic, which hampers the work quality of the developer

- Developing a product without verifying the existence of a market for it and without verifying the marketing abilities

- Parallel development of too many alternative solutions

- Unnecessary responses to requests for proposals

Reducing this wasted time, the methods presented in earlier chapters can greatly improve the performances of the development department.

Make/Buy Decisions

One of the important value drivers in development is deciding whether to buy a ready-made product ("off the shelf") as opposed to developing it. There is no doubt that self-development of a product or subsystem will better address needs and allow appropriate integration into the system. However, in many instances, buying a ready-made product saves efforts of the permanent development bottlenecks and drastically reduces development times.

Summary

The R&D department is the heart of a knowledge-intensive organization. The methods presented in this chapter can reduce response times and greatly increase the R&D throughput of the organization. It is possible to achieve these goals using the existing resources of the organization.

22

The Focused Management Approach in Logistics

The desire of customers to get a large variety of products customized to their needs, in a short lead time, at lower prices, and in high quality, forces firms to constantly improve their logistic capabilities.

What Is Logistics?

Logistics is a managerial system that ensures that the right service or product will be delivered to the right place, on time, in the right quantity. Logistics manages the following aspects of materials, products, and services:

- Purchasing

- Raw materials inventory

- Finished goods inventory

- Transportation and transfer

- Warehousing

- Distribution

- Integrated logistic support (ILS)

A good logistics function in an organization contributes to its value. The major logistics-related value drivers are:

- *Proper management of inventories.* Logistics focuses mainly on the raw materials and finished goods inventories. Value enhancement on the part of logistics is achieved via:

  —*Inventories reduction.* Improves the cash flow of the organization, prevents unused inventories, and improves quality. Proper management of inventories implies that their reduction does not damage throughputs.

  —*Elimination of lost sales.* Usually you are able to reduce the overall level of inventory and yet prevent lost sales by eliminating surplus inventories, increasing to some extent those inventories that were previously too short, and better managing the existing inventories in terms of transportation, batch sizes, and so on (see also Chapter 11 for lost sales measurement).

  —*Increasing customers' satisfaction.* Improved service level and availability of products and services.

- *Reduction of the costs of purchased materials and services.* In a typical industrial firm, about 50 percent of the costs are from purchasing materials, components, services, and subcontractors. Better purchasing methods can reduce these costs substantially.

- *Lead time reduction.* Better management of the finished goods and fast transfers and transportation. As seen later in this chapter, lead time reduction results in the reduction of inventory levels and the reduction of lost sales.

- *Decrease in the costs of logistics garbage plant.* This garbage plant includes:

  —Delayed deliveries

  —Unused inventories and slow moving inventories

  —Double handling—transfer, recounting, sorting

  —Damage to products and materials

  —Product returns

  —Surplus inventory

  —Re-service

  —Product expiration

  —Customers' dissatisfaction

  —Unnecessary transfers

  —Tied-up cash

Reduction of the garbage plant increases throughputs, reduces operating expenses, and reduce inventories. This leads to an improved cash flow and value enhancement.

Typical Issues in Logistics Management

The following questions are commonly asked to determine issues that might be affecting management of logistics:

- What is the level of inventory that a supermarket should hold?

- How do we measure the purchasing department?

- Should we have a central warehouse or several warehouses?

- What is the level of spare parts for a given system that should be kept in stock?

- What should be the size of the purchasing lots?

- Is it right to reduce the level of raw materials and/or finished goods?

- How do we protect sales from fluctuations in demand?

- How do we protect throughput from uncertainty in the supply of materials and components?

The resources of logistics are capital, materials, time, space, equipment, information, and trained staff.

The Focused Management View on Logistic Systems

We will now examine the logistic systems from the Focused Management perspective: a global view, focusing on the main issues, and simple tools.

A Global View

A global view of the logistic system has two dimensions:

1. Taking into consideration the total life cycle of the product or service in terms of its life cycle costs.

2. Broadening the boundaries of the system through global analysis of the effects of logistics on the value of the organization. For that matter, you should not consider the performance improvements of the purchasing department but rather consider the value enhancement of the organization as a whole achieved by applying more effective methods to this department. Similarly, we are not trying to achieve inventory reduction per se, but rather we are interested in

an improved cash flow for the organization resulting from the reduction of finished goods or the elimination of lost sales.

Focusing on the Main Issues

Logistics has to focus on the following value drivers:

- Conforming to inventory levels requirements as a value driver

- Purchasing costs as a dominant factor in value enhancement

- Lead time reduction as a strategic edge to the organization

- Reduction of the logistics garbage plant

Simple Tools

On top of several logistics methods presented in previous chapters (small batches, the Complete Kit concept, and so on), we introduce the following simple tools for managing logistic processes:

- The global inventory management model

- The buffer management approach

The Global Inventory Management Model

The three types of inventory (raw materials, work in process, and finished goods) are different in their nature and in the way they should be managed (Figure 22.1). Each form of inventory has different purposes and different management methods. Generally speaking, any inventory that does not contribute to the value of the organization is unnecessary. Inventory that contributes to throughput is viewed as a buffer and its levels should be planned and adjusted to the needs.

Suppliers

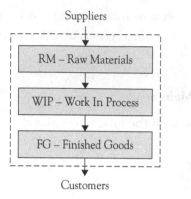

Customers

Figure 22.1 A simplified logistics system

Work in Process Management

As we have seen before, the level of work in process should be near zero except for buffers in front of bottlenecks. Use of the various management methods outlined in this book, drastically reduce work in process, and at the same time shorten lead times.

Finished Goods Inventory Management

A finished goods inventory permits the customer to get the product within a lead time that is shorter than the production lead time of this product.

For example, if an airline needs an airplane six months from now, and the lead time for assembly and integration is four months, there is no reason to keep an inventory of airplanes in stock.

On the other hand, the purchase of a candy bar is a spontaneous-impulsive decision by a customer; hence, the availability has to be immediate. The production and the distribution processes require several days. In this case, a proper inventory of candy bars should be kept in stock.

To sum up, the shorter the production lead time, the smaller the required inventory should be. For example, one company held a 14-week consumption of finished goods inventory in its distribution center in Europe. That makes sense because the lead time for production was 12 weeks. Following a production lead time reduction to three weeks, the inventory of finished goods in Europe was reduced to five weeks of consumption.

The factors that govern the level of finished goods inventory are the following:

- *Product costs.* The lower the product cost—the higher the inventory level can be in order to reduce the risk of shortage. In one multinational company, the shortage of a 10¢ diode caused a delay in the supply of a system whose total value was several millions of dollars.

- *Uncertainty in demand.* The higher the uncertainty, the higher the required finished goods inventory is.

- *Internal uncertainty.* High rate of breakdowns in production and frequent quality problems in the internal system put the system supply at high risk. This can be protected by high levels of finished goods. Such a situation dictates a higher level of finished good inventory.

- *Production lead time.* As seen earlier, reduction in production lead time enables a reduction in the level of finished goods.

- *Transportation lead time.* The higher the transportation time—the larger the amount of finished goods that is tiedup and unavailable for delivery to the customers.

Each of these factors can be dealt with in the following ways:

- *Products costs.* Smart management of the finished goods inventory implies the classification of the finished goods inventory according to their value.

The inventory of the A products (in the Pareto classification by value) should get most of the managers' attention. At the same time, the rate of shortages in B and C products should be drastically reduced by requiring higher safety stocks for these products.

- *Uncertainty in demand.* To overcome this difficulty, buffers of finished goods have to be placed close to the customers. These buffers are the regional warehouses that are intended to beat the fluctuations in the demand.

- *Internal uncertainty.* A central finished goods warehouse, next to the production site, overcomes the fluctuations in the production process.

- *Production lead time.* Reduction of the production lead time according to the methods discussed enables the reduction of finished goods inventory levels.

- *Transportation lead time.* These lead times can be shortened by alternative transportation channels and fewer delays in ports and customs.

A large food producer found that 13 raw materials (A items) constituted about 90 percent of the raw materials costs. The management created a team to analyze the logistics of these items. One of the most important decisions of this team was to ship part of these 13 items by air freight rather than by sea, and thus save about three weeks. The team found an airline that was involved in agricultural products shipments to the locations of the origins of the raw materials for the food producer. As a result of the negotiations, the airline was ready to match the sea transportation costs since its freight airplanes were usually returning empty.

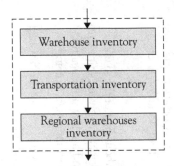

Figure 22.2 Finished goods elements model

A model that describes the elements of the finished goods inventory (Goldratt and Goldratt, 2003) is depicted in Figure 22.2. Table 22.1 summarizes the elements of finished goods inventory, their characteristics, and methods for treatment.

Raw Material Inventory Management

Raw materials inventory serves as a buffer and protects the system's throughput. The level of this inventory is influenced by several factors:

- *Frequency of shipments.* The higher this frequency is, the lower raw materials can be set without undermining the throughput, as demonstrated in Figure 22.3

  For example: If the average demand for a certain raw material is 100 units per month and 600 units are purchased every six months, then the average level of this raw material is 300 units. Changing the frequency of shipment such that 300 units will be shipped every three months will reduce the average inventory to 150 units. In many cases, the increase in shipment frequency leads to fast improvements, especially if it is done by focusing first on the A items of the raw materials inventory.

Table 22.1 Finished goods elements

	Central Warehouse Inventory	Transportation Inventory	Regional Warehouses Inventory
Protection against uncertainties (fluctuations)	Protection against internal fluctuations	Does not protect against fluctuations	Protection against fluctuations in transportation and demand
Parameters that dictate the inventory levels	• Demand levels • Production lead time • Level of internal uncertainty	• Demand levels • Transportation lead time	• Demand levels • Transportation lead time • Transportation frequency
Inventory level	The average demand during the production lead time and safety stock against internal fluctuations	The average demand during the transportation lead time	About half of the average demand between shipments and a safety stock against fluctuations in demand
Its share in the total finished goods inventory	A substantial part of the finished goods inventory	Proportional to the transportation lead time	A small part of the finished goods inventory
Required treatment	• Reduction of production lead time • Buffer management	• Reduction of transportation lead time	• Increase of transportation frequency • Improved demand forecasts • Buffer management
Ease of treatment	Relatively easy	Medium	Medium

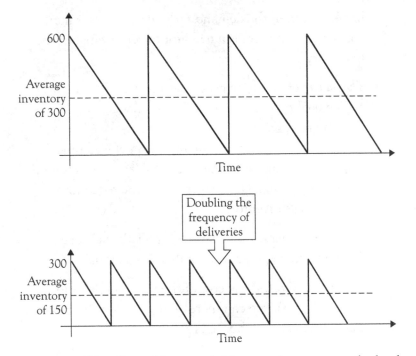

Figure 22.3 The effect of increased shipments frequency on the level of raw materials inventory

- *Supplier reliability.* If the suppliers are reliable, you can keep smaller levels of raw materials inventory. Supplier reliability has several aspects:

  - Reliability of the due date ("it was promised for March 1 and arrived on March 30")

  - Reliability of quantities supplied ("ordered 100 units but only 90 arrived")

  - Quality of materials supplied ("the last shipment had 0.1 percent defects, while this time there are more than 3 percent defects")

- *Internal system reliability.* If the internal system is reliable, stable, has less quality problems and less breakages, then the demand for raw materials is more consistent and there is a need for lower raw material inventory.

- *The quality of the raw materials demand forecast.* The better the quality of the forecast is, the smaller the required inventory.

  As mentioned earlier, the reduction of lead time improves the quality of the forecast. Hence, lead time reduction has an additional effect on the reduction of raw materials inventory.

- *Supplier lead time.* The lower the supplier's lead time is, the lower the required level of this raw material.

- *Raw material cost.* If the cost of the raw material is low (e.g., a C item), you can increase the level of this raw material to prevent shortages.

If none of these methods (higher shipments frequency, working with more reliable suppliers, and so on) were used, an arbitrary reduction of the raw materials inventories is risky and can cause decrease of throughput, delayed deliveries, lost sales, and lost customers.

In What Form Should Inventories Be Kept?

An intriguing issue related to inventory management is the preferred form of inventory. Which is best: raw material inventory, work in process inventory, or finished goods inventory?

Keeping a high level of work in process is destructive—all the problems (evils) of work in process do occur when too many semifinished products wait at that phase. The result is diminished throughput, increase in operating expenses, undermined quality, longer lead time, poor due-date performance, and weaker control over the system. Therefore, you have to reduce the amount of work in process and thus reduce lead time of the process—be it production, service, development, or sales. It is crucial, however, to create appropriate buffers in front of bottlenecks.

Keeping inventory in the form of finished goods is preferred over keeping it as work in process. Finished goods products are well packed and kept in a warehouse, the space requirements are low and, in most cases, they can be sold even if the market has been changed or if the customer has changed his mind.

Nevertheless, the best way of keeping inventory is in the form of raw materials: raw materials are versatile—you can use them in a variety of products/services, and also they can be more easily sold if the market is changed or the customer cancels the order.

To sum up, the preferred way to manage inventory is as follows: keep a controlled level of raw materials as a buffer against fluctuations in supply, reduce lead time such that the level of work in process will be minimal except for buffers in front of bottlenecks, and keep an inventory of finished goods in cases where the expected lead time of the customers is shorter than the system's lead time for production.

Table 22.2 summarizes the advantages and disadvantages of each inventory form.

Leveraging Logistics for Improved Performance—Buffer Management

Buffer management is an approach suggested by Goldratt and Fox (1986) for the effective and efficient management of systems. It is based on the continuous monitoring of the status of the various buffers in the organization. Schragenheim and Ronen (1991) studied this concept and turned it into a simple and applicative tool.

Generally speaking, we can identify several types of buffers in the organization:

- Raw materials buffer
- Finished goods buffer

Table 22.2 Advantages and disadvantages of each inventory form

	Raw materials (RM) inventory	Work in process (WIP) inventory	Finished goods (FG) inventory
Advantages	• Low carrying costs • High flexibility • Quality not impaired	• Only buffers in front of bottlenecks do guaranty the throughput of the system	• Protects the system against lost sales in cases where production in longer than the customer expected lead time • Quality not impaired
Disadvantages	• Purchasing and carrying costs	• High carrying costs • Limited flexibility • Risk of impaired quality • Longer lead time	• Demand levels • Transportation lead time • Transportation frequency

- Buffers in front of bottlenecks

- Feeding buffers after each branch in the process that is feeding a bottleneck

- Time buffers in front of the project due date and contractual milestones

In this discussion, we focus on the first three. Buffer management has three main functions:

1. To protect the system throughput without adding more inventory. As a matter of fact, buffer management usually leads to a reduction of inventory levels.
2. To serve as a warning system that detects problems in the process. This system also gives management the right priorities for treating the problems.
3. A tool for the planning and control of inventory levels.

The Buffer Management Mechanism in Bottleneck Management

The buffer management acts as a protection, diagnosis, and planning and control tool. The size of the buffer is defined in terms of consumption days of the constraint (bottleneck). The use of buffer management involves two steps as illustrated in Figure 22.4:

1. Buffer planning
2. Monitoring and gap analysis

Buffer Planning

Department 2 is the bottleneck and you have to create a buffer in front of it. To exploit the constraint, plan the time of entrance

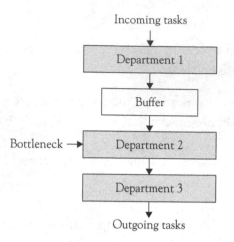

Figure 22.4 An example of a 1-2-3 process with a buffer

for each task into the buffer (Table 22.3). The products to be produced are A and B. We can see that for hours 1, 2, 3, 4, and half of 5 the bottleneck is planned to work on A units. Later, it will work on B units, and during the ninth hour it will start working again on A units.

Table 22.3 The planned buffer in the example

Hour →										
Minutes within the hour	1	2	3	4	5	6	7	8	9	10
0–15	A	A	A	A	A	B	B	B	B	A
15–30	A	A	A	A	A	B	B	B	A	A
30–45	A	A	A	A	B	B	B	B	A	A
45–60	A	A	A	A	B	B	B	B	A	A
Zone		Red			Yellow			Green		

Monitoring and Gap Analysis

The actual content of the buffer (see Table 22.4) is as follows: A units are available for the first, second, third, and half of the fourth hours of the bottleneck. B units are available as planned. The units of A, planned for the ninth and the tenth hours of bottleneck work are missing in the buffer.

We divide the buffer into three zones. The size of the zones is determined individually for each case. As a default, the buffer is divided into three equal-sized zones:

1. *The red zone.* The first third of the buffer that covers the forthcoming working hours of the bottleneck. If some or all of the units that are planned to be in the buffer (according to the work plan of the bottleneck) are missing, this is an alert situation that calls for expediting of the missing units.

2. *The yellow zone.* The interim zone. If the units planned for this zone are missing, corrective action should be taken.

Table 22.4 Actual content of the buffer in the example

Hour → Minutes within the hour	1	2	3	4	5	6	7	8	9	10
0–15	A	A	A	A	Ⓐ	B	B	B	B	Ⓐ
15–30	A	A	A	A	Ⓐ	B	B	B	Ⓐ	Ⓐ
30–45	A	A	A	Ⓐ	B	B	B	B	Ⓐ	Ⓐ
45–60	A	A	A	Ⓐ	B	B	B	B	Ⓐ	Ⓐ
Zone		Red			Yellow			Green		

3. *The green zone*. The latest third, the units in it are planned to be processed last at the bottleneck. If these units are missing, no action is required other then recording the event for further statistical analysis.

Buffer Management in Bottleneck Management

The buffer protects the system's throughput against fluctuations or disturbances, caused by some disruptions in working centers preceding the bottleneck. Reasons for disruptions include quality issues, breakdowns in equipment or computers, absenteeism of workforce, shortage of materials or components, and so on. The buffer is intended to ensure that the bottleneck will not cease to work.

A too-small buffer results in lost throughput, whereas a too-large buffer prolongs the lead time of the system and increases the amount of the work-in-process inventory.

The objective is to find the buffer size that will overcome most possible disruptions but not all of them. The size of the buffer can be assessed by three methods:

1. *Trial and error*. Usually, the initial buffer in the system is larger than required. Moreover, buffers observed in many cases (in development, production, and sales) are much too large. In such cases, you can cut the size of the buffer by half and the level of protection is reexamined after several weeks. This is a very practical way to adjust the size of the buffer that is practiced by many organizations. In many development organizations, we find, in front of the bottleneck resource, buffers that represent several months work. The mechanism described earlier can be used to bring down the size of such huge buffers.

2. *The reliability level method*. According to this method, the buffer is formed such that it will protect the bottleneck in a

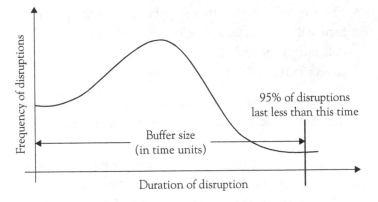

Figure 22.5 Determining the buffer size by the reliability level method

reliability level of 95 percent (or any other arbitrary level) against disruptions. This method requires a data collection mechanism that gathers statistical data about the durations of disruptions in the materials and intermediates supply to the bottleneck. Figure 22.5 presents an example of buffer size determination using this method.

3. *The optimization approach to buffer sizing.* Buffer size can be optimized taking into account the cost of holding the various inventory items and the effect on the lead time against the penalty resulting from the shortage of materials in front of the bottleneck. Examples for such optimizations were presented by Ronen and Trietsch (1988) and Levy and Ronen (1989).

Buffer Management as a Warning System

The game rules for buffer management are as follows:

- Shortage of materials that are planned for the green zone will be noted but no immediate action should be taken.

- Shortage of materials that are planned for the yellow zone will start an examination about the causes for the delay in the arrival of these materials and possible ways to rectify the disruptions.

- Shortage of materials that are planned for the red zone demands immediate expediting of the missing materials.

The information gathered on the availability of materials and intermediates in the various zones, and the causes for the delays is used for analysis of the origins of disruptions and possible corrective actions.

Buffer Management as a Tool for Inventory Levels Management

The statistics gathered on the availability of materials in the various zones of the buffer (red, yellow, and green), can be used as a basis for the determination of the proper size of the buffer. If in the long run there are nearly no shortages in the green zone then the buffer is too large and it should be decreased. On the other hand, if there are shortages in the red zone too often, you have to increase the size of the buffer. A simultaneous study of the disruption events will lead to a reduction in their amount.

Buffer Management in the Management of Finished Goods Inventory

Management of the finished goods inventory has a large potential as a value driver. An effective and efficient mode of finished goods inventory management according to the buffer management method can lead to a substantial reduction in inventory levels and at the same time to a reduction in the extent of shortages. The buffer management approach is suitable for products whose demand is relatively stable and it absorbs the disruptive effect of random fluctuations in demand. However, this approach is not suitable for the management of finished goods in situations where the demand in not stable (and randomly distributed) but rather there is a spiky demand.

In the case of finished goods, it is difficult to precisely forecast the market demand for each product. Forecasts regarding the near future can be reasonably good, but the quality and accuracy of forecasts deteriorate for later periods. Namely, the shorter the system lead time, the higher the forecast quality and accuracy (Goldratt and Fox, 1986).

Prior to the implementation of buffer management to finished goods inventory, you have to classify the products into A, B, and C classes according to their throughput volume using the Pareto analysis. The A products (the hot products) will be produced and kept in stock according to the buffer management mechanism. The B products (the cold products) will be made to order and will not be kept in stock. C items can either be made to order or (usually) kept in stock.

Finished goods inventory management using the buffer management method requires short production lead time. In this method, there are two levels to be monitored:

1. *The minimum level.* Determined according to the lead time of the production system. For example, if the system is able to supply typical demands within 10 days, then the minimum finished goods inventory level can be set at 10 days demand.
2. *The maximum level.* Determined according to the batch sizes policy of the company for the products involved.

The directives for buffer management in finished goods inventory are as follows:

1. The level of inventory should be kept between the minimum and the maximum levels.

2. The percent occurrences of the finished goods level within the buffer limits will be a major performance measure for the COO.

3. Production orders will be given to the production manager according to the current inventory levels. The production manager will decide on the batch sizes.

4. Buffer management is suitable for stable and random demands and not for spiky demand.

5. Management will update the minimum and maximum levels of the finished goods buffer according to seasonality, average demand, and the amount of previous deviations (above the maximum or below the minimum). If no deviations are experienced, buffer decrease should be considered. If there were too many deviations, buffer increase should be considered.

Buffer Management of Finished Goods Inventory

The firm's value can be enhanced using buffer management of finished goods:

- *Protection of the system's throughput.* Management of the finished goods inventory according to the buffer management method reduces the extent of lost sales and increases the throughput of the company.

- *A warning tool for the detection of problems.* Buffer management enables the analysis of the causes for shortages in finished goods and leads to the rectification of disruptions.

- *Ensures the proper inventory level.* Companies that used buffer management for their finished goods inventory reduced the levels of inventory and at the same time improved the availability of their products and the throughput.

Buffer Management for the Raw Materials Inventory Management

Raw materials and purchased items can be divided into two categories:

1. *Standard raw materials that are used for the production of numerous products.* Management of the inventory of these materials can be achieved by buffer management.
2. *Specific raw materials and components.* Such raw materials and purchased items usually serve a few products and have to be managed via different methods that are based either on the actual demand or on the forecasted demand for the corresponding finished products.

Buffer management of raw materials and purchased components is done in a manner similar to the buffer management of finished goods.

Summary

Proper management of logistics results in the improvement of the corresponding value drivers. These value drivers are relatively easy to implement. Inventories management according to the methods described in this chapter usually leads to substantial improvement in a relatively short time.

Part V

Perspective and Implementation

23

Our Managerial Credo

It is difficult to determine what is "right" and "not right" in management, and what management style is best. In a world of uncertainties in markets, technology, and politics, it is important to adapt trade conditions, management methods, and tools to the changing situations.

However, we must design a managerial concept that will help increase competitiveness, enhance the firm's value for its owners, and improve the performance measures of the organization.

This chapter lays out the managerial framework that we feel is the most suitable one for the twenty-first century.

The World Is Simpler Than It Seems

The business world is complex and complicated. It is affected by dozens, perhaps hundreds, of factors. It is filled with uncertainty in demand for services, technology and politics. The various management functions are in permanent conflicts (marketing versus development, development versus operations and so on). Life cycles of services and products are becoming shorter and shorter. New technologies appear almost daily, and competition puts pressures on all departments in the organization.

As previously shown in this book, viewing the managerial world through a different prism makes us realize that this world is simpler than it seems. The approach to simplicity is *focus*. Things seem simpler through focused eyes.

For example:

- *Focusing on core problems.* Any organization faces a multitude of problems. Trying to solve them one by one will take up most of the managers' time, and will probably not yield the desired results because we are solving symptoms rather than solving the problems themselves. Every organization has only a small number of core problems and focusing on them simplifies matters. Solving these core problems may, even partially, relieve most of the symptoms and problems of the organization.

- *Focusing on the system's constraints.* A system has many resources that contribute to its complexity. However, if we focus on the relatively few true system constraints, things will become clearer and simpler.

- *Focusing on type A items in the Pareto analysis.* An organization has many failures and quality problems, many suppliers and service providers, a large variety of services and products, various customers, various raw materials and components, and many performance requirements in every service. If we focus on the few and important type A items, the world will be simpler.

- *Focusing on the critical path or the critical chain.* A typical project consists of hundreds of activities. Careful control and monitoring of many activities concurrently make management complex and complicated. Focusing on the critical path or the critical chain that contains only a limited number of activities can greatly simplify the project management.

- *Focusing on key points.* Most processes are complex and complicated. They usually have many stages that add to the complexity, especially if they cross various departments of the organization. Focusing on key points, such as gating at the beginning of the process, generates fewer control points that require less effort to handle. Other key points like buffer management make the issues simpler and more controllable.

- *Focusing on uncertainty.* Processes in research and development are complex and complicated. Focusing on the factors that contribute most to the uncertainty simplifies the picture and focuses attention on the essentials.

All Organizations Are "Sick"

There is no such thing as a "healthy" organization. Organizations operate only at 10 percent to 20 percent of their potential value or performance. This rather dismal situation, presents opportunities for dramatic improvements.

A situation where a system operates at low effectiveness and utilization, is not rare. This is analogous to engineering/thermodynamics where many engines operate at single digit utilization.

An organization is a collection of people, resources, and tools that are working to provide a certain need or have gathered to achieve a certain goal. The low organizational effectiveness stems from several reasons inherent in the mere existence of the organization and its processes:

- Inherent conflicts

- The goals of the individual and the goals of the organization

- Internal and external uncertainty

- Technological innovation

- Ongoing competition

- The *garbage plant* of the organization

The inherent conflicts in an organization emerge from the inherent conflicts in the ways that the different functions of the organization operate. It would be nice if this friction would be a constructive one, but it usually is not, leading to a reduction of performance.

For example, the development-marketing conflict: Marketing wants to develop for every customer a unique product with features as close as possible to "tailor made." Development wants to generate unique leading edge technology products, ones that are also "fun" to develop.

There is also the development-production conflict: The production department prefers to produce one product at a time. The development department wants to develop many products and prototypes with short life cycles.

These conflicts and others create tension between people and the organization, and thus reducing the organization's overall performance.

The inherent conflicts in an organization also manifest themselves in incomplete measurement of various functions. It is very difficult to find local performance measures that are all congruent with the organization's goals. Thus, there is a gap between the local performance measures (of a project manager, head of an area, operations manager, marketing director, and so on) and the performance measure of the whole organization. This gap, known as the *performance measures' gap*, causes deviation from the desired performance of the organization. After all, every system is a subsystem of a broader system, and optimization of a smaller system is liable to result in suboptimization of a larger one.

Goals of the Individual and the Organization. In the ideal setting, the goals of the individual coincide with those of the organization.

The individual usually has goals of self-fulfillment, depending on his or her personality. The organization consists of tens, hundreds, or even thousands of individuals who are in daily contact with management and with each other. Lack of communication and conflicting objectives may lead to low effectiveness of operation.

External and Internal Uncertainty. This is a critical factor in reducing organizational effectiveness. External sources of uncertainty include demand, regulation, competition, legislation, politics, quantities and prices of outputs, costs and availability of inputs, and so on. Internal sources of uncertainty include failures in computing services; production failures; quality problems; worker absenteeism; processing time of information, services, and products; and technological uncertainty. All these inhibit organizational effectiveness.

Technological innovation accelerates competition and leads to a reduction of the life cycle of all technological systems. By the time a technology had been diffused into the organization, it already needs to be improved, changed, or replaced. Before an organization has gotten comfortable in providing a service or producing a product, it needs to consider designing a new one. Technological innovation occasionally forces an organization to provide incomplete services or to market products that require extensive support and maintenance.

Ongoing competition forces the organization to operate less effectively than had it been a monopoly.

All these as well as other issues combine to create a considerable *garbage plant*—all activities that do not add value to the organization in general and particularly to the customers, the products, services, or processes. The size of the garbage plant is usually dozens of percentages of labor hours as well as the costs of materials and other inputs. The garbage plant expresses itself in repairing defects, correcting mistakes, system integration that may last from days to weeks, many unnecessary development cycles, conflicts with dissatisfied customers, hours of meetings and discussions to figure out what went wrong and why, unnecessary inventory, unnecessary conveyance, unneeded activities, repeat performances, and other types of waste.

It is thus not surprising that organizations work only at 10 percent to 20 percent of their potential. How do such organizations survive? Their competitors undoubtedly have similar problems.

Improvements in an organization can create a competitive edge, and these improvements can be best achieved by *focusing*.

Global View

Viewing the system as a whole is just part of the managerial outlook. Every employee and manager must view the whole system from the perspective of top management, who must keep a global view all the time.

Global vision reduces the phenomenon of suboptimization, where optimizing a subsystem with an objective function that may be different than that of the whole organization, reduces the value of the organization.

Managerial Maturity

As we have seen, organizations suffer from a lack of resources, especially in the permanent bottlenecks. There is a need for managerial maturity to understand this phenomenon and to manage resources properly. Managerial maturity permits the organization to knowingly forgo tasks, projects, products, services, and customers in order to be able to focus efforts on more profitable ones. For example, an organization wishes to develop four new innovative products, each one with a potential of being a breakthrough in the market. However, development resources are limited and are sufficient for the development of only two products. Management has to decide to forgo the development of two of the products and focus on the two that have the highest potential for enhancing value for the organization. The dilemma is serious because of the underlying uncertainty: maybe one of the forgone products would be the one that would launch the organization beyond its competitors? Managerial maturity is the ability to make brave decisions in the face of uncertainty when it is clear that there is always the possibility of an error in judgment. The decision must be made using the best information available to the decision makers.

Human Resources

Every manager must devote much of his or her time to manage the human resources needed to extract the potential of the organization. Human resources have the highest potential for improvement, on the one hand, and have the highest variability, on the other. Hence, there is a need to devote special managerial attention both for extracting the potential and for realizing the variability among the human resources in the organization.

Satisficer Principle

Nobel laureate, H. A. Simon, recognized in the 1960s one of the major managerial problems that stands in the way of decision makers: Managers tend to behave as optimizers. An optimizer is one who aspires to reach the best possible decision, regardless of timeframe considerations.

There is no doubt that leaning toward being an optimizer will lead to better decisions, but the decision may take too long. In a dynamic world and where time to market is critical, the world of the optimizers is becoming extinct.

Simon proposes that we behave as satisficers and make "satisfactory," good enough, decisions: establish a reasonable level of aspiration that must be achieved to reach a substantial improvement in performance. With the satisficer approach, there is no objective of maximizing or minimizing a performance measure, but rather achieving a predetermined satisfactory aspiration level. The objective of modern management is not to find the ideal solution to a problem but rather to achieve significant improvement.

Using Performance Measures

People and systems behave according to how they are measured. "Tell me how you behave and I will tell you how you are being measured." Choosing and implementing appropriate performance measures will greatly assist the value enhancement of the firm.

Simple Tools

Modern management approaches are based on simplicity and common sense. Experience shows that "what is not simple—simply will not be."

The 85/15 Rule—Importance of Process

The modern manager must monitor processes and improve them. The 85/15 rule states that 85 percent of problems result from the processes, and are management's responsibility. Only 15 percent of problems are the employees' responsibility. Thus, focus should be aimed at improving the process.

The 10 Times Rule

A failure that is not detected at an early stage of the process will cause damage 10 times more harmful if detected at the next stage. As a result, we must focus on the early stages of the process.

Differentiation

The modern managerial outlook stresses differentiation—different policies for different cases and different managerial situations.

Implementing Focused Management Methods

In the process of improving organizational value, three questions must be addressed (Goldratt, 1990):

1. What to change?
2. What to change to?
3. How to make the change?

What to Change?

The goal is to enhance the value of the firm or improve performance in not-for-profit organizations. We exploit the value drivers to enhance the value of the organization on the one hand, and treat the value inhibitors (policy constraints, dummy constraints, weaknesses and threats) on the other. The idea is to focus on a small number of factors that we try to improve. It is simply impossible to properly focus on too many issues simultaneously, as management time is a bottleneck.

What to Change to?

We want to utilize the value drivers and enhance the value of the firm along time.

How to Make the Change?

This is the key question. The principles discussed in this book seem simple, but it takes time and effort to fully implement them in an organization. This is a result of the need to change the minds of many people in the organization and create a work environment that is open to new ideas and their implementation.

The Process of Change

The process of change has several stages:

- *The business/functional diagnosis of the organization.* The business diagnosis of the organization involves identifying the business environment and identifying value drivers. These are performed as follows:

  —Conduct in-depth interviews with managers and workers.

  —Examine financial reports, marketing and sales reports, operational and development reports.

  —Examine other improvement endeavors (external and internal) done by the organization.

  —Collect external information regarding the organization.

  Once the value drivers have been identified, they are sorted so we can focus on the more important ones:

- *Preparation of an implementation plan draft.* After the business/functional diagnosis has been completed, a draft is prepared for a value enhancement implementation plan.

- *Training and knowledge transfer.* Knowledge about new and novel management approaches and tools that were described in this book is transferred to management through an interactive workshop lasting several days. During this workshop, management identifies the value drivers and prepares a detailed implementation plan. At a later date, the knowledge is transferred to middle management and the rest of the workers.

  The guiding principle is that implementing a change is done by the management and workers themselves. This reduces resistance to change because it is done internally and not by external agents.

- *Establish value enhancement teams.* Management should establish value-enhancement teams that will deal with the various value drivers. The value enhancing process is carried out in the spirit and with the tools presented in this book.

- *Performance monitoring and control.* Management serves as a steering committee for the project. Its role is to oversee and manage the work of the value enhancement teams, meet with them on a regular basis, and approve their findings and recommendations for implementation.

Introducing Changes and Reducing Resistance to Change

Several principles should guide management when it plans to enhance the value of the organization or improve its performance:

- Implementation will be performed by people within the organization.

- The role of an optional external body will be to introduce methodology, transfer knowledge to management and employees, and facilitate the implementation process.

- The value enhancement teams will include managers as well as rank and file people of the organization.

- The number of teams should be small. They will be responsible for suggesting changes and for the actual implementation.

- Areas for enhancement will be chosen by their contribution to value and the difficulty in implementing them, using the focusing matrix.

- Value enhancement is a central role of the duty and work of management, and is not a side project.

- All the organization's employees should gradually join the knowledge transfer circles.

- Follow-up and control of the implementation of value enhancement will be done using the tools presented in this book.

Role of Information Systems in the Change Process

Information systems play a central role in the change process. However, the idea that implementing an information system will by itself solve the organizations' problems needs clarification. Implementing an information system in an organization should be done according to a two-stage model (Ronen and Pass, 1997) as follows:

1. *Change the managerial approaches and the managerial processes of the organization.* First, there is a need to implement approaches such as management by constraints, the Complete Kit concept, the VFM model, the GDM methodology for decision making, global measuring and control, project management methodology, management of research and development and more.

2. *Design an information system that will support these approaches.* After the work processes have been designed, and the managerial approaches have been implemented, an information system must be adapted to support these approaches. The resulting information systems, designed in a satisficer frame of mind, will be highly effective, yet simple. Building information systems to support these approaches is a necessary condition for a continuation of value enhancement processes along time.

Summary

What will management look like in the future? Management will reflect the business, economic, social, technological, and political environments. Management approaches will adapt themselves to changing environments. We believe that the principles presented in this book serve basic building blocks. In the future, new managerial innovations will arise that will illuminate existing and new problems in a light that will provide additional insight on the management world.

References

Borovitz I., and P. Ein-Dor. 1977. Cost/utilization: A measure of system performance. *Communications of ACM* 20 (3): 185–191.

Burbridge, J. L. 1968. *The principles of production control*, 2nd ed. London: Macdonald and Evans.

Coman, A., G. Koller, and B. Ronen. 1996. The application of focused management in the electronics industry: A case study. *Production and Inventory Management*, (2): 65–70.

Coman, A., and B. Ronen. 2001. *The ARENA strategic model: A theory of constraints approach to strategic analysis.* Working paper, Tel-Aviv University, Faculty of Management, Tel-Aviv, Israel.

Cooper, R., and R. S. Kaplan. 1988. Measure costs right: Make the right decisions. *Harvard Business Review.* Vol. 66, Issue 5: 96–103

Copeland, T., T. Koller, and J. Murrin. 2005. *Valuation: Measuring and managing the value of companies, 4th Edition.* New York: John Wiley & Sons.

Cox, J. F. III, and J. H. Blackstone Jr., eds. 1998. APICS *dictionary*, 9th ed. Falls Church, VA: APICS.

Cox, J. F. III, and M. S. Spencer. 1998. *The constraints management handbook.* Boca Raton, FL: St. Lucie Press.

Crosby, P. B. 1979. *Quality is free.* New York: McGraw-Hill.

Deming, W. E. 1986. *Out of the crisis.* Cambridge, MA: MIT Center for Advanced Engineering Study.

Dettmer, H. W. 1998. *Breaking the constraints to world-class performance.* Milwaukee, WI: ASQ Quality Press.

Eden, Y., and B. Ronen. 1993. Improving workflow in the insurance industry: A focused management approach. *Journal of Insurance Issues.* Vol. 16, Issue: 49–62.

435

Eden, Y., and B. Ronen. 2002. Activity based costing and activity based management. *Articles of Merit 2002 Competition, FMAC Award Programs for Distinguished Contribution of Management Accounting, International Federation of Accounting*: 47–58.

Feigenbaum, A. V. 1983. *Quality costs in total quality control*. New York: McGraw-Hill.

Geri, N., and B. Ronen. 2005. Relevance lost: The rise and the fall of activity-based-costing. *Human Systems Management* 24: 133–144.

Goldratt, E. M. 1990a. *The haystack syndrome: Sifting information out of the data ocean*. Croton-on-Hudson, NY: North River Press.

Goldratt, E. M. 1990b. *What is this thing called theory of constraints and how should it be implemented*. Croton-on-Hudson, NY: North River Press.

Goldratt, E. M. 1994. *It's not luck*. Croton-on-Hudson, NY: North River Press.

Goldratt, E. M. 1997. *Critical chain*. Croton-on-Hudson, NY: North River Press.

Goldratt, E. M., and J. Cox. 2004. *The goal: A process of continuous improvement*, 3rd ed. Croton-on-Hudson, NY: North River Press.

Goldratt, E. M., and R. E. Fox. 1986. *The race*. Croton-on-Hudson, NY: North River Press.

Goldratt, E. M., and A. Goldratt. 2003. *TOC insights into distribution*. www.eligoldratt.com.

Hillier, F. S., and G. J. Lieberman. 2002. *Introduction to operations research*, 7th ed. New York: McGraw-Hill.

Horngren, C. T., G. Foster, and S. M. Datar. 2000. *Cost accounting: A managerial emphasis*, 10th ed. Englewood Cliffs, NJ: Prentice-Hall.

Johnson, H. T., and R. S. Kaplan. 1987. *Relevance lost: The rise and fall of management accounting*. Cambridge, MA: Harvard Business School.

Juran, J. M. 1989. *Juran on leadership for quality*. New York: Free Press.

Karp, A., and B. Ronen. 1992. Improving manufacturing operations: An entropy model approach. *International Journal of Production Research* 30 (4): 923–938.

Kendall, E. I. 2004. *Viable vision: Transforming total sales into net profits*. Fort Lauderdale, FL: J. Ross Publishing.

Kim, W. Chan, and R. Mauborgne. 2005. *Blue ocean strategy: How to create uncontested market space and make the competition irrelevant*. Harvard Business School Press, Boston, MA.

Koch, R. 1997. *The 80/20 principle*. London: Nicholas Brealey Publishing.

Lechler, T. L., B. Ronen, and E. Stohr, Critical chain: A new project management paradigm or old wine in new bottles? *Engineering Management Journal*, Vol. 17, No. 4, December 2005.

Leshno, M., and B. Ronen. 2001. The Complete Kit concept: Implementation in the health care system. *Human Systems Management* 20 (4): 313–318.

Levy, N. S., and B. Ronen. 1989. Purchasing and raw materials management in science-based industries. *International Journal of Materials and Product Technology* 4 (1): 1–9.

Livne, Z., and B. Ronen. 1990. The component chart: A new tool for purchasing and production. *Production and Inventory Management* 1990 (3): 18–23.

Mabin, V. J., and S. J. Balderstone. 2000. *The world of the theory of constraints: A review of international literature*. Boca Raton, FL: St. Lucie Press.

Pass, S., and B. Ronen. 2003. Managing the market constraint in the hi-tech industry. *International Journal of Operations Management* 41 (4): 713–724.

Project Management Institute. 2004. *Project management body of knowledge*. 3rd ed. Newtown Square, PA: Project Management Institute.

Ronen, B. 1992. The Complete Kit concept. *International Journal of Production Research* 30 (10): 2457–2466.

Ronen, B., A. Coman, and E. Schragenheim. 2001. Peak management. *International Journal of Production Research* 39 (14): 3183–3193.

Ronen, B., and S. Pass. 1997. Manufacturing management information systems require simplification. *Industrial Engineering* 24 (2): 50–53.

Ronen, B., and Y. Spector. 1992. Managing system constraints: A cost/utilization approach. *International Journal of Production Research* 30 (9): 2045–2061.

Ronen, B., and M. Starr. 1990. Synchronized manufacturing as in OPT: From practice to theory. *Computers and Industrial Engineering* 18 (8): 585–600.

Ronen, B., and D. Trietsch. 1993. Optimal scheduling of purchase orders for large project. *European Journal of Operational Research* 68: 18–195.

Schonberger, R. J. 1986. *World class manufacturing: The lessons of simplicity applied*. New York: Free Press.

Schragenheim, E., and B. Ronen. 1990. The drum-buffer-rope shop floor control. *Production and Inventory Management* 31 (3): 18–23.

Schragenheim, E., and B. Ronen. 1991. Buffer management: A diagnostic tool for production control. *Production and Inventory Management* (2): 74–79.

Shenhar, A. J. 1998. From theory to practice: Toward a typology of project management style. *IEEE Transactions on Engineering Management* 41 (1): 33–48.

Shingo, S. 1996. *Quick changeover for operators: The SMED system*. Cambridge, MA: Productivity Press.

Simon, H. A. 1957. *Models of man*. New York: John Wiley & Sons.

Stern, J. M., and J. S. Shiely. 2001. *The EVA challenge.* New York: John Wiley & Sons.

Stewart, G. B. III. 1994. EVA: Fact and fantasy. *Journal of Applied Corporate Finance:* 1078–1196.

Taguchi, G. 1986. *Introduction to quality engineering: Designing quality into products and processes.* Cambridge, MA: Productivity Press.

Recommended Readings

Aacker, D. A. *Developing Business Strategies*, 6th ed. New York: John Wiley & Sons, 2001.

Anderson, D. J. *Agile Management for Software Engineering*. Upper Saddle River, NJ: Prentice-Hall, 2004.

Coman, A. *The ARENA Model*. Presented at the International Association for the Management of Technology Conference, Orlando, FL, 1999.

Deming, W. E. *The New Economics*. Cambridge, MA: MIT Center of Advanced Engineering Study, 1993.

Forsberg, K., H. Mooz, and H. Cotterman. *Visualizing Project Management*, 2nd ed. New York: John Wiley & Sons, 2000.

Gleason, M. "High Level of Operating Equipment Efficiency Requires Overall Effort." *Pulp and Paper* 69(7) (1995): 79–84.

Grosfeld-Nir, A., and B. Ronen. The Complete Kit concept: Modeling the managerial approach. *Computers and Industrial Engineering* (3) (1998): 695–701.

Juran, J. M., and F. M. Gryna. *Quality Planning and Analysis*, 3rd ed. New York: McGraw-Hill, 1993.

Leach, L. P. *Critical Chain Project Management*. Boston, MA: Artech House, 2000.

Newbold, R. C. *Project Management in the Fast Lane*. Boca Raton, FL: St. Lucie Press, 1998.

Ronen, B., and I. Speigler. "Information as Inventory: A New Conceptual View." *Information and Management* 21 (1991): 239–247.

Shtub, A., J. F. Bard, and S. Globerson. *Project Management: Processes, Methodologies, and Economics (2nd Edition)*. Englewood Cliffs, NJ: Prentice-Hall, 2004.

Woehr, W. A., and D. Legat. *Unblock the Power of Your Salesforce!* Vienna: NWV, 2002.

Index

CPSIA information can be obtained
at www.ICGtesting.com
Printed in the USA
LVHW080830220722
723259LV00001B/11